THE ERA OF GOOD INTENTIONS

James A. White

ARNO PRESS

A New York Times Company
New York • 1978

Editorial Supervision: JOSEPH CELLINI

◆

First publication 1978 by Arno Press Inc.

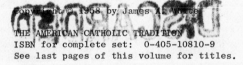

Copyright © 1958 by James A. White

THE AMERICAN-CATHOLIC TRADITION
ISBN for complete set: 0-405-10810-9
See last pages of this volume for titles.

Manufactured in the United States of America

◆

Library of Congress Cataloging in Publication Data

White, James Addison.
    The era of good intentions.

    (The American Catholic tradition)
    Originally presented as the author's thesis,
Notre Dame, 1957.
    Bibliography: p.
    1. American literature--Catholic authors--
History and criticism. I. Title. II. Series.
PS153.C3W5 1978   810'.9'9222   77-14631
ISBN 0-405-10866-4

THE ERA OF GOOD INTENTIONS
A Survey of American Catholics' Writing Between the Years 1880-1915

A Dissertation

Submitted to the Graduate School of the

University of Notre Dame in Partial Fulfillment

of the Requirements for the Degree of

Doctor of Philosophy

by

James A. White, M.A.

Aaron V. Abell
_____
Director

Department of History

Notre Dame, Indiana

TABLE OF CONTENTS

PREFACE

The Era of Good Intentions surveys the careers of many American Catholics writing between the years 1880-1915. Although it possibly may be mistaken for a literary lifeboat rescuing writers from oblivion, The Era of Good Intentions, above all, is a record of a manigicent effort to do good. It is the chronicle of well-intentioned men and women in an age of do-gooders and of their desire to lead their fellow Americans and co-religionists to a finer appreciation of culture, education, and religion. The survey reveals that almost every literary form was used in recording their impressions of life in the United States and in their suggestions for its improvement. It includes reminders of one's loyalty to God and Country, of the necessity for more and better education, and of the advisability of abandoning degrading habits.

Several reasons prompt the selection of 1880 as the point of departure for this study. By that year, the Catholic young man's societies clearly exhibited their interest in literature, while the astute observer, Bishop John Lancaster Spalding demanded a greater creative literary effort from his co-religionists. Again, by using 1880, a before and after perspective develops. Although Catholicity in the United States made remarkable gains from 1865-1880, this progress pales before the acceleration of Catholic activities following the momentous Third Plenary Council of Baltimore (1884).

The year 1915 concludes the study, as the First War brings the
realization that an age confident in its own ability to fashion
reform recognized its failure.

The dissertation's order is topical with the topics arranged in
a chronological sequence. The "pioneer women" writers, with their
virtue-triumphant, problem-solving novels, first exhibited the
tendency to guide their co-religionists. In a natural sequence,
they headed the order, followed by other fiction makers and the
poets. Both fiction and poetry preceded the essay, since some
essayists were apt to criticize fiction and poetry. In this manner
the reader becomes somewhat familiar with the objects under
scrutiny.

The hierarchy also employed its critical franchise, since the
busy prelates adhered to the theme that the printed word influenced
their contemporaries. These bishops and archbishops, colorful in
personality and vigorous in administration, did not always repeat
their personal triumphs in writing. Yet, their effort was sufficient to give them national recognition in the secular and religious
journals. However, it remained for the editors of the Catholic
magazines and newspapers to bring the bulk of criticism before the
Catholic public. Straight forward with truth, bitter with animosity,
the editors highlighted the cultural, social, educational, and
political defects of their co-religionists. Then, they alleviated
this condition with well-written articles involving literary
criticism, historical narrative, scientific description, and

religious truth. Some suggestions were frank, ironic, humorous; but, in this fashion, the Catholic editor hoped to help his reader.

The Era of Good Intentions concludes with a chapter outlining the supporting background. The writers' impulse to do good was shared by many other Catholics, who were anxious to contribute to the commonweal. Their contributions: learned societies, reading circles, summer schools, anthologies, and encyclopedias formed but a part of this healthy, encouraging condition.

Between 1880 and the First War, Americans saw their laissez-faire optimism being refined with realism. The resulting change became evident: the better day is not going to evolve naturally; intervention is necessary to bring a more perfect existence in these United States. The American Catholics adapted this prevailing, optimistic outlook to suit their own purposes during the years 1880-1915. The spirit of reform did not escape them and they needed look no further than to their own co-religionists to find a worthy object for their efforts. Frequently, the writers' better literary inclinations were submerged in this desire-to-help motive; and, the resulting fiction, poetry, essay, and editorial endeavored to mold opinion, to inspire and correct the Catholic populace, and to declare loyalty to God and Country. Admittedly, the writing of these authors varies from excellent to mediocre. Yet, the magnificent motives which inspired this great outpouring, leads one to believe this is THE ERA OF GOOD INTENTIONS.

The writer is deeply indebted to Dr. Aaron I. Abell, Professor of History, University of Notre Dame, for the encouragement and counsel given him in the preparation of this dissertation. He is grateful to the Reverend Thomas T. McAvoy, C.S.C., head of the Notre Dame History Department, for perceptive criticism and encouragement. Finally, the writer is indebted particularly to his parents and to his friends from the various stations and persuasions of this life, who kept him at this pleasant task.

James Addison White
South Bend, Indiana
May, 1956

CHAPTER I

THE PIONEER WOMEN NOVELISTS

Van Wyck Brooks, in the last volume of his American literary
survey, labeled the years 1885-1915, The Confident Years. A
dominating characteristic of the period, the pyramiding growth of
railroads, industries, and investments, lent substantial support to
such a contention, although the Granger Movement, Populism, the
Agitation for Free Silver, and the panics of 1884 and of 1893
clearly indicated imperfections in our country's economic system.
Following the turn of the century, the Progressives and the
Muckrakers partially refined and reformed the abuses attending the
growth of Big Business. All the while, Americans were conscious of
the country's progress. The opening of the Twentieth Century,
January 1, 1901, was an occasion for reviewing the past and surveying the future.

As literary America moved through romanticism towards realism,
the optimistic note persisted that the material needs of the people
never were better served. "At no period in earth's history has it
been possible to have all the legitimate wants of civilization well
ministered to," wrote The Arena's editor, Benjamin Orange Flower,
"with such short days as to afford men and women ample time for
growing upward, for developing all that is finest, truest, and

most worthy in their natures, and for enjoying life."[1] The World's
Work predicted that the best was still to come.

> Sanitary science and preventive medicine, the more extended
> use of electricity, the still greater and more revolution-
> ary applications of machinery——in a dozen different direc-
> tions tasks are in hand that will make a new earth of the
> planet that we are yet only beginning to know.[2]

The Century magazine forthrightly declared that it was not
"immoderately hopeful to cherish the faith that Americans in the
coming century" would see a further bettering of the working class'
condition and "a still higher sense of responsibility on the parts
of the guardian of Capital." All this was to be accomplished "by
evolution instead of by revolution."[3] More sobering in thought
was the opinion of the Literary Digest that the inheritance be-
queathed by the 'dead century' revealed the inadequacy of 'mere
trade and wealth to develop international amities and to elevate
the spiritual capacities of man.'[4] This same magazine, poll conscious even then, stated: ..."the consensus of opinion centers
upon imperialism and war as being the greatest dangers confronting
humanity at the present day."[5] More critical in tone was Elizabeth
Bisland's indictment of the tyranny of commercialism and milita-
rism. It was plain that the old formula would not serve the new
generation. She wondered, "Will the new generation evolve some

---

Benjamin O. Flower, "The Last Century as a Utilitarian Age,"
The Arena, XXV (March, 1901) 280.
[2] J. D. Whelpley, R. R. Wilson, "Great Tasks of the New
Century." The World's Work 1 (January, 1901) 285.
[3] "The Twentieth Century," The Century, LXI (January, 1901) 473
[4] The Literary Digest, XXII (January 5, 1901) 6.
[5] Ibid., XXII (January 12, 1901) 35.

thought undreamed of, some new and happier guess at the great
central truth which forever allures and forever eludes our
grasp?"[6] The American in 1901, in regarding his country, was proud
of its progress, critical of abuses, and still hopeful for "the
better day."

Although the new century could serve as our period's dividing
line with twenty years before 1901 and fourteen years following,
others have suggested that the 1890's constituted the watershed.
Correctly appraising the Turner thesis, Harold U. Faulkner wrote:

> For three centuries the national social, economic, and
> political life had been dominated by one outstanding
> influence, an abundance of unoccupied and fertile land...
> Already in 1890 the unsettled area was so broken into
> that the frontier line had ceased to exist, and by the
> close of the decade the nation faced a situation unlike
> that had gone before.
>   The rapidly diminishing supply of good free land,
> while only one of the forces destined to mold social
> growth in the new century, was probably the most impor-
> tant.[7]

Thomas Beer saw "the Gay Nineties" as The Mauve Decade, while
Fred Lewis Pattee wrote of them:

> ... the decade was a culmination; it was the end of an
> era; it was an equinox between two creative periods, a
> moment of pause, of sterility, an Indian summer, silent,
> hectic with colors, dreamy with the past, yet alive with
> mighty gathering forces. The vital twentieth century
> was opening; in reality it began in the nineties.[8]

-----

[6]Elizabeth Bisland, "The Time-Spirit of the Twentieth Century,"
The Atlantic Monthly, LXXXVII (January, 1901) 22.
    [7]Harold U. Faulkner, The Quest for Social Justice, 1898-1914, p.
2.
    [8]Fred Lewis Pattee, The New American Literature, 1890-1930, p.
3.

In the same vein, the nineties were significant years for the
Catholic Church in America for the Catholic layman continued to
emerge from his passive role in Church affairs; and the results of
his cooperation with the clergy could be seen in the lay congresses
the Catholic exhibit at the Chicago Columbian Exposition, and the
various Catholic "Chautauquas" (also known as Summer Schools)
established during the decade. (Such was the enthusiasm among
certain Catholics for promoting things both American and Catholic,
that it occasioned a reprimand from Rome.[9]) For those Catholics
professing to be writers, this particular decade was not markedly
outstanding. No sharp line, such as Pattee envisioned, penetrated
their efforts, since, during this entire period, the several representative works could hardly overcome the handicaps imposed upon
Catholic literature (if it existed at all[10]) by the voluminous
exertions of the hopeful. None the less, a relationship existed
between these writers and their times. The creators of apologetic
fiction—— good advice and catechism lessons fabricated to tell a
moral tale—— were in accord with the older American Romanticism in
the 1880's; while the founders of The Dolphin, The America, and The
Catholic Encyclopedia were attuned to their contemporaries' desire
for presenting the facts to the new century. Throughout the entire

---

[9]Rev. Thomas T. McAvoy, C.S.C., "Americanism, Fact and
Fiction," American Catholic Historical Review, XXXI (July, 1945)
145-146.
     [10]Rev. Stephen J. Brown, S.J., Thomas McDermott, A Survey of
Catholic Literature, p.147.

period, Catholics shared the belief of their fellow Americans in the power of the printed word to bring about great change and reform.

As early as 1876, one of the many ambitious Irish editors, Peter Hickey, advertised, in keeping with Pope Pius IX' plea, to inundate the country with good literature;

> A special feature of the Catholic Review will be its notices of Catholic books as well as of the chief secular works of the day. We shall urge, in season and out of season, Catholics to read more largely Catholic litera- ture, to aid in establishing libraries and book clubs.[11]

Father Francis Weninger, S.J., a great missionary, that same year declared "every Catholic in America" ought to be able, both publicly and privately, to give testimony of his faith. Yet, few were able to do this in spite of "the many books of instruction written for this purpose."[12] Four years later, the Catholic World, one of the great uplifting journals of any generation, suggested a solution:

> The light and active operations of the periodical press are most especially suited to the present and immediate exigencies for the cause we have in hand, the diffusion of Catholic knowledge, the disspiation of popular errors, the general promotion of religion, virtue, intellectual, moral, social, and political well-being, by the inculcation of Catholic principles.[13]

Jose Rose Greene Hassard advanced the further concern (1882) that the sale of Catholic books published within the last ten years lagged far behind the "copies sold of similar books twenty years

---

[11] Rev. Francis X. Weninger, S.J., Centennial Address to the Catholics of the United States, p.17.

[12] Ibid., p.5.

[13] "Introductory" Catholic World, XXXI (April, 1880) 4.

ago."[14] The Catholic publishers had tried hard to find material
appealing to the Catholic public but the response was discouraging.
One critic observed that men whose reading was confined to the
daily papers, could not be considered as having "literary inclinations."[15]

Happily, a nucleus organized in various societies for young men
did have literary inclinations. Isolated at first in particular
parishes and cities, the pioneer literary societies exposed their
members to debates, the reading of essays, and to the discussion
of authors. The fortunate maintained a reading room and library.
The National Union of Young Men's Catholic Associations, in 1875,
asked these various societies to unite in order to perfect their
cultural aspirations and to indoctrinate them further in Catholic
traditions and beliefs. The Union's success and strength varied
with the years; but, its faith in good reading never wavered and,
in 1881, it urged that Catholic reading matter be supplied to
American military posts.[16] Although the young men's organized
literary societies probably preceded those of the Catholic young
ladies by some twenty-eight years,[17] one had to admire the efforts

[14]John R. G. Hassard, "Literature and the Laity," Catholic
World, XXXVI (October, 1882) 6.
[15]"Book Review, The Constitution and Proceedings of the
Catholic Young Men's National Union," Catholic World, XXXV (April,
1882) 136.
[16]James A. White, The Founding of Cliff Haven, Early Years of
the Catholic Summer School of America, p.5.
[17]Ibid., p.3.

of the distaff side. Borrowing the enthusiasm of the young men and adopting the very successful methods of the Chautauqua Reading Circles, the Catholic young ladies, in forming the Ozanam Reading Circle in 1886, inaugurated a trend which saw many similar societies organized within the succeeding fifteen years. It was these enthusiastic men and women of the Catholic sponsored reading circles, who supported the Catholic Summer School of America during its formative years. For the student of the Reading Circle and Summer School, reading was important. The Paulist Fathers indicated as much in advertising their Reading Circle "Union," (1892)

> The Columbian Reading Union is intended to be a useful auxiliary to the Catholic reading public. It endeavors to counteract wherever prevalent the indifference shown toward Catholic literature, and to suggest ways and means of acquiring a better knowledge of standard authors. The desired result can be advanced by practical methods of co-operation among those in charge of libraries, managers of Reading Circles, and others.[18]

The Columbian Reading Union was fortunate in securing the services of Father John Talbot Smith, author and historian. The opinions of the versatile Father Smith were extremely valuable because of his active interest in so many of the worthwhile Catholic interprises of this period. At the various Congresses and Summer School gatherings, he was an enthusiastic participant. Actors and actresses regarded him as a friend and protector. Moreover, his

---

[18]Rev. John Talbot Smith, List of Catholic Writers of Fiction, p. 2.

critical insight into American affairs attracted the attention of
editors on both sides of the Atlantic. Actually, Father Smith was
well aware of the needs of his co-religionists. With these needs
in mind, Father Smith drew up a list of the Catholic Writers of
Fiction (1892) for the purpose of aiding the Columbian Reading
Union members in their search for Catholic reading material. It
was an imperfect list, Father Smith warned, relying on publishers'
catologues and possibly out-of-print books. Nonetheless, a purpose
was served. A further tribute to reading was made by the editor of
the Catholic Citizen of Milwaukee, Humphrey J. Desmond. In his
booklet, A Reading Circle Manual (1903), he wrote:

> Risen from the ranks. Poor boy becomes rich man. Little
> schooling, nevertheless——statesman! Cooper, Greeley,
> Lincoln——the procession is endless...
>   But how did they rise? Primarily, the cause lay in
> the fact that they had brains...Where did these men get
> their brains, their ideas, their mighty conceptions, aims,
> purposes?
>   These men read. Their fund of information was not
> gathered at the corner grocery, but from the great books
> of the world.[19]

In the Nineties, that decade revered by Pattee and rebuffed by
Beer, at least three "how and what to read" books were published
under Catholic auspices. "We must choose those books which will
teach us the right in principle and the good in taste," (1893)
wrote the Jesuit Father John Francis Xavier O'Conor.[20] A similar

---

[19]Humphrey J. Desmond, A Reading Circle Manual, p.77.
[20]Rev. John Francis Xavier O'Conor, S.J., Reading and the
Mind, with Something to Read, p.12. (Revised Fifth Edition)

sentiment was shared by the Paulist, Rev. James Louis O'Neil,
writing in 1893, "Not as a panacea for humanity's ills would I offer
literature, but surely as a great element in elevating, refining,
and reforming man."[21] The scholarly layman, Brother Azarias
Mullany advised (1896) that since "we cannot read everything...we
must confine ourselves to a selection of subjects, small in number
and limited in range."[22] Continuing with the common sense, Brother
Azarias counselled that subjects selected should be in accord with
"both our mental acquirements and our daily occupations." All
three writers referred their readers to not only acceptable works
of Catholics but to such time-tested favorites as Tennyson, Ruskin,
and George Eliot as well. As for reading non-Catholic works, the
Pastoral Letter of 1884 set the temper.

> Happily the store of Catholic literature, as well as works
> which, though not written by Catholics nor treating of
> religion, are pure, instructive, and elevating is now so
> large that there can be no excuse for running risk of
> wasting one's time with what is inferior, tainted, or
> suspicious.[23]

Early in the decade, the Boston _Pilot_ exultantly queried. "What
Catholic has not blessed GOD for the art of printing?"[24] The
Milwaukee editor and publisher, Humphrey J. Desmond, was not so sure

[21]Rev. James Louis O'Neil, O.P., _Why, When, How, and What We
Ought to Read_, p.6.
[22]Brother Azarias Mullany, F.S.C., _Books and Reading_, pp.8-9.
[23]Rev. Peter Guilday, (ed.) _The National Pastorals of the
American Hierarchy_, (1792-1919) p.249.
[24]_The Pilot_, Boston, (January 6, 1892.)

of printing's bounty and at least twice during the ten-year period

he evaluated the woes of American Catholic literature[25] and the

accomplishments of Catholic authors and publishers.[26] Catholic

publishers often emitted junk instead of literature. At Harvard,

admittedly no citadel of Catholicism, John La Farge found the

situation discouraging. (Circa 1897)

> In my sophomore year I was given two hundred dollars to
> spend on furnishing the Catholic room with suitable
> reading matter. I bought a supply of books from Kenedy
> and Benziger but after I'd put them on the shelves I
> noticed that nobody ever used them.[27]

This despondency did not end with the century, although the

belief in a book's ability to achieve either good or evil continued

unabated. To the question, "What constitutes an evil book?", the

Catholic World was of the opinion, "...that what lowers the

standard of belief in the existence of purity and honor in men and

women, holds the marriage bond and the sanctity of the family up to

scorn is poisonous."[28] Exactly two years later, the Catholic

World, after admitting that money had been lavished on "second and

third rate productions"[29] expressed the hope that enlightened

Catholics would "shake off the idea that good literature is a

---

[25] The Catholic Citizen, Milwaukee (July 29, 1893)
[26] Ibid., (January 29, 1896)
[27] Rev. John La Farge, S.J., The Manner is Ordinary, p.67.
[28] "The Columbian Reading Union," Catholic World, LXXIV (November, 1901) 276.
[29] Ibid., LXXVIII (November, 1903) 280.

fortuitous accident."[30] The remedy, of course, resided in reading.

You must begin at once with your suitable Catholic literature, with your guild, your society, your club, your good
advice... In my opinion, to teach the young to read is one
of the most essential parts of pastoral work... So, by
degrees, with the habit of reading would come the demand
for reading, and the Catholic boy would stir itself more
and more to supply better and better reading.[31]

As the century advanced, the organized assault on the lack of

reading declined. Humphrey Desmond noticed that a "periodic

lethargy" had overtaken the Reading Circle as early as 1903.[32] "The

death of Warren E. Mosher, March 22, 1906, reduced the number of

magazine editors who printed the activities of the various Reading

Circles in their journals."[33] After October, 1909, "The Columbian

Reading Union" department was discontinued by the Catholic World.

Still, Catholics were urged to read. The Rev. Charles L.O'Donnell,

C.S.C., wrote in the Catholic Educational Review that the main

problem confronting Catholic schools, academies, and colleges was

the promotion of the "right kind of reading."[34] Reading, for him,

was more than a mere acquaintance with facts, titles, names, dates;

it could be the cornerstone of knowledge. Later (1914), Father

O'Donnell with George N. Shuster, compiled a ten-page list of

[30]Ibid., LXXVIII (November, 1903) 280.
[31]Ibid., p.282.
[32]Desmond, op.cit., p.6.
[33]White, op.cit., p.94.
[34]Rev. Charles L. O'Donnell, C.S.C., "Reading in Secondary
Schools and Colleges," Catholic Educational Review, II (December,
1911) 898.

readings of special appeal for Catholics. The selections were
grouped under such designated topics as Devotional, Education,
History, Social Questions, Autobiography, Biography, Travel, Essays,
Poetry, Fiction. In the list, which included such distinguished
artists as Cardinal Newman and Henri Sienkiewicz, there was a strong
American representation. Named were Bishop Spalding, Brother
Azarias, Carleton Hayes, Father John A. Ryan, Agnes Repplier, Louise
Imogen Guiney, Marion Crawford, Maurice Francis Egan, Christian
Reid, Anna Sadlier and numerous others.[35] In spite of the sustained
interest in reading on the part of some right-thinking Catholics,
the general response was not heartening. In 1915 at the Twelfth
Annual Meeting of the Catholic Education Association at St. Paul,
Minnesota, the Rev. James J. Daly, S.J., lamented:

> Who will seriously maintain that a disregard or a contempt
> for books, among the rank and file of our Catholic popula-
> tion, helps them individually in their morals or their
> faith? Who will deny that it is an obstacle which pre-
> vents the Church from engaging the respectful attention of
> thousands who need most what the Church has to give?[36]

Reading, then, with its ability to instruct, was held to be a
most desirable habit to be acquired by the American Catholic. At
various intervals during these thirty-five years, various Catholics
had declared their high regard for good reading. During this time,
equally well-intentioned Catholics believed that they, through

---

[35]Rev. Charles L. O'Donnell, C.S.C., George L. Shuster,
Catholic Literature: A Reading List.
[36]Rev. James J. Daly, S.J., "Reading and Character," The
Catholic Mind XIII (December 22, 1915) 662, 663.

their writings, could provide reading material of particular
interest for Catholics.

Among those who held this latter belief were the "two honored
pioneers of the Catholic novel in America,"[37] Mrs. Mary Anne
Sadlier and Mrs. Anna Hanson Dorsey. Mrs. Sadlier, and Mrs. Dorsey,
converts to Catholicity, both had a sense of mission to stimulate
their coreligionists with the proper regard for faith, country, and
good behavior. Since Mrs. Dorsey was the elder by five years (an
ungentlemanly revelation), her work was treated first in this study.
She, the daughter of a naval chaplain, was born December 17, 1815.
Influenced by the Church's revival in England,[38] she and her
husband, Lorenzo, became Catholics in 1840. Several years later,
she began writing; and, in 1847, The Student of Blenheim Forest,
her first considerable work was published. This novel depicting
the conversion of a rich, young Virginian to Catholicity, indicated
the trend of the author's writings for the next forty years. Her
intentions were expressed in a preface to one of her novels.

> The object of this little narrative is to eulogize and as-
> sist in sustaining the great Catholic truth, that confi-
> dence in the mercy and wisdom of God is the best preserva-
> tive from temptation and despair, amid the tearful and
> sudden mutations of life.[39]

---

[37]Brother Azarias Mullany, F.S.C., op.cit., p.55.
[38]John D. Wade, "Anna Hanson Dorsey", V (Dictionary of American
Biography) 385.
[39]Mrs. Anna Hanson Dorsey to Rev. Daniel E. Hudson, C.S.C.,
Oriental Pearl, p.7.

In this same vein, she wrote to her friend, the Rev. Daniel E.
Hudson, C.S.C., the diminutive, extremely able editor of the Ave
Maria, that she hoped by blending religion with dramatic incident,
the interest of the young would be retained.[40] In her opinion, if
a stronger love of country was cultivated in the children, a much
better generation of citizens would result. Prompted by this
reasoning, Mrs. Dorsey introduced historical sketches into her work
Tangled Paths (1885) for that generation who did not remember anything concerning the Civil War.[41]

Nor did Mrs. Dorsey neglect the foreign-born in portraying the
lives of good, practicing Catholics. Oriental Pearl (1848), for
instance, disclosed the fortunes of a newly arrived, German immigrant family. Gustav Conradt, his daughter Marie, and his son-in-
law Henrich were able, through prayer and hard work, to realize a
"handsome net (sic) profit"[42] from their farm in this haven, the
United States of America. Naturally, Oriental Pearl praised the
German people. There was a general commendation for their industry
which had its own reward, material success. Specifically, Casper
Krunfeldt was noted for his kindness to newly arrived immigrants;[43]

---

[40]Ltr. (Undated. Year 1879 assigned by UND archivist). Mrs.
Anna Hanson Dorsey to Rev. Daniel E. Hudson, C.S.C. The columinous
correspondence of those writing to the Rev. Daniel E. Hudson is
housed in the archives of the University of Notre Dame, Notre Dame,
Indiana. Henceforth, the Notre Dame Archives will be designated
UNDA.
[41]Anna Hanson Dorsey to Rev. Daniel E. Hudson, C.S.C., (March
27, 1877) Hudson Papers, UNDA.
[42]Anna Hanson Dorsey, The Oriental Pearl, p.161.
[43]Anna Hanson Dorsey, op.cit., p.51.

Mrs. Scheff, the grocer's wife, for aiding her destitute country-women;[44] and Marie Conradt for her benignity to the orphan Katrine.[45] The German priest in America, also, fared extremely well in a comparison with the venerable old paster in the Fatherland.[46] Thus, the overall effect of this piece was to urge upon the German people the realization that the United States held many, brilliant promises for them, especially if they remained loyal to their God.

Like the German immigrant in <u>Oriental Pearl</u>, the Irish immigrant was singled out for particular treatment in <u>Nora Brady's Vow</u> (1869). Again, the virtues of thrift and industry were lauded:

> With a few boarders, a small grocery, and two cows, they not only lived comfortably, but had saved money and pur-chased property, affording another proof that with equal opportunities, the Irish are as thrifty as any people under the sun.[47]

Then, too, some of the prosperous Irish in America gladly helped the newly arrived. Mr. Donahoe of the <u>Pilot</u> befriended many a poor girl who was looking for a situation. One Boston Irishman said of Mr. Donahoe: "He's got the warm side left for his countrymen, sure, an' never thinks of trouble when he can do'em a good turn."[48] On the darker side, mention was made of those "bad Catholics" who gave "those outside" such a poor opinion of the Church.[49] Equally gloomy was the notice that some Irish Catholics were ashamed of

---

[44]Ibid., p.18.
[45]Ibid., p.131.
[46]Ibid., p.24.
[47]Anna Hanson Dorsey, Nora Brady's Vow, p.89.
[48]Anna Hanson Dorsey, op.cit., p.90.
[49]Ibid., p.95.

their religion.[50]

Mrs. Dorsey did not reserve her talents exclusively for the
Irish and the German. The Flemings (1869) showed how good example[51]
converted a New England Puritan family to Catholicity. Though for
a time, it cost them friend and fortune, the Flemings at the end of
foud hundred and forty-four pages were a success materially and more
important spiritually. The Old Gray Rosary[52] viewed events south
of the Mason-Dixon line illustrating the influence of a Catholic
slavewoman, a Catholic girl friend, and a good Catholic husband upon a fine Protestant wife. The necessity for making substantial
Catholic marriages was the theme of Warp and Woof (1887). Inter-
woven with its major ideal was the interesting problem of mis-
cengenation.[53] The quadroon's son, the image of his white father,
refused to give up his suit for the hand of the white girl. He
persisted in such a course in spite of his mother's protest, and
only a fatal horseback accident[54] prevented this Catholic man for
marrying. Two other stories, Palms and The Mad Penitent of Todi
(1887) differed from the rest by telling tales of Christianity
before its division into Catholicism and Protestantism. Palms
depicted the clash of pagan and Christian in ancient Rome. The Mad
Penitent of Todi, on the other hand, related the marvelous

[50] Ibid., p.109.
[51] Anna Hanson Dorsey, The Flemings, pp. 42, 63.
[52] Anna Hanson Dorsey, The Old Gray Rosary, p.134.
[53] Anna Hanson Dorsey, Warp and Woof, p. 144.
[54] Ibid., p.213.

transformation of Todi's most famous citizen from a worldly
degenerate into pious monk.

Mrs. Dorsey in her writings did not hesitate to review certain
problems. Consequently, slavery at its best was a miserable system
full of dread evil.[55] As for the taboo on waltzing, the Church had
said nothing.* "It's only some of the clergy who have made a fuss
about it."[56] In an Emily Post-like role she wrote, "She (the
bride) was dressed as a Catholic bride should always be——
modestly."[57] True to her dictum, historical personages such as
Jefferson, Adams, Burr, Clay, Randolph,[58] friends of Daniel
Boone,[59] and Sherman's Army[60] made brief one-line appearances on
her pages.

One result of Mrs. Dorsey's great writing effort was world-wide
recognition. Oriental Pearl, for example, was translated into
German and published in Vienna. In fact, the royal household of
Franz Joseph read and enjoyed the book.[61] In addition to the German
translation, other works were translated into French and Hindu-
stani.[62] In England, Cardinal Nicholas Wiseman and the Catholic
Earl of Shrewsbury admired her works.[63] The Scots wrote to her

---

[55]Anna Hanson Dorsey, Zoe's Daughter, p.410.
[56]Anna Hanson Dorsey, Warp and Woof, p.75.
[57]Anna Hanson Dorsey, Zoe's Daughter, p.596.
[58]Op.cit., p.206.
[59]Ibid., p.201.
[60]Anna Hanson Dorsey, Warp and Woof, p.242.
[61]New York Freeman's Journal, (January 2, 1897)
[62]The New World, (January 2, 1897), The Catholic News, (January 6, 1897)
[63]The Catholic News, (January 6, 1897)

American publisher that her <u>May Brooke</u> was the first Catholic book
published in Edinburgh since the days of John Knox.[64] Other honors
included tributed from both Pope Pius IX[65] and Pope Leo XIII[66] for
whom she expressed a great admiration. A personal friend was
Cardinal James Gibbons. It was Gibbons, then an Archbishop, who
planned to present <u>Tangled Paths</u> and some of her other works to the
Holy Father.[67] The Laetare Medal, the University of Notre Dame
annual award to Catholics prominent in promoting the Church's
welfare in America, was awarded her in 1889.[68]

Notre Dame, which honored Mrs. Dorsey, was nonetheless a source
of criticism of her writings. On one occasion, she threatened to
cease writing for the <u>Ave Maria</u> because the University's president,
the Rev. Edward Sorin, C.S.C., had criticized her work.[69] That
threat never materialized, for two years later, Mother Angela
Gillespie, C.S.C., president of Saint Mary's Academy, Holy Cross,
Indiana, criticized Mrs. Dorsey's <u>Adrift</u> as being fit only for a
sensational romance magazine and not appropriate for the pages of
the <u>Ave Maria</u>.[70] Since many of the author's stories appeared in

---

[64] Ibid.

[65] <u>New York Freeman's Journal</u>, (January 2, 1897)

[66] Anna Hanson Dorsey to Rev. Daniel E. Hudson, C.S.C., (March
13, 1878) Hudson Papers, UNDA.

[67] Dorsey to Hudson, (February 11, 1880) Hudson Papers, UNDA.

[68] <u>The Laetare Medal: America's Golden Rose</u>, (Pamphlet) UNDA.
Laetare Medalist Dossier.

[69] Dorsey to Hudson, (January 2, 1887) Hudson Papers, UNDA.

[70] Dorsey to Hudson, (May 20, 1879) Hudson Papers, UNDA.

that magazine in serial form, it was not surprising to learn of Mother Angela's complaint of the 'never ending story.'[71] Mrs. Dorsey's favorite editor, Father Hudson, thought some of her serials were lengthy;[72] and, on one occasion, advised her to omit the Italian phrased[73] in the future installments of one serial.

Mrs. Dorsey, therefore, had her critics as well as her admirers; and she had one particular contemporary, Mary Anne Sadlier, with whom she shared the literary limelight. This other pioneer of the American Catholic novel was born Mary Anne Madden in Cootehill, Ireland, December 30, 1820. The daughter of a merchant, she was suitably educated for her future role of author and translator. Her first work, translations, appeared in La Belle Assemblee,[74] a London publication. Eventually, she migrated to Canada and in November, 1846, she married James Sadlier,[75] the Montreal branch manager of D. and J. Sadlier and Company. For the next fourteen years, she lived in Montreal[76] and accomplished much of the work that brought her fame. Three divisions marked Mrs. Sadlier's literary efforts: the historical Irish romances; the devotional religious pieces, both originals and translations; and

---

[71]Dorsey to Hudson, (June 10, 1879) Hudson Papers, UNDA.
[72]Dorsey to Hudson, (June 27, 1879), (April 1, 1886) UNDA.
[73]Dorsey to Hudson, (March 13, 1886) Hudson Papers, UNDA.
[74]Richard J. Purcell, "Sadlier, Mary Anne Madden," Dictionary of American Biography, XVI (1935) 284.
[75]Thomas F. Meehan, "Sadlier, Mary Anne Madden," The Catholic Encyclopedia, XIII (February, 1912) 322, 323.
[76]Ibid.

fiction for the immigrant.[77] In all, she wrote about sixty novels treating with Irish historical episodes and the social, religious, and educational problems of the Irish in America.

> To the latter, she strongly recommended pride of background, reconciliation of the customs of the New World, Americanization without secularization, and compromise between the old folks and the American born children. Thus, she performed a real service beyond entertainment, and as social studies some of her books retain a pronounced value.[78]

Furthermore, one observer was doubtful whether a single author could be found "whose works exerted in their day...a wider, deeper, or more beneficial influence than those of Mrs. James Sadlier."[79] Other fictionists, it was admitted, were more artistic, but few more effective.[80] Thus, she embraced the rapidly growing Irish-American community, and slanted her writings to protect her countrymen from temptation and the Church from assault. Several of her books, aimed at solving the current religious-social problems, were done at the request of other prominent Catholics. Hence, Bessie Conway (1885), illustrating the plight of the Irish girl in domestic service, was written at the suggestion of the great Paulist leader, Father Isaac Hecker.[81] The New York Catholic Protectory, a project of the warm-hearted convert, Dr. Levi Silliman Ives,[82] was at his bidding, promoted in Aunt Honor's

---

[77] The Catholic News, (April 11, 1903)
[78] Richard J. Purcell, op. cit.
[79] William D. Kelly, "A Benefactress of Her Race," Notre Dame Scholastic, XXVIII (March 23, 1895) 405.
[80] Ibid.
[81] Ibid., p. 407.
[82] Ibid.

Keepsake (1890). Different in nature was her translation of a life
of the Blessed Virgin Mary to fulfill the request of Archbishop
John Hughes[83] of New York.

Here, it should be noted that the range of Mrs. Sadlier's
literary ability extended beyond fiction and translation. She contributed essays and editorials as well as fiction to such periodicals as the New York Tablet, New York Freeman's Journal, Boston
Pilot, The American Celt, and The Literary Garland. After his
death, she edited the poems of Thomas D'Arcy McGee;[84] and, for a
time, she was an editor of the New York Tablet,[85] when it was
controlled by the Sadlier's. With Mother Angela Gillespie, C.S.C.,
she compiled a Catechism of Sacred History and Doctrine;[86] and she
alone revised (1889) an American edition of Dr. I. Schuster's,
Illustrated Bible History of the Old and New Testaments for the Use
of Catholic Schools.[87] The Young Ladies Reader (1885), a compila-
tion, was presented to the teachers of the more advanced classes in
Catholic Female Schools "to help elevate the literary taste of our
young girls, and inspire them with a love for really good reading
in prose and poetry."[88]

----

[83]Ibid.
[84]The Catholic News, (April 11, 1903)
[85]Ibid.
[86]Richard J. Purcell, op.cit.
[87]I. Schuster, Illustrated Bible History of the Old and New
Testaments for the Use of Catholic Schools, (New York, Wm. H.
Sadlier, 1889)
[88]Mrs. James Sadlier, The Young Ladies Reader, Compiled and
Arranged for Advanced Classes, VI.

Concerning the author's translations, many were of a religious nature treating such subjects as Our Lord, Jesus Christ, the Blessed Virgin Mary, Saint Joseph, and Saint Elizabeth of Hungary. Studies of the doctrinal problems of the Immaculate Conception and of the existence of the devil along with a French catechism and Father Auguste Riche's sociological treatise on The Family also were translated. At least two French novels appeared in her translation and both were in keeping with Mrs. Sadlier's desire of being an inspiration for Catholics. She emphatically declared in the preface to The Orphan of Moscow (1849):

> Should even one young heart be weaned from the career of folly and dissipation by the sage precepts here laid down ...then will the translator's trouble be well repaid.[89]

This novel revealed the fortitude of the pious French families of Moscow, which enabled them to endure the successes and reverses of Bonaparte's Russian campaign. Suffering was also the keynote of The Knout, A Tale of Poland[90] (1856) which portrayed the plight of the Poles during the Russian occupation of the 1830's. Mrs. Sadlier believed that Catholics could read this latter translation "with safety, if not profit."

Toward this same end, the author directed her fictional efforts. Admittedly, Mrs. Sadlier's fiction had two aspects: one telling the tales of Old Ireland, the other portraying the life of

---

[89]Madme. Woillez, The Orphan of Moscow, tr. Mrs. James Sadlier, V.
[90]The Knout, A Tale of Poland, tr. Mrs. James Sadlier, V.

the Irish in North America. The purpose of the former was to glorify those living in the "old country." The preface to New Lights or Life in Galway (1885) stated this admirably.

> To the faithful and much enduring people of Ireland, to
> those who still cling with undying love to the beautiful
> land of their birth, enduring all things rather than
> break asunder the tie which binds them to the Niobe of
> Nations!, and to those who, like myself, have left the
> graves of our fathers to seek a home beneath foreign
> skies all alike bound together by one glorious bond: our
> ancient, our time honored, our never changing faith --
> to them do I dedicate this little work.[91]

To serve this purpose, particular pieces described Galway, the Claddagh of Galway, Cashel, and the perilous times of the Irish under Queen Elizabeth and during the rebellion of 1641. These were the tales of the one true Faith, of strife, of plots against authority, of trials allegedly unjust, of Protestant proselytizing Catholic school children, of the cottage, potato garden and poverty. From this and "bearing all things with resignation," the true Irish emerged: brave, pious, "chaste as the snow," humble, patient, temperate, kind, generous and hospitable. Typical of these tales was The Fate of Father Sheehy (1863). Father Sheehy "turned to the bag" (assumed a beggar's disguise) to evade being captured by Orangemen. Eventually, however, he was brought to trial and convicted, thanks to the perjury of Moll Dunlea and Jácky Lonergan, the devil's own boy. The doom of Father Sheehy was

---

[91]Mrs. James Sadlier, New Lights or Life in Galway, V.

spelled in Mrs. Sadlier's words. "By the power, if Saint Peter himself came down an' proved Father Sheehy innocent, his oath wouldn't be believed agin Moll Dunlea's or Jacky Longergan.[92] The unfortunate priest was hanged, his body drawn and quartered, his head hung from a pole. Shortly after this event, Moll Dunlea fell down cellar to her death— "the thread of life cut short by the avenging hand of God."[93] Ill fortune befell Jacky Lonergan[94] and the jury also as Father Sheehy's innocence was proven.

This religious struggle with necessary modifications was featured in Mrs. Sadlier's North American fiction. Added to it was her desire to establish a true standard for the Catholic Irish in America. She wrote in 1855:

> It is needless to say that all my writings are dedicated to the one grand object: the illustration of our holy faith by means of tales or stories.[95]

Thirty years later, she continued to admonish the descendants of the Catholic Irish in America for lending themselves to the senseless folly, "the un-Catholic prejudice that here makes the word Irish synonymous with disgrace."[96] Mrs. Sadlier carefully added that she would not have them love America less but she would have them more respectful of Ireland and their Irish ancestry.

---

[92] Mrs. James Sadlier, The Fate of Father Sheehy, p.127.
[93] Ibid., p.123.
[94] Ibid.
[95] Mrs. James Sadlier, The Blakes and Flanagans, VI.
[96] Mrs. James Sadlier, Old and New, p.485.

The economic, social, and religious ideals for the Irish in
America were contained in her "stories" as she called them. Old
and New (1885) scorned those Irish who, ashamed of kith and kin,
imitated Yankee ways and Yankee speech.[97] On the other hand,
Con O'Regan (1885) praised the effort to get the immigrants out of
the crowded cities and on to the farms in the interior, in Con's
case Iowa.[98] Aunt Honor's Keepsake (1890) did more than indicate
the need of Catholic institutions for destitute children. Tenement
life with its attending evils of crowded rooms,[99] filth, drinking
(of gin), and the poverty which prompted the boys to steal a loaf
of bread were a part of this story. The convicted bread thieves[100]
were sent to the House of Refuge where no priest could penetrate
either on Sunday or at the hour of an inmate's death.[101] Under the
eye of superintendent Mr. Watchem,[102] the Catholicity was trained
out of Honor O'Grady's nephew, Charley. Poor little Kevin O'Byrne
was tormented by Mr. Watchem's insistence upon calling him King
O'Byrne.[103] The author in a footnote told how a New York House of
Refuge sent boys and girls West where they were sold at auction.[104]
This fact appeared in the narrative as Charley was sent to the
Illinois frontier. Not so surprisingly, Charley, through the

[97]William D. Kelly, op.cit., p.407.
[98]Mrs. James Sadlier, Con O'Regan, p.226.
[99]Mrs. James Sadlier, Aunt Honor's Keepsake, p.26.
[100]Ibid., p.49.
[101]Ibid., p.139
[102]Ibid., p.56.
[103]Ibid., p.133.
[104]Ibid., p.160.

influence of good Catholics and the genius of Mrs. Sadlier's pen,
was won back to the Church.

The danger of permitting Catholic children to attend the
"Godless public schools" exposed itself in The Blakes and the
Flanagans,[105] (1873) a work contrasting two Irish families and
their adjustment to the American way. The one remaining faithful to
the Irish traditions was rewarded with prosperity, satisfactory
Catholic marriages, and a houseful of grandchildren. The other,
having gone American, suffered mixed marriages, indifference and
disrespect from the children, the son's embracing free masonry, an
unhappy death, and loneliness. Concerning specific school pro-
plems, the book declared that New York could boast of Catholic
schools as good as any on the Western Continent,[106] that the school
house was second only to the House of God,[107] and finally, that the
children's religious instruction depended upon parental instruction.[108]

Bessie Conway[109] warned the girls of the perils awaiting them
in domestic service. The serving girl Bessie, through her excellent
demeanor, converted and eventually married the young master, Henry
Herbert. "That was the making of the Conway's, as the neighbors
used to say."[110] The book, furthermore, urged the girls to win the

---

[105]Mrs. James Sadlier, The Blakes and the Flanagans, pp.22-38.
[106]Ibid., p.377.
[107]Ibid., p.391.
[108]Ibid., p.390.
[109]Mrs. James Sadlier, Bessie Conway, III, IV.
[110]Ibid., p.315.

confidence and respect of their employers;[111] send some money
home[112] and not be spending it all on clothes.[113] Savings were to
be preferred to pawn shops.[114] As for saloonkeepers, they were not
to take a drop too much as did Neddie Finnigan,[115] the proprietor
of that fine public house Ardfinnan Castle.

Mrs. Sadlier's writings, like Mrs. Dorsey's, passed judgment on
certain situations. Not all Irishmen "were so fond of the
drink."[116] Tim Reilly drank neither mint juleps nor sherry-
cobblers, in fact, he eschewed all other bacchanalian devices.[117]
(He was good to his mother, you may be assured.[118]) As for dancing,
there would not have been a curse on it if they had stuck to jigs
and reels.[119] She was equally appalled at the vandalism of the
Irish mobs on New Year's[120] and the affectation of some saying Bon
Soir for Good Night.[121] Above all, she cited the good example of
her fellow Catholics that did so much to win an understanding for
the one, true, Faith. Mrs. Sadlier's stories approached authenti-
city since they were based on existing conditions which so harassed

---

[111] Ibid., V.
[112] Ibid., p.137.
[113] Ibid., p.135.
[114] Ibid., p.136.
[115] Ibid., p.135.
[116] Mrs. James Sadlier, Aunt Honor's Keepsake, p.27.
[117] Mrs. James Sadlier, The Blakes and The Flanagans, p.387.
[118] Ibid., p.388.
[119] Ibid., p.151.
[120] Ibid., p.263.
[121] Ibid., p.152.

the Irish in their adopted land. Her dialogue, also attempted
to be real. Hence the ailing Mrs. Dillon "was not long for this
world;"[122] or, to the confusion was added a "whole rigimunt of
children runnin' in and out of the street."[123]

For this great effort in aiding and guiding her co-religionists, Mrs. Sadlier achieved prominence in her time. She received
the Laetare Medal[124] in 1895 and a special blessing from Pope Leo
XIII[125] in 1902. The Blakes and The Flanagans went through a
German edition entitled Alt Irland und America.[126] In this
fashion, Mrs. Sadler joined Mrs. Dorsey in a writing campaign to
improve the cultural backgrounds of Catholics in America. They were
the pioneers and following them, equally purposeful Catholics
inundated this country with their literary good intentions. One of
the more productive writers of this later generation was Frances
Christine Fisher Tiernah who wrote under the name of Christian
Reid. She was born south of the Mason-Dixon line is Salisbury,
North Carolina, July 5, 1846. An aunt, Miss Christine Fisher,
raised Frances, her brother and sister, since the children's mother
had died prior to the war and their father had been killed in

---

[122]Ibid., p.216.
[123]Mrs. James Sadlier, Aunt Honor's Keepsake, p.27.
[124]Richard J. Purcell, op.cit.
[125]Ibid.
[126]Ibid.

action leading his regiment at Manassas.[127] Fortunately,
Miss Fisher was another convert to Catholicity.

> The influence of their aunt's fine example of Christian
> womanhood did not leave the children long undecided, but
> in each case the decisive step was not taken until the
> years of maturity had been attained.[128]

Consequently, Frances Christine Fisher herself was a convert; and
she was confirmed December 15, 1868, by the Vicar-Apostolic of
North Carolina, James Gibbons.

Two years later, this young Catholic author, under her pseudo-
nym Christian Reid, published Valerie Aylmer (1870), a novel
selling eighteen thousand seven hundred copies in a few months.[129]
Christian Reid, in this and several other novels gave the impression unmistakably that the best life in the United States had been
in the "Old South." A letter written to Father Hudson protesting
the inaccuracy of a serial currently appearing in the Ave Maria
attested to this conviction.

> There is no Southerner who would not be indignant at the
> revival of old anti-slavery slander contained in that
> effusion. They are so absurd as they are false to one
> who knows the truth of the old relations between master
> and slave... Catholics who know so well what it is to be
> slandered should be able to realize that the bitter
> enemies of a system or a people are not exactly fitted to
> describe either with truth.[130]

---

127 Kate Harbes Becker, Biography of Christian Reid, p.10.
128 Ibid., p.15.
129 Ibid., p.20.
130 Christian Reid to Rev. Daniel Hudson, C.S.C., (February 9,
1886) Hudson Papers, UNDA.

Naturally, not all of her settings were in the South. After her marriage in 1887, she and her husband James M. Tiernan traveled to Mexico[131] where Mr. Tiernan reopened several silver-lead mines. Mexico, obviously, became the background for Carmela (1891), The Picture of Las Cruces, The Land of the Sun, A Daughter of Sierra and others. The Old World,[132] specifically Paris, Rome, Switzerland, Europe in general or Bohemia as she called this playground also served as settings. Christian Reid in all wrote nearly fifty novels.[133]

Her writings expressed varied degrees of Catholicity. Some novels made only casual but favorable reference to things Catholic such as a pretty church, a good priest, the peace reflected in a nun's face. Others were piled, page upon page, with explanations of the Faith. The Plantation Series fell into the first category. Morton House (1871) depicted the anything but triumphant return from abroad of Pauline Morton. Society shunned her while covetous eyes were cast at her house. After her son killed her husband,[134] she gave Morton House to the one young relative who had befriended her. Mabel Lee[135] (1871) told of a "violet eyed darling" who suffered mesmerism, insanity, and abduction before she fell swooning into the arms of her intended at the end. A young man's

---

[131]Kate Harbes Becker, op.cit., p.77.
[132]Ibid., p.52.
[133]Sara G. Bowerman, "Tiernan, Frances Christian Fisher," Dictionary American Biography, XVI (1936) 531, 532.
[134]Christian Reid, Morton House, (New York, D. Appleton, 1871) p.260.
[135]Christian Reid, Mabel Lee.

dilemma of being engaged simultaneously to a girl and her step-sister was the featured problem of A Daughter of Bohemia[136] (1873). Two others, Bonnie Kate (1878) and Hearts and Hands (1875) composed this series of five.

The strictly Catholic novels included A Child of Mary, Secret Bequest, and The Light of the Vision (1911). In A Child of Mary (1885), a young French Catholic heiress came to live with her uncle in a strictly Protestant southern town. Her good example converted a divinity student while her fortune built the town's first Catholic Church, Our Lady of the Sacred Heart.[137] Secret Bequest (1915) viewed the plight of another heiress who was required to win her cousin away from Catholicity as a condition of her inheritance. Needless to say, the temporary heiress married the Catholic and happily renounced the fortune.[138] The Light of the Vision con-scientiously related the conversion of a young divorcee and her subsequent good influence upon an erring husband and a none too Catholic suitor.[139] This theme of divorce and Catholic marriage appeared again in Vera' Charge (1907) and His Victory (1887).

In her novels, Christian Reid gave vent to her opinions. It was not easy, she declared, for a Catholic to have a spectacular time in this world.[140]

[136]Christian Reid, A Daughter of Bohemia.
[137]Christian Reid, A Child of Mary, p.219.
[138]Christian Reid, Secret Bequest, p.341.
[139]Christian Reid, The Light of the Vision, p.291.
[140]Christian Reid, His Victory, p.70.

Life is meant for something better than mere living for
one's own interest or one's own pleasure; and I think we
both see that the other existence is within our reach.[141]

Americans were foolish to live abroad while their homes here

decayed.[142] Equally violent was her reaction to bachelor-girls

living in crowded New York apartments.[143] Moreover, little

children should not be permitted to drink brandy.[144] More important

than her opinions expressed above were her continual expoundings of

Catholic ideals. She wrote of prayer:

> The end was no doubt near and those who were Catholic, as
> they turned away, dropped into the nearest church to pray
> for this soul in its agony.[145]

Forty Hours Devotion in Saint Peter's, Rome, was deemed beauti-

ful[146] and there was wonder in the strained windows of Chartres

Cathedral.[147] The author commented on the Pope's being the central

head[148] of the Church and upon the delightful custom of having

religious statues in a room in the house.[149]

In addition to this religious content, she like Mrs. Dorsey,

introduced historical events into her fiction. So, allusions to

the adventurous Conquistadores in Mexico (especially to the Noche

Triste),[150] and to the Piedmontese[151] storming the Vatican in 1870

---

[141] Christian Reid, Armine, p.359.
[142] Christian Reid, Morton House, p.15.
[143] Christian Reid, Vera's Charge, p.170.
[144] Christian Reid, Morton House, p.34.
[145] Christian Reid, Heart of Steel, p.530.
[146] Ibid., p.535.
[147] Christian Reid, The Light of the Vision, p.7.
[148] Christian Reid, A Child of Mary, p.86.
[149] Ibid., p.35.
[150] Christian Reid, Carmela, p.348.
[151] Christian Reid, Armine, p.6.

were not unusual. Included, also, was the fact that not all of

Scotland had abandoned the "old religion."[152]

Contemporary criticism concerning her novels varied. For in-

stance, Maurice Francis Egan wrote:

> The truth is that Christian Reid did not appeal to the
> great public because she lived in a dreamland, a very
> beautiful dreamland, an exquisite and lovely and unap-
> proachable country which existed just as little as the
> land of the "Princess Lointaine."[153]

The critics further felt that her writings lacked deep intellectual

perception, that her characters were not well developed,[154] and that

she possessed no humor.[155] On the other hand, they praised the

excellence of her narrative and the wit of her dialogue.[156] Some of

this dialogue, nonetheless, tended to be theatrical. For example,

"You are my sun— the only one thing which can give light and

fragrance to my life."[157] This was surpassed in another novel:

> They looked into each other's eyes and they read there the
> love and faith that had never faltered with either, and
> were forever beyond the things of Earth and Time.[158]

Contrarily, John Gilmary Shea, when editor of Leslie's Weekly,

admitted, "I am publishing the best novel I have ever printed but I

can not make it go."[159] (Bonnie Kate (1878) was the novel in

---

152Christian Reid, A Little Maid of Arcady, p.10.
153Maurice Francis Egan, "Christian Reid: A Southern Lady,"
America, XXII (April 24, 1920) 18,19.
154Ibid., p.18.
155Sara G. Bowerman, op.cit.
156Maurice Francis Egan, op.cit.
157Christian Reid, A Daughter of Bohemia, p.222.
158Christian Reid, Valerie Aylmer, p.221
159Maurice Francis Egan, op.cit.

question.) More positive was the opinion of Ella L. Dorsey, Anna
Hanson Dorsey's talented daughter, who wrote to Father Hudson, "we
are all charmed with Christian Reid's Carmela."[160] Anna T.
Sadlier,[161] Mrs. Sadlier's equally talented daughter, reported that
Doctor Orestes Brownson praised Morton House while Catholics and
non-Catholics alike enjoyed Valerie Aylmer, A Daughter of Bohemia
(1873), and Ebbtide (1872). The University of Notre Dame, as it
did in the cases of Mrs. Dorsey and Mrs. Sadlier, bestowed upon her
its Laetare Medal[162] in 1909. This was in recognition, no doubt,
that the fifty some novels, which flowed from her pen, had fulfilled
in some measure, her expressed intention of furnishing Catholics

> with reading matter which while amusing the fancy, will
> also instruct the mind and lead it to the contemplation
> of the beauty and holiness of religion.[163]

These three women, then, were representative of that group of
aspiring Catholics writing during this period 1880-1915. The convert played a key role in this effort as illustrated by Mrs. Dorsey
and Christian Reid, while Mrs. Sadlier gave evidence that those
born in the faith did not neglect their conceived obligation to
their fellow Catholics. Father John Talbot Smith thought Mary

---

[160]Ella L. Dorsey to Rev. Daniel Hudson, C.S.C., (July 18,
1890) Hudson Papers, UNDA.
[161]Anna T. Sadlier, "Christian Reid, The Tribute of a Fellow
Worker," Ave Maria, XI (April 17, 1920) 688.
[162]Sara G. Bowerman, op.cit.
[163]Christian Reid, Grace Morton, Preface.

Agnes Tincker a worthy contemporary of these three ladies. Miss

Tincker (1831-1907), however, only wrote three Catholic novels

before turning to write for the general public. This caused Father

Smith to lament:

> Miss Tincker had all a convert's enthusiasm, which deepened
> finally during her stay in Rome. Its temper may be seen
> in her Catholic novels which I have already quoted. What a
> grief it must have been to her, the suppression of her re-
> ligious emotions and thoughts in the novels which were
> written for the general public and which brought her fame
> and income.[164]

Miss Tincker in Rome, probably, anticipated Marion Crawford by a

decade. She liked the Italians and yielded to the telling of a

story from the Italian point of view, which was not always consis-

tent with true Catholic principles. However, her earlier works,

The House of Yorke (1872), Grapes and Thorns (1874), and A Winged

Word earned for her a place in Catholic letters and the deep regard

of Father Smith.[165] Mary Agnes Tincker, then, joined Mrs. Sadlier,

and Christian Reid to form the advance party of a group of

ambitious American women professing to be writers.

---

[164]Rev. John Talbot Smith, "Mary Agnes Tincker," Ave Maria,
LXIX (July 31, 1909) 146.

[165]Father Smith, in reviewing the career of Miss Tincker,
commented on the contemporary scene.

> And whereas the Catholic body in 1875 had noble representatives
> among the literary guild, in the year 1909 the number has
> diminished, because the Catholic writers have turned from their
> own people, who neither paid nor honored them, to a secular
> world which has honors and gold, appreciation and applause for
> such workers.

Smith, ibid.

CHAPTER II

STILL MORE NOVELISTS

Sadlier, Dorsey, Reid, and Tincker and the Catholic writers
following them did not become involved in the realists' effort to
dethrone romanticism as the guiding principle for American novelists. While Howells, Crane, Norris, and Dreiser proclaimed themselves to be realists, many other writers professed to be content
with romanticism and its trappings; and, Catholics found themselves
favoring (though not allied to) the latter group. The desire to
tell a good story, to guide and inspire adults as well as children,
and to illustrate some tenet of faith in an historical setting
seemed better served and achieved with the romantic forms. The
Catholics' good intention of showing their countrymen the ideal
American life was better adapted to the romantic style of writing
than to the realists' earthy observations. Moreover, those sharing
this fine intention, the talented writers and the merely ambitious
ones, constituted a sizeable section of Catholicism. Unfortunately,
some of the anthologists were attracted by the quantity of writers.

A contemporary tribute (1897) to the number of women writing
was fashioned by the Ursuline Nuns of New York who selected sample
writings of sixty-three women and presented these along with minute
biographies of their creators in a volume entitled Immortelles of

Columbian Literature[1] (1897). (Versatility seemed to be a prevalent fact for these women attempted prose, poetry, the short-story as well as the novel.)[2] Two years prior to the Ursuline publication, a literary Adirondacks physician, William A. McDermott, using the pen name Walter Lecky, honored a dozen of his co-workers by reviewing some of their contributions to Catholic letters. Benziger Brothers, keeping apace in 1896, published A Round Table of the Representative American Catholic Novelists,[3] a collection of shorter stories written by well known authors of the day, six women and five men. This list of twenty-one formed by Lecky's Down at Caxton's[4] (1895) and the Benziger selections shifted the emphasis from quantity to quality. Among the Benziger choices were two talented priests: the famed Father Francis J. Finn, S.J.; and the Rev. John Talbot Smith, novelist, editor, historian. Lecky's sound judgment prompted him to sing the praises of the novelists Richard Malcolm Johnston and Marion Crawford. (Of all the American novelists who professed Catholicity at this time, the convert Crawford enjoyed the greatest universal literary reputation.)

---

[1] Mother Seraphine, O.S.U., Immortelles of Catholic Columbian Literature.

[2] Annette S. Driscoll, Literary Convert Women. Mrs. Driscoll gives further testimony of the zeal and versatility which enabled converts on both sides of the Atlantic to contribute so much to their Church.

[3] Benziger Brothers, publishers, A Round Table of Representative American Catholic Novelists.

[4] William A. McDermott, Down at Caxton's.

As for Father Finn, according to George N. Schuster, eminent
educator and critic of Catholic affairs, the Jesuit priest "created
a Catholic juvenile literature in English."[5] Finn's contemporaries
were even more enthusiastic as one labeled him "the foremost
Catholic writer of fiction for young people."[6] Furthermore, he was
the first author "to give a picture of the American Catholic boy."[7]
Francis James Finn was born in St. Louis, Missouri, October 4, 1859.
Although a siege of malaria curtailed his youthful physical exertions, the compensating factor enabled him to pursue without dis-
traction his avid interest in literature. This interest, of course,
never deserted him.

Young Finn entered the Society of Jesus where he astounded his
fellow novices with his admitted ambition of becoming a novelist.

> I carried with me an intimate consciousness from the joys
> of romance of the power which the noble characters of
> fiction could exercise upon the young reader.[8]

The ambitious instructor found the inspiration and opportunity to
write while he was stationed at St. Mary's College, Kansas,— "at
that time an obscure and struggling preparatory school."[9]

> One of my duties was to supply the boys with reading for
> the refectory. I found it difficult to procure them fic-
> tion which would at once interest and elevate. There
> were few Catholic books of the kind I desired. It was

---

[5] George N. Schuster, "Finn, Francis James," _Dictionary_
American Biography, VI (1931) 392.
[6] Georgina Pell Curtis, _The American Catholic Who's Who_, p.204.
[7] Ibid.
[8] Francis X. Talbot, S.J.; _Fiction by Its Makers_, p.190.
[9] Schuster, _op.cit._

then the thought came to me that it would be a fine thing
to take Catholic boys as I found them—American boys with
Catholic training—and put them into stories.[10]

These early stories, Percy Wynn (1889) and Tom Playfair (1892),

usually acknowledged his best, attained "vast and almost immediate

popularity." Tom Playfair, the Michigan Catholic proclaimed as

"the best boy's book that ever came from the press."[11] Claude

Lightfoot (1893) evoked the warm praise of the Catholic World.

> But for a real bright, live book of the present day,
> redolent of youthful life and gaiety, faithful as the
> reflection of a mirror to the originals of modern boy
> life as beheld in many of our Catholic institutions, we
> have not as yet seen anyone who approaches this fine work
> of Father Finn....in this take the author has solved a
> problem which has often vexed the minds of other writers—
> the problem how to make a religious book as interesting to
> the average literary cormorant, boy or girl, as pirate or
> highwayman, or love-smitten imitator of Romeo.[12]

For nearly forty years, Father Finn continued to write—blending

"pranks, fun, shrewd observation, idealism, and deft moral teach-

ing."[13] Such books as Harry Dee (1893), Mostly Boys (1897), New

Faces and Old (1896), That Football Game (1897), His First and Last

Appearance (1900), That Office Boy (1915) helped him fulfill his

ambition of giving the "American Catholic small boy the kind of hero

he would like and strive to imitate."[14] More than twenty fiction

---

[10]Talbot, op.cit.
[11]Curtis, op.cit.
[12]"Talk About New Books," Catholic World, LVIII (December,
1893) 438.
[13]Schuster, op.cit.
[14]Talbot, op.cit., p.192.

pieces flowed from his pen. Naturally, the power of writing to influence others was readily recognized by the talented Jesuit.

> There are priests and Religious throughout the country who owe their vocations to the reading of Catholic books for Catholic boys, written by such authors as Father Copus, Spalding, Boyton, Holland, Gross, Conroy, McGrath, and Mrs. Waggaman and others.[15]

The Mrs. Waggaman, to whom Father Finn referred, was an amazing and gifted woman. Nearly all of her adult life (and she lived to be eighty-five) was spent in writing; so, it was not at all surprising that she should at the age of seventy-seven (1923) win a secular short-story contest over three thousand other writers.[16] (Irwin S. Cobb, humorist and author, had high praise for her prize-winning story.)

Mary Theresa Waggaman, however, had made her mark long before this in the realm of juvenile fiction.

> Few women have identified themselves so closely with childhood and youth. To begin with, she reared eleven sons and daughters of her own, in true Southern style. Then she turned nursery entertainment into story writing of her own, and published one book after another for the pleasure of Catholic children.[17]

Instead of being a detriment to the author's efforts, her large family proved to be a source of inspiration. Unable to find satisfactory books, those that "would 'sugar coat' piety and yet be interesting,"[18] to augment her eldest son's preparation for First

---

[15] Ibid., p.193.
[16] Mathew Hoehn, O.S.B., (editor) Catholic Authors, Contemporary Biographical Sketches, 1930-1947, p.756.
[17] "One Who Loved Children," Commonweal, XIV (August 26, 1931) 393.
[18] Hoehn, op.cit.

Communion (circa 1894), the resourceful Mrs. Waggaman wrote Little
Comrades, A First Communion Story, which was an instant success.[19]
Her family also served as the "proving ground" for her work as she
wrote to her editor, Father Hudson: "I hope you will like the
story. My 'home critics' who have read its opening prefer it to
Billy Boy (sic)— but that is of course a matter of taste."[20]
(Incidentally, in reference to Billy Boy (1912), a self-professed
script writer for that new medium, the movies, asked her permission
to adapt it for the "flickers.")[21] In another letter to Father
Hudson, a year later, Mrs. Waggaman admitted she was creating
another story which she hoped would be pleasing both to boys and
girls but "specially boys."[22] This preference suggested, perhaps,
either boys read more than girls, or were more in need of her
inspiration and guidance.

Billy Boy related the adventures of a young lad sent to
Colorado to regain his health at the Bar Cross ranch operated by his
older brother, Jack. Little did the boy suspect that his idolized
brother had taken to "evil ways" and that Jack's "next morning
Malaria"[23] was nothing more than a gargantuan hangover. (Billy, of

---

[19] Ibid.
[20] Mary T. Waggaman to Rev. Daniel E. Hudson, C.S.C., (December
7, 1911) Hudson Papers. UNDA.
[21] Herman Masters to Mary T. Waggaman, (February 10, 1915)
Hudson Papers. UNDA.
[22] Mary T. Waggaman to Rev. Daniel E. Hudson, C.S.C., (December
12, 1912) Hudson Papers. UNDA.
[23] Mary T. Waggaman, "Billy Boy," Ave Maria, LXXII (1911)
286.

course, at confirmation, had taken the pledge not to drink until he
was twenty-one.)[24] Through good example, heroism, prayers to the
Blessed Virgin Mary,[25] and blossoming business acumen, Billy Boy
reformed "Rackety" Jack and routed evil on all fronts. This tale
was quickly followed by the Secret of Pocomoke (1914), which the
"home critics" liked so well. Miss Pat, the young mistress of the
destitute Pocomoke plantation, was taken into the home of her
guardian. Here, wrote Mrs. Waggaman, she was introduced

> into cold worldly ways that she has never known.
> How this impulsive... little lady of Pocomoke bears
> this chilling environment and finally helps and serves
> will, I think make an interesting and lively story.[26]

In the process of being an inspiration to her guardian and his
family, the heroine expounded several of Mrs. Waggaman's ideas
concerning the contemporary scene. Social climbing,[27] the
exorbitant prices for clothes (ten dollars was too much to pay for
a hat),[28] parents permitting young men to drink[29] were objects of
her scorn. On one occasion, Miss Pat refused to read about the
Reformation after announcing to her teacher and classmates at the
fashionable Miss Benson's School, "I am a Catholic."[30] These two

---

[24] Ibid., p.412.
[25] Ibid., pp.125, 539.
[26] Mary T. Waggaman to Rev. Daniel E. Hudson, C.S.C., (December 7, 1911) Hudson Papers. UNDA.
[27] Mary T. Waggaman, "The Secret of Pocomoke," Ave Maria, LXXIV (1912) 381.
[28] Ibid., p.349.
[29] Ibid., p.446.
[30] Ibid., p.477.

stories, then, set the pattern for Mrs. Waggaman's fiction— a
pattern which was followed for many years according to one observer:
"Her books in later years were written with a desire to strengthen
the religious faith of young Catholic readers."[31]

Mrs. Waggaman took her mission to her fellow Catholics
seriously. For her, juvenile writing was not light, easy work. 'I
can truthfully say that I have given by juvenile writings the best
that is in me.'[32] This great effort did not go unnoticed. At
least on two occasions,[33] Ella Lorraine Dorsey, the daughter of
Anna Hanson Dorsey and an author in her own right, wrote to Father
Hudson and chattily informed him of Mrs. Waggaman's excellence. A
critic of a later day wrote of her various works:

> Most of these appeared serially in the Ave Maria, during
> the many years when that periodical was edited by the
> great, generous, discerning Father Hudson. As a result,
> Mrs. Waggaman gained an extraordinary wide reading public,
> though her work continued to be a labor of love in the
> sense that financial reward was never heaped high.[34]

Miss Dorsey also wrote for children and like Mrs. Waggaman, she
held this particular task in high esteem. It was nothing to be done
hastily. "I'll be glad to make a story for the children when I pull
together a bit," she wrote to her editor.[35] Midshipman Bob (1887)

[31]Hoehn, op.cit., p.756.
[32]"One Who Loved Children," op.cit., p.394.
[33]Ella Lorraine Dorsey to Rev. Daniel E. Hudson, C.S.C.,
(September 10, 1910), (August 19, 1914) Hudson Papers, UNDA.
[34]"One Who Loved Children," op.cit., p.394.
[35]Ella Lorraine Dorsey to Rev. Daniel E. Hudson, C.S.C.,
(September 2, 1888) Hudson Papers. UNDA.

was dedicated

> To Boys in General But Particularly to those who are
> pluckily Fighting their way against the World, the Flesh,
> and the Devil, Towards a Manhood worthy of their Faith,
> Their country and Themselves.[36]

In the same vein, Jet the War Mule (1894) was dedicated "to every

one of my dear Catholic boys and girls who is standing, or trying

to stand guard on the line of duty."[37] Miss Dorsey introduced

Catholicity into her stories in various ways. A fragment of

dialogue concerning a severely injured man illustrated the fact.

> 'Is it wise to excite him so by praying and — or —
> that?' asked the captain uneasily. 'Well, I do not
> know,' said the doctor thoughtfully. 'These Catholics
> are such queer fish, it seems to settle rather than
> upset them.'[38]

Other vestiges of her religion included an affirmation of the "Real

Presence"[39] in the tabernacle, of the duty to obey the Church's

teachings,[40] and the reminder that Our Lord did not die that we

might "get on" in Society.[41] A general observation was that

"...every well bred young person, white and colored, called the old

and respectable darkies, 'Uncle' and 'Auntie.'"[42] One remark might

have sorely tested the credulity of her young readers, when she

---

[36]Ella Lorraine Dorsey, Midshipman Bob, (Notre Dame, Indiana,
Joseph A. Lyons, 1887)
[37]Ella Lorraine Dorsey, Jet the War Mule, Ave Maria, (Notre
Dame, Indiana, 1894)
[38]Ella Lorraine Dorsey, Midshipman Bob, p.202.
[39]Ibid., p.215.
[40]Ibid., p.220.
[41]Ibid., p.231.
[42]Ella Lorraine Dorsey, Jet the War Mule, p.115.

declared that Catholics in battle, oftentimes, were saved as their
religious medals deflected bullets from their fatal course.[43]

Miss Dorsey, Mrs. Waggaman, and Father Finn were only three of
the many Catholics writing for juveniles. Maurice Francis Egan,
author, editor, college professor, diplomat, wrote The Watson Girls
(1900) in answering the plea, "Mr. Egan must write a book for
girls."[44] Laced between the girls' adventures was the sound advice
that Catholics' good example made converts for the Church,[45] and
that there was much profit to be gained from the daily reading of
the New Testament.[46] Egan, naturally, did not write juvenile
fiction exclusively; yet, he represented those many Catholics, who
attempted to expose the Catholic viewpoint in as many ways as
possible. Two letters written to Father Hudson explained the
motivation that prompted the creation of a fiction guaged to attract
the Catholic girl and boy. Mollie Elliott Seawell, who admitted
that she wrote historical romances for young people with great
success, maintained that a boy should be incited to idealize a girl
with the effect of elevating and purifying the boy.[47] That was the
purpose of her fiction. Mary Josephine Brown wrote in detail.

---

[43]Ibid., p.61.
[44]Maurice Francis Egan, The Watson Girls, p.7.
[45]Maurice Francis Egan, The Watson Girls, p.194.
[46]Ibid., p.49.
[47]Mollie Elliott Seawell to Rev. Daniel E. Hudson, C.S.C.,
(July 29, 1911) Hudson Papers. UNDA.

Of course I am writing another book (juvenile) but it is
to be one complete story in itself, and what I want to
know is; ought I to come out decidedly Catholic in it, or
would it be better not to mention religion in any particular
way at all? Some people say it will sell better and do
perhaps more good among different denominations if I do the
latter. For my own part, I hardly know which is right and
which is wrong, though I feel sure that I cannot put my
heart and soul into my work, without making it Catholic in
tone. And there is a certain pride in trying to build up
a Catholic literature and show the non-Catholics that we
can write as well and even better than they.[48]

This problem confronting Mary Josephine Brown presented itself

many times to other Catholic authors.[49] Their solutions varied

from those who studiously injected Catholic belief into their

stories to the others who made only a casual reference to the point

of ignoring Catholic practices. It was evident, then, that some

preferred to tell a good story rather than constantly burden their

work with the baggage of religious implications.[50]

Falling into this latter category was one of the greatest

story-tellers of his generation, Francis Marion Crawford. A

contemporary wrote, "Other romances come and go, but Mr. Crawford

goes on forever." His new novels frequently appeared on the "six

best selling lists," often "twice a year with tiresome

---

[48]Mary Josephine Brown to Rev. Daniel E. Hudson, C.S.C.,
(August 26, 1888) Hudson Papers. UNDA.

[49]The discussion of the possibility of creating a substantial
Catholic literature was reserved for a later chapter so that poems,
essays, and other works of non-fiction as well as fiction could be
reviewed.

[50]It was erroneous to declare, as some did, that those
content to tell a good story were lax in their Catholicity.

regularity."[51] A later day critic designated him "the most versatile and prolific novelist of his day,"[52] writing some forty novels in less than twenty-five years.

> He wrote undoubtedly too much; more than hald of his voluminous product could be spared, but the other half, especially those novels like the Saracinesca series which deal with the Italian life he knew so well, has won a secure place.[53]

The creator of these romances was born in Bagni di Lucca, Italy, August 2, 1854. In the process of acquiring an education, he attended St. Paul's School, Concord, New Hampshire; Harvard; Trinity College, Cambridge; the universities of Heidelberg and Rome. Crawford, a student of languages, mastered French, Turkish, Russian, German, Swedish, and Spanish among others. His interest in Sanskrit took him to Bombay, where, eventually, "he did editorial work on the Indian Herald of Allahabad.[54]

> During his stay in India, Marion changed not only his signature but his religion, joining the Catholic Church, in whose fold he remained to the end. When we contrast the service in the cold, little Protestant church on the Via Nazionale with the splendid pageantry of the Roman Church, its traditions, its pomp and circumstance, its glamour and glow, his change of faith seems quite natural.[55]

---

[51]"Marietta, a Maid of Venice," The Critic, XL (January-June, 1902) 178.
[52]Edward Wagenknecht, Cavalcade of the American Novel, p.166.
[53]Frederick Lewis Pattee, "Crawford, Francis Marion," Dictionary American Biography, IV (1930) 520.
[54]Arthur Hobson Quinn, American Fiction, An Historical and Critical Survey, p.385.
[55]Maud Howe Elliott, My Cousin, Marion Crawford, p.63.

His sojourn in India (1880) also had another positive influence on his career. Crawford, after returning to the United States, told his uncle, "Samuel Ward, and George Brett of MacMillan's about a diamond merchant, Mr. Jacob, whom he had met in India."[56] Ward and Brett realized that this was a story worth publishing; so, at their suggestion, the young cosmopolite wrote Mr. Isaacs (1882) in about six weeks time. Immediately, it was a popular success.[57] This, then, was the beginning of the fabulous career of F. Marion Crawford.

Success followed success. In 1884, Elizabeth Berdan became his bride; the year following, they moved to Sorrento, Italy, where the author worked, lived, and died. However, he was no ex-patriate; the United States was his home and he made almost yearly pilgrimages there, sometimes in his own yacht.[58] Indeed, this was expensive living; and suggested, perhaps, the reason for writing an annual novel or two.

It has been said, Crawford "never wrote a book that was not entertaining."[59] He was the supreme entertainer, rarely dull. His historical romances treated such characters as Darius the Persian, Eleanor of Aquitaine, and Philip the Second of Spain's proud years.

---

[56]Quinn, op.cit., p.386.
[57]Ibid.
[58]Pattee, op.cit.
[59]Wagenknecht, op.cit., p.169.

Life in Spain, France, Germany, and the United States was the subject for many of his works. Yet, it was for his revelation of the
Italian character that he was praised most often. Laudable, also,
were the action and dialogue of his romances, although, they often
tended to be melodramatic.[60] Vernon Louis Parrington, the literary
historian, however, declared that Crawford had no conception of the
American political novel;[61] thus, he successfully resisted the un-
dertow of Realism that gripped some of the other American novelists
of his day.

For Marion Crawford "the novel was a 'pocket theater' exclusively for entertainment: propaganda, or moral teaching, or the
shedding of light on the meaning of life was no part of its
province."[62]

'For my part, I believe, that more good can be done by
showing men what they may be, ought to be, or can be, than
by describing their greatest weaknesses with the highest
art.'[63]

In spite of this proclamation, Marion Crawford was not
alienated completely from those who desired to "do good." Yet,
some of his fellow Catholics, after reading Casa Braccio, felt that
he had deserted them and that his religious faith was in jeopardy.

---

[60]Ibid., p.170.
[61]Vernon Louis Parrington, The Beginnings of Critical Realism
in America, 1860-1920, Vol. III of Main Currents in American
Thought, 172.
[62]Pattee, op.cit.
[63]Wagenknecht, op.cit., p.168.

A more acute observer, such as the novelist Hugh Walpole, called
Casa Braccio (1894) "a great novel" and reported that Crawford, as
a "Roman Catholic" depicted the full horror of the "elopment of a
nun from a monastery and her flight with her lover."[64] On another
occasion, a reviewer noted that the writer's first three books gave
no "internal evidence" of his being a Catholic. Nonetheless, this
same reviewer acknowledged of the third book, To the Leeward
(1884): "the influence of the work is for the good."[65] Many times,
reviewers made no mention of Crawford's Catholicity.

Happily, the novelist's able, contemporary vindicator existed
in the person of Father Hudson. The little editor wielded a big pen
in denouncing "certain American Catholic circles" for "harsh not to
say unjust criticism of some of his books, notably Casa Braccio."[66]

> Although eminent Catholic friends in Rome found no serious
> fault with this novel understanding its purpose — 'to show
> the effect of crime in successive generations,' — and re-
> membering that Marzori's masterpiece also deals with abuses
> also connected with monastic life, which ecclesiastical
> discipline has long since done away with and prevented the
> recurrence of, Mr. Crawford expressed to us his perfect
> Willingness to suppress "Casa Braccio," (sic) declaring that
> he deeply regretted its publication, since its influence was
> considered harmful. Living abroad for the most part, he
> had not understood the supersensitiveness of Catholics in
> this country on the subject of convent life, — a super-

---

[64]Hugh Walpole, "The Stories of Francis Marion Crawford,"
Yale Review, XII (July, 1923) 685.

[65]"Two New Novelists," Catholic World, XXXVIII (March, 1884)
792.

[66]Rev. Daniel E. Hudson, C.S.C., "A Word in Defense of a Dead
Author," Ave Maria, LXVIII (May 8, 1909) 591.

sensitiveness created by the travesties and calumnies of
anti-Catholic writers of the Maria Monk order. He was
genuinely surprised to learn to what an extent Americans
were still swayed by bigotry and ignorance.[67]

The defense continued pointing out that he wrote for the general
public —"he was not free to do otherwise"— and that he made
"honest efforts to benefit his readers as well as to entertain
them." His Rose of Yesterday (1897) firmly portrayed the Catholic
position on divorce.

He was happy to have written that book; and there can be no
question of its good effect on a host of readers, who, had
it borne the imprint of a Catholic publisher would not have
looked at it.[68]

Father Hudson declared that the author's own favorite, Marzio's
Crucifix (1887), had a beneficent purpose and that Via Crucis
(1898) fittingly presented an accurate pen-picture of St. Bernard.
As though this was not enough to dispel the critics, Father Hudson
further revealed that Marion Crawford was contemplating a lecture,
"Why I am a Catholic," when death intervened. The conclusion of
this apology was unmistakable: Francis Marion Crawford was an
"estimable Catholic gentleman."[69] The author's widow Elizabeth,
appreciative of the above article, wrote to its creator stating her
husband's Catholicity had been "staunch and very good."[70]

---

[67] Ibid., p.592.
[68] Hudson, op.cit., p.591.
[69] Ibid.
[70] Elizabeth Marion Crawford to Rev. Daniel E. Hudson, C.S.C.,
(May 29, 1909) Hudson Papers. UNDA.

Entertainment was the aim of Crawford's novels and his large following indicated how well he had achieved his goal. Another talented American shared this ideal of telling a good story, but she was virtually unread. Kate O'Flaherty Chopin wrote short-stories, excellent ones. Yet, she was a "genius in eclipse destined to be total."[71] It should be remembered, however, that her work was significant "not in terms of quantity but of quality. Her output was not large, but she carried the art of the short-story to a height which even Cable did not surpass."[72]

Kate O'Flaherty Chopin was born February 8, 1851. Her mother, Eliza Paris, was French and her father, Irish. Her youth was spent in St. Louis, Missouri, where Captain Thomas O'Flaherty, her father, was the friend and adviser of Archbishop Peter Richard Kenrick.[73] Young Kate developed a voracious reading habit which ultimately carried her through the works of Scott, Fielding, Spencer, Daudet, Flaubert, De Maupassant, and Moliere. Following her graduation from Sacred Heart Convent in 1870, she married Oscar Chopin, banker and prospective plantation manager. The young couple shortly moved onto a plantation at Cloutiersville, Natchitoches Parish, Louisiana. Here, she raised her family and observed the people about her. Time

---

[71]Frederick Lewis Pattee, The Development of the American Short Story, p.325.
[72]Quinn, op.cit., p.354.
[73]Daniel S. Rankin, Kate Chopin and her Creole Stories, p.27.

did not exist for writing. Not until after Oscar Chopin's sudden

death (1882) and her subsequent return to St. Louis, did Kate Chopin

begin to write. Youth's Companion, Wide Awake, and Harper's Young

People published her juveniles.[74] Nevertheless, she was best known

for her short-stories.

The local color of Natchitoches Parish formed the background

for the Creole, Acadian, and Negro characters created by Mrs. Chopin.

They were people she knew, loved, understood. Writing spontane-

ously,[75] emphasizing character rather than situation,[76] the widowed

author captured a segment of life in Louisiana.

> What Hamlin Garland did for the Middle West, Mary Wilkins
> Freeman for New England, Thomas Nelson Page for the middle
> South, and Miss Murfree for the Tennessee mountain folk,
> Mrs. Chopin did for the dwellers along the sluggish, marshy
> streams that meander among the sugar plantations of up-
> state Louisiana.[77]

Bayou Folk (1894) and A Night in Acadie (1897) formed the short-

story collections which attracted the critics.

> ...there are few pieces in the American short-story collec-
> tions that surpass in restrained intensity, in finesse, in
> the inevitableness of startling climax, some of the best of
> her tales.[78]

For example, the acknowledged masterpiece, Desiree's Baby, first

published in Vogue, told the tale of a white couple whose first-born

---

[74]Dorothy Ann Dondore, "Chopin, Kate O'Flaherty," Dictionary
American Biography, IV (1930) 90.
[75]Pattee, op.cit., p.325.
[76]Joseph J. Reilly, "Stories by Kate Chopin," Commonweal, XXV
(March 26, 1937) 606.
[77]Ibid.
[78]Pattee, ibid.

was colored. The irate father, after banishing the broken-hearted
wife and their child from the house, tried to remove all traces of
their existence. The husband, while in the attic to gather his
wife's letters to burn, stumbled across a letter written by his
mother to his father. There, in one shattering sentence, the
wounded man learned of his mother's fond desire—— that her son
would never know that his mother was born to an "enslaved race."

In addition to their general excellence, Kate Chopin's stories,
usually, presented a picture of people influenced by the Catholic
religion. She was superior to both George Washington Cable and
Grace King in this respect. Sr. M. Callista Long, O.S.U., in a
detailed study—— an unpublished master's dissertation—— offered
the following conclusions:

> Mrs. Chopin's Creoles are profoundly Catholic. Firmly
> rooted in the Faith, they possess a true concept of the
> purity of womanhood—— factors which make for strong
> family ties and consequently love of home.[79]

The Creoles were disdainful of most things new, and all things
American, refusing to relinquish their French tongue, clinging to
their original mode of life. Mrs. Chopin's Acadians, according to
Sr. Callista,

> ...are a simple, passionate, hospitable people, clinging
> for the most part to the customs, language, and Catholic
> Faith of their eighteenth century ancestors.[80]

---

[79]Sr. M. Callista Long, O.S.U., Kate Chopin: Artistic Interpreter of Creole, Acadian, and Negro Culture, (Unpublished Master's Dissertation, Notre Dame, Indiana, University of Notre Dame, July, 1941) p.121.
[80]Ibid.

Mrs. Chopin, there, after making the distinction between Creole and Acadian revealed the influence of the Faith upon them. This was not the work of a conscientious propagandist, but rather that of a keen observer with a marked, creative writing ability. The Catholic tone of her work was unmistakable in spite of her personal aloofness to her faith. One of Mrs. Chopin's biographer's remarked, "She never openly repudiated the faith of her youth; she remained merely indifferent to the practical duties of the Catholic religion."[81]

Unfortunately for Americans, both non-Catholic and Catholic alike, Mrs. Chopin's writing career altered because of the cool reception given to her novel, The Awakening (1899). This tale of a mixed marriage and the wife's love of another man told in sensuous language subtle with symbolism caused provincial critics to cry out asking the author to cease writing.[82] (Actually, she was twenty years or so in advance of the time.)[83] Publishers refused to handle her material. She continued to write but the spark was gone. Yet, she had written enough to earn the toga, "greatest American short-story writer of her sex."[84] No other Catholic save Richard Malcolm Johnston could even approach her local color stories.

Colonel Richard Malcolm Johnston was born in Powelton, Georgia, March 8, 1822. Although he was a lawyer, he preferred to teach

[81]Daniel S. Rankin, Kate Chopin and her Creole Stories, p.106.
[82]Dorothy Ann Dondors, "Chopin, Kate O'Flaherty," Dictionary American Biography, IV (1930) 91.
[83]Ibid.,
[84]Reilly, op.cit., p.607.

rhetoric and belles lettres at the University of Georgia in Athens.
During the Civil War, he acquired the honorary "Colonel" although he
was a non-combatant. A significant national event and a turning-
point in his own personal life brought an end to the educational
institutions conducted by Colonel Johnston. Sherman's famous march
dismissed his private school at Rockby,[85] Georgia; while Johnston's
conversion to Catholicism (1875) brought the decline of his Pen
Lucy School in Maryland.[86]

His professional career developed from the sketches he wrote for
his own amusement. The South's famed poet, Sidney Lanier, read them
and urged Johnston to publish with the result that the Southern
Magazine had a new contributor. He was nearly sixty when "the North
discovered he could write[87] "as Harper's (1883) and later Appleton's
(1892) published a collection of his magazine articles. The best
known of his works, The Dukesborough Tales (1871), based on the
antebellum days in Powelton, were "rambling talks about folks, and
places, and manners."[88] Plotless almost, without action, these
tales were "loving, nostalgic studies."[89] Humor was preferred to
tragedy and they were free from bitterness and hatred.[90] Although

---

[85]Stanley J. Kunitz, Howard Haycroft (editors) American Authors
1600-1900, p.422.
[86]Jay B. Hubbell, The South in American Literature, 1607-1900,
p.779.
[87]Pattee, op.cit., p.276.
[88]Ibid.
[89]Kunitz, Haycroft, ibid.
[90]Hubbell, ibid., p.781.

"Moll and Virgil" and "Mr. Absalom Billingslea" were good short stories,[91] his fond tales were more aptly classified as humorous sketches rather than as artistically contrived short stories.[92] Nevertheless his work qualified him as a local color humorist, one talented enough to win the recognition of the better known Southern writer, Thomas Nelson Page, who considered "The Colonel" a better dialect writer than himself.[93]

The importance of his conversion should not be ignored; for in Johnston, Catholicism had acquired a striking personality and an excellent literary instructor. This friend of Mark Twain, Lanier, and Joel Chandler Harris hurled himself into the Catholic Summer School movement giving lectures and writing for its magazine. As a public reader and lecturer, Richard Malcolm Johnston attained considerable status[94] appearing at John Hopkins in Baltimore as well as Cliff Haven on Lake Champlain. His daughter wrote the best one-line description of the grand enthusiast, "My father's personality was greater than his writings."[95] Johnston's friend and contemporary, Joel Chandler Harris, was another convert; but, whereas "The Colonel" had been within the fold for twenty-three years, Harris "put off his entrance into the Church until a few weeks before his

[91]Ibid.
[92]Ibid.
[93]Walter V. Gavigan, "Two Gentlemen of Georgia," Catholic World, CXLV (August, 1937) 588.
[94]Ibid.
[95]Hubbell, op.cit., p.782.

death, possible, one suspects, by making his isolation as brief as possible."[96] Although the creator of the beloved "Uncle Remus" died in 1908, his interest in Catholicism was traceable as far back as 1890 when he attended Mass of his own accord.[97] His writings, however, kept his secret.

> As has been pointed out that religious tone is by no means lacking in much that Harris wrote for publication, especially in his later years, and yet when one surveys his works as a whole there is little that is specifically Catholic in his fiction or his poetry. The few tales and sketches that do have authentic Catholic atmosphere are negligible.[98]

Harris, Johnston, Chopin, Crawford were writers professing Catholicism to some degree. As a professional class they deemed it their duty to entertain the American public with their best fiction. Nor, did they indulge in the studied effort to fill fiction with pro- Catholic propaganda as did their co-religionists such as Mrs. Dorsey, Mrs. Sadlier, Father Finn, and Mrs. Waggaman. The members of this latter group, nonetheless, were admirable in their persistence (oftentimes at a considerable personal sacrifice) of flooding Catholic periodicals with their Faith-fortifying literature. These, then, formed the two extremes of fiction by Catholics: one, aiming primarily at entertainment; the other at religious edification and exposition.

---

[96]Calvert Alexander, The Catholic Literary Revival, p.201.
[97]Walter V. Cavigan, op.cit., p.584.
[98]Ibid., p.586.

More noteworthy was the surprising number of Catholics,
particularly the converts, attempting fiction. Some had the gift
for it. Many times a publicist, a poet, or an essayist would stray
into fiction and contribute his or her bit. Among these enter-
prising people were found more Catholics of good intentions.

Father John Talbot Smith rightfully belonged in this category.
Priest, editor, drama critic, founder of the Catholic Actors'
Guild, Catholic Summer School Camp director, Father Smith did many
things to promote the welfare of the Church. His A Woman of Culture
(1897), an intriguing romance of Canada, contrasted scepticism with
Catholicism and revealed an "eleventh hour" imperfect recognition of
God.[99] Saranac (1897) praised the Irish and French Canadians for
inter-marrying[100] and showed the younger generation's abandoning
some of the customs and prejudices held so firmly by their parents.
Phases of the social progress of the Irish-American element formed
the bases of His Honor the Mayor and Other Tales (1891). In this
collection of short stories, the Irish and the French Canadians
learned to appreciate each other as they were fused together by
economics and religion.[101] The Irish were guilty of calling the
French, "nagurs."[102] Father Smith, furthermore, hit out against the
Irish tendency to be in style, loaded with jewelry. Brave man that

---

[99] John Talbot Smith, A Woman of Culture, p.353.
[100] John Talbot Smith, Saranac, pp. 57-58.
[101] John Talbot Smith, His Honor the Mayor and Other Tales,
p.235.
[102] Ibid., p.242.

he was, Father scored their abominations in machine politics.[103]

Somewhat different from Father Smith was the convert Henry
Harland. Better known, perhaps, as the co-editor of The Yellow Book,
a London literary periodical, and the author of several books
depicting the life of the Jew in East Side, New York, Harland, in
My Friend Prospero (1904) and The Cardinal's Snuff Box (1900),
exhibited a familiarity and respect for Catholicism. Concerning
My Friend Prospero, a reviewer wrote:

> There is a healthful atmosphere about this story which
> Catholic readers will not fail to observe. Mr. Harland
> writes as one who knows and it is pleasing to meet among
> modern writers of fiction one who can touch upon matters
> pertaining to Catholic customs and belief without blun-
> dering.[104]

The Albany Argus was of the opinion that The Cardinal's Snuff Box
had few equals in giving "so broad and beautiful picture of the
Catholic as this garden idyll."[105] His Eminence Egidio Maria
Cardinal Udeschini, not a saint—not a prig, worked as hard as any
parish priest visiting the sick, comforting the afflicted, coralling
the alcoholics, and collecting the stilettos of the belligerent.[106]
This snuff-using churchman was instrumental in bringing happiness to
a young English widow who proudly boasted, "I hear it (Mass) on
every morning of my life."[107] Moving human beings like chesspieces

---

[103] Ibid., p.216.
[104] "The Latest Books," Catholic World, LXXIX (April, 1904) 126, 127.
[105] Henry Harland, The Lady Paramount, p.293.
[106] Henry Harland, The Cardinal's Snuff Box, p.119.
[107] Ibid., p.97.

with the aid of his snuff-box, the cardinal brought the widow and
the "right man" together for the romance's prescribed happy ending
to the approval or disapproval of eighty-five thousand readers or
so.[108]

Harland, in relation to the general literary trend of the United
States, presented the oddity of approaching realism first, only to
abandon it. His local-color conception of the Jewish, East Side,
New York gave some indication of the true problems facing the
immigrant's adjustment to a new life. Moving abroad, Harland became
part of the American ex-patriate colony of London, where he edited
(along with Aubrey Beardsley) the unique, bizarre, fashion-setting,
"art for art's sake" Yellow Book. However, his popularity rested
on the picturesque romances, My Friend Prospero and The Lady
Paramount.

Whereas Harland preferred to depict life abroad in his romances;
Frank Hamilton Spearman, also a convert, was extremely successful
with two American themes, the railroad and the western. Spearman's
great zeal was more readily detected in his letters to Father
Hudson[109] but Catholicism was well served in Robert Kimberly (1911)
and a later work The Marriage Verdict (1923) which revealed the

---

[108]Ibid., p.2.
[109]Frank H. Spearman to Rev. Daniel E. Hudson, C.S.C.,
(February 16, 1908) (May 17, 1908) Hudson Papers. UNDA.

Church's position regarding the sanctity of matrimony[110] and
divorce. Spearman also had the pleasant habit of dedicating his
books to clergyman such as his son, Rev. Arthur Dunning Spearman,
S.J.,[111] and Francis Clement Kelly, Bishop of Oklahoma City and
Tulsa.[112] He was better known, however, as the author of "popular"
books, of which two at least, Whispering Smith (1906) and Nan of
Music Mountain (1916), were adapted for the movies. Laramie Holds
the Range (1921) was a well-written "western." This spirit which
prompted Catholics to write in the popular idiom was defined in
Madeline Vinton Dahlgren's letter to Father Hudson. Mrs. Dahlgren
wrote to her friend that she had submitted her latest novelette to
a non-Catholic magazine because "her public seems to be there."[113]
Although Mrs. Dahlgren used secular themes such as the social and
political life in Washington, Mother Seraphine avowed that her work
often was "Catholic in spirit."[114]

Some Catholics writing fiction, directly or indirectly, gave
favorable notice to their chosen faith. In juvenile fiction (and
some adult) this Catholic promotion studiously appeared; while a
more subtle approach to religious issues attended the work of

---

[110]Frank H. Spearman, The Marriage Verdict, pp. 73,251.
[111]Frank H. Spearman, Flambeau Jim, p.111.
[112]Frank H. Spearman, Carmen of the Rancho,p.111.
[113]Madeline Vinton Dahlgren to Rev. Daniel E. Hudson, C.S.C.,
(September 19, 1885) Hudson Papers. UNDA.
[114]Mother Seraphine, O.S.U., Immortelles of Catholic Columbian
Literature, p.73.

Crawford, Chopin, Harland, and Spearman. Combined, the two
extremes, probably attained a greater audience since those repelled
by lengthly expositions of Catholic devotion and conduct might
have been attracted by the Catholic undertones of the better written
and less labored novels.

CHAPTER III

INSPIRATION AND ADVICE IN POETRY AND VERSE

roetry in the United States during these years 1880-1915 did
not undergo any great change until extremely late in the period.
For the greater part, the traditional poetic forms, romantic and
sentimental, dominated the output. Before the turn of the century,
the fine, experimental poetry of Emily Dickinson and "The Poet of
the South," Sidney Lanier, remained obscure; while the popular
James Whitcomb Riley reminded Americans of the pleasant life in
rural Indiana. Yet, at the appearance of Harriet Monroe's widely
acclaimed magazine Poetry (1912), the realist revolt was consummated
in a "new poetry" characterized by freer forms of expression and an
interpretation of American civilization far removed from Riley's
folksy nostalgia. An American school of poetry emerged in the
figures of Carl Sandburg, Edgar Lee Masters, Vachel Lindsay, Robert
Frost, and others.

The Poetry of Catholics, then (1880-1915), adhered to the traditional forms. For the few, true poets among them, the older,
conservative forms served well in expressing lofty concepts of God
and nature. Many Catholics aspiring to write poetry were not
particularly interested in form, instead, for them, poetry became a
medium for promoting the notions that their co-religionists were
Christian, patriotic, culturally minded citizens. Whether for true

expression or for promotion's sake, the Catholic interest in poetry
was considerable.

Volume, which was a characteristic of the Catholics' attempt in
fiction, certainly was not lacking in their poetic endeavors. Many
now-obscure names affixed to equally obscure poems graced the pages
of such magazines as the Ave Maria, Donahoe's, The Catholic World,
The Globe, The Magnificat, The Rosary, and such newspapers as the
Catholic Telegraph, The Monitor, New-York Freeman's Journal, and The
Pilot. The editors of these various periodicals should be recognized for publishing, praising, and otherwise encouraging these
poets. Fragments from two letters of Louise Imogen Guiney, a poet
of true value, to Father Hudson illustrated this fact. Miss Guiney
wrote in 1909, "I am forwarding to my old friend Mr. Gosse your
complimentary citing of his lovely lyric in the issue of Jan. 16."[1]
Two years later, she pleaded:

> I have ventured to send you the enclosed, hot from the non-
> professional author's desk. It is a bit prosy, as most
> modern blank verse is, but it is also clear, comprehensive,
> dignified, is it not? and rubrically it covers the ground.
> I wonder if you will print it next November? I hope so. I
> am going to tell you privately that if you care to do so,
> Mr. Hilton, I know, would be glad enough to receive the
> small quid pro quo on acceptance; he is poor, one of the
> say-nothing-about-it kind.[2]

---

[1]Louise Imogen Guiney to Rev. Daniel E. Hudson, C.S.C.,
(January 22, 1909) Hudson Papers. UNDA.
[2]Louise Imogen Guiney to Rev. Daniel E. Hudson, C.S.C., (July
13, 1911) Hudson Papers. UNDA.

(Incidentally, A. J. Hilton's poem "Advent" appeared in the Ave
Maria, December 2, 1911.)[3]

Likewise in this vein of encouragement, the poetry appearing in
the various periodicals was accompanied often by the by-lines
"written for the Pilot,"[4] "written for the Telegraph,"[5] "written for
the Ave Maria,"[6] and "for the New-York Freeman's Journal."[7] Further
encouragement was added by San Francisco's Charles Phillips, editor
of The Monitor, who wrote:

> But American Catholic poets, or American poets who are
> Catholics, have been few. However, they are increasing in
> numbers. The race did not die with John Boyle O'Reilly...[8]

Phillips, an interesting critic, after praising some twenty American
Catholic contemporaries including Charles J. O'Malley, Thomas Walsh,
Miss Guiney, Eleanor Donnelly, and Katherine E. Conway, concluded:
"We want more Catholic poetry. The possibilities are vast beyond
comparison."[9] This enthuastic article appeared both in the Catholic
World and in The Monitor.[10] Maurice Francis Egan[11] and editor
Phillips shared the opinion that Charles J. O'Malley was America's
foremost Catholic poet.[12] Mr. O'Malley, interestingly enough, also

---

[3]A. J. Hilton, "Advent" Ave Maria, LXXXIII (December 2, 1911)
714,715.
[4]The Pilot, (May 1, 1886. June 19, 1886. January 6, 1894)
[5]Catholic Telegraph, (January 24, 1884. February 21, 1884)
[6]Ave Maria, LVII (January 1, 1881) 1.; LVII (May 7, 1881) 367.
(New-York Freeman's Journal, (February 28, 1903)
[8]Charles Phillips, "The Year's Catholic Poetry," Catholic
World, XC (January, 1910) 445.
[9]Ibid., p.461.
[10]The Monitor, (January 29, 1910. February 5, 1910)
[11]Phillips, Ibid., p.447.
[12]The Monitor, (April 2, 1910)

was an editor[13] of Catholic periodicals, The Midland, Review, and The New World; and his wife, Sallie M. O'Malley penned an entertaining and informative literary column, "Under the Library Lamp" for The Monitor.[14] Among then living poets, Mrs. O'Malley had high regard for Eleanor Donnelly and Judge Daniel J. Donahoe.[15] The Pilot publicized Miss Guiney in an article with the general title, "Literary Workers Who Are Catholics."[16] Incidentally, this admirable poet was the fourth figure so honored by The Pilot.[17]

Although these periodicals emphasized the verse-making efforts of American Catholics, their pages were not devoted exclusively to poets Catholic and American. Thus, works of such European artists as Coventry Patmore,[18] William Butler Yeats,[19] Aubrey de Vere,[20] and Rudyard Kipling[21] made an occasional appearance. With great pride, The New-York Freeman's Journal, announced the reigning pontiff Leo XIII had written another poem, this one being dedicated to a friend.[22] James Whitcomb Riley,[23] William Cullen Bryant,[24]

13 Ibid.
14 The Monitor, (February 3, 1912)
15 Ibid., (February 10, 1912)
16 The Pilot, (January 20, 1894)
17 Ibid.
18 Coventry Patmore, "The Toys," Ave Maria, XVII (June 4, 1881) 441.
19 New-York Freeman's Journal, (May 9, 1903)
20 Aubrey de Vere, "Wordsworth's Prophecy," Ave Maria, XXXVII (October 27, 1894) 449.
21 The Pilot (January 27, 1894)
22 New-York Freeman's Journal (February 14, 1903)
23 Ibid., (May 9, 1903). Catholic Telegraph (September 20, 1894)
24 The Pilot (September 1, 1894)

John Greenleaf Whittier,[25] Ella Wheeler Wilcox,[26] and Eugene
Field.[27] were non-Catholics whose works received this additional
recognition. Furthermore, The Pilot published the lines both of
Catholics and non-Catholics in a column entitled "Rich Words from
Many Writers"[28] to which readers were invited to send in the
selected pieces of their favorite writers. The Catholic Telegraph,[29]
Joseph Schwenenberger editor, also liberally borrowed poems from the
secular press.

It was only natural, however, that these periodicals were filled
with the writings from their co-religionists' pens. Some seemed
almost to write exclusively for one particular magazine or paper
while others had more diffused outlets for their efforts. John
Boyle O'Reilly, while editing The Pilot, did not hesitate to give
that paper a full injection of his poetry.[30] The 1896 index[31] to
Donahoe's revealed at least six men and women whose poetry had
appeared in the magazine the year previous.[32] The Globe was
partial to Caroline D. Swan,[33] printing her poems and her criticism

---

[25] Ibid., (April 10, 1886)
[26] Ibid.
[27] Catholic Telegraph (December 20, 1894.) New-York Freeman's
Journal (February 7, 1903)
[28] The Pilot (April 10, 1886)
[29] Catholic Telegraph (July 12, August 30, December 20, 1894)
[30] The Pilot (May 8, 1886; May 29, 1886)
[31] Donahoe's, XXXV (1896) Index.
[32] Ibid., XXXIV (1895) 3.
[33] Caroline D. Swan, "Christmas Morn," The Globe, XII (December,
1902) 365. Ibid., "Easter Glory", XII (March, 1902) 23. Ibid., "A
New Poet," XI (March, 1901) 29.

of a new English poet, Stephen Phillips. On the other hand, the
Catholic Telegraph evidenced a strong liking for Henry Coyle[34] and
George Harrison Conrad.[35] Among the Ave Maria favorites were the
converts Eliza Allen Starr[36] and William D. Kelly.[37] Such established poets as Father Abram Ryan[38] and Eleanor Donnelly[39] found
their writings in more than one Catholic journal.

A partial explanation of the considerable poetic volume might
be offered in the fact that the poetic form constituted an expres-
sive outlet for current and popular feelings. In this fashion, the
Irish journals were loaded with patriotic and nostalgic verses,
high in praise of the Emerald Isle while some were correspondingly
severe with the British Lion. When the Mississippi overflowed its
banks in 1884, it was duly recorded in verse.[40]

> O great and mighty river
> Where is thy valley now
> Where are the beauteous landscapes
> That dotted vale and brow?
> Where are the towns and cities
> That flourished on thy shore
> They're buried 'neath thy bosom
> Perhaps to rise no more.

[34]Catholic Telegraph, (April 12, 1894; December 20, 1894)
[35]Ibid., (September 13, 1894; October 18, 1894)
[36]Ave Maria, XXII (January–June, 1886) vii; XXXI (July–December, 1890) vii.
[37]Ibid.
[38]Catholic Telegraph, (April 19, 1894)
[39]The Pilot, (January 6, 1894) Eleanor Donnelly, "The Cannon in the Convent Grounds" Ave Maria, XVII (March 19, 1881) 227.
[40]Catholic Telegraph, (February 21, 1884)

> Ah, pitying Heaven help us!
>   Should darker hours come,
> And teach us, in humility
>   To say, Thy will be done.
> And bless our generous brothers
>   Of many creeds and types
> Brave hearts that beat in union
>   Beneath the Stars and Stripes.

A further use of poetry was to honor the living and the dead. The following were among lines in praise of Miss Eliza Allen Starr:[41]

> Striving thro' Art and Literature to move
> The Young-eyed souls to pure and high endeavor.

Mother Angela Gillespie, C.S.C., and the Sisters of the Holy Cross, who had labored in Civil War hospitals, were donated two shattered cannons by their grateful government. This occasion, of course, did not escape poetic notice and, consequently, "The Cannon in the Convent Grounds"[42] made its appearance in 1881. It was a much sadder task for the Cincinnati Catholic Telegraph to record (in poetry) the death of a Polish immigrant killed in an excavation accident.[43] In general, many of these poems sang the praises of God and treated various subjects such as patriotism, death, love, the lives of the saints, and Ireland.

A Catholic whose patriotic poetry overshadowed his religious, was the Reverend Abram J. Ryan. Louise Manly wrote (1895) of his

---

[41]"Sonnet to Eliza Allen Starr," Ave Maria, XVII (October 15, 1881) 821.

[42]Eleanor C. Donnelly, "The Cannon in the Convent Grounds," Ave Maria, XVII (March 19, 1881) 227.

[43]Catholic Telegraph, (January 24, 1884)

poetry: "His patriotic poems are among the best known and most admired that the South has produced."[44] Another critic writing eight years later, was less cautious in acclaiming this Franciscan Tertiary as "the most popular of Southern poets,"[45] and placing him on a plane with Poe, Hayne, Timrod, and Lanier.[46] Although doubt existed as to the exact place and year of his birth,[47] still, there was considerable agreement that Abram J. Ryan was born in Norfolk, Virginia, August 15, 1839. His parents, recent immigrants[48] from Ireland, moved to St. Louis where he received his early education from the Christian Brothers. He acquired his theology at Niagara, New York, and at Loyola College, Baltimore.[49] "He was ordained a priest at St. Louis just after he became of age, at a time when he was in such delicate health that he was obliged to sit through the ceremony."[50] Naturally, some of Father Ryan's poetry reflected his Irish ancestry as witnessed by his "Erin's Flag."[51]

> Lift it up, Lift it up! the old Banner of Green
> The blood of its sons had but brightened its sheen;
> What though the tyrant has trampled it down,
> Are its folds not emblazoned with deed of renown?

[44]Louise Manly, Southern Literature: From 1579-1895, p.392.
[45]F.V.N. Painter, Poets of the South, p.115.
[46]Ibid., p.4.
[47]Benjamin Francis Musser, Franciscan Poets, p.214.
[48]F.V.N. Painter, op.cit., p.104.
[49]Benjamin Francis Musser, ibid.
[50]Edwin Anderson Alderman, Joel Chandler Harris, Charles William Kent, (editors), Library of Southern Literature, X, p.4624.
[51]Painter, ibid., pp.104,105.

Father Ryan, however, being an American and a Confederate
chaplain had a much more vivid experience to sing. As a true
Southerner, he felt the defeat of the Confederacy with a marked
intensity. "He felt a little more deeply what all were feeling and
gave adequate expression to that common emotion."[52] This feeling
versified became "The Conquered Banner" which was accepted
immediately as the poem of defeat.[53] Of this universal acceptance,
Hannis Taylor declared:

> Only those who lived in the South in that day and passed
> under the spell of that mighty song can properly estimate
> its power as it fell upon the victims of a fallen cause.[54]

A letter from Father Ryan to Francis Fisher Brown added this information:

> I wrote "The Conquered Banner" at Knoxville, Tennessee, one
> evening after Lee's surrender, when my mind was engrossed
> with thoughts of our dead soldiers and dead cause. It was
> first published in the New-York Freeman's Journal. I never
> had any idea that the poem, written in less than an hour,
> would attain celebrity. No doubt the circumstances of its
> appearance lent it much of its fame.[55]

This poem, then, became the "requiem" of the Lost Cause.

> Furl that Banner, softly, slowly;
> Treat it gently- it is holy,
>   For it droops above the dead;
> Touch it not- unfold it never;
> Let it droop there, furled forever,
>   For its peoples hopes are fled.[56]

---

[52]Edd Winfield Parks, Southern Poets, cxii.
[53]Ibid.
[54]Alderman, Harris, Kent, op.cit., X, 4623.
[55]Francis Fisher Browne, Bugle Echoes, p.278.
[56]Abram J. Ryan, Poems: Patriotic, Religious, Miscellaneous,
(1896 ed.) p.168.

Although, he wrote other poems Confederate in theme, none quite achieved the success of "The Conquered Banner," a fadeless song. Yet, "The Sword of Robert E. Lee," reverently praising the great general, received an enthusiastic reception[57] as did his "A Land Without Ruins."[58] The Confederacy also "loved" him for "March of the Deathless Dead" and for the "Lost Cause."[59]

As verified by the title of his bound volume, Poems: Patriotic, Religious, and Miscellaneous, Father Ryan sang primarily of the Southern Confederacy and of the Catholic Church. The appearance of his poems in the periodicals testified to this latter phase.[60] Furthermore, the Reverend Matthew Russel, S.J., editor of The Irish Monthly, Dublin, commented:

> His tributes to the Blessed Virgin are frequent and
> fervent for he felt as he sang,
> > Ah, they to the Christ are the truest
> > Whose hearts to the Mother are true.[61]

One writer noted that the "Poet-Priest of the South"[62] found subjects in distinctive Roman Catholic dogma and declared:

> "The Feast of the Sacred Heart" is in parts, too prosaically
> literal in its treatment of tran-substantiation for any but
> the most believing and devout of Roman Catholics.[63]

---

[57]Parks, op.cit., cxii.
[58]Ibid.
[59]Benjamin Francis Musser, op.cit., p.211.
[60]The Pilot, (January 16, 1886) Catholic Telegraph, (February 15, 1894; April 19, 1894; April 26, 1894)
[61]Matthew Russel, "Our Poets. No. 25, Rev. Abram Ryan," The Irish Monthly, XIX (December, 1891) 637.
[62]The Pilot, (January 16, 1886)
[63]Painter, op.cit., p.107.

Perhaps Father Ryan reached his spiritual heights in the "Song of the Mystic," "Here we have...the soul given in utter abandon to the Divine Love."[64]

And I have seen Thoughts in the Valley,
    Ah me, how my spirit was stirred!
And they wear Holy veils on their faces,
    Their footsteps can scarcely be heard;
They pass through the Valley like Virgins
    Too pure for the touch of a word.[65]

Several esteemed this his best religious effort. Another was undecided in his preference between "Song of the Deathless Voice" and "The Poet."[66] However, the mystic quality of his religious poetry was generally noted, although, one man remarked that he "was a mystic who could never rid himself of reality."[67]

Obviously, the poetry of this priest had its limitations. His was not polished poetry and he forthrightly acknowledged that "these verses" were written always in a hurry "with little of study and less of art."[68] Possibly, more perfection might have been attained had not his priestly duties and precarious health consumed so much of his time. In a letter to Father Russel, he humorously wrote:

---

[64]Benjamin Francis Musser, op.cit., p.209.
[65]Rev. Abram Ryan, op.cit., p.1.
[66]Benjamin Francis Musser, op.cit., p.210.
[67]Parks, ed., op.cit., cxviii.
[68]Rev. Abram J. Ryan, op.cit., Preface.

My Bishop has promised me, time and again, to give me
release from duty for awhile in order that I might give
the world a little book; but unfortunately in this country,
however it be in youts, the promises of Bishops are not
exactly like those of Our Lord.[69]

One critic thought that, with Father Ryan, message counted for more

than did rhythm and rhyme;[70] and, furthermore detected an undue

fondness for alliteration and assonance.[71] This latter fault could

be seen readily in the first stanza of the famous "The Conquered

Banner." Frankly, his poetry seldom rose above the cultured

commonplace[72] as he failed to

... break through with one striking metaphor, or hew away
the verbal padding or polish the rough line, or subdue the
cliche, or so gain in craftsmanship of the technician...[73]

Other critical adjectives assigned were too rhetorical, too

verbose, too sing-song, too facile and too sentimental.[74]

In spite of these defects, there was no disputing the

popularity of these verses which had at least twenty-four printings

by 1907.[75] Part of his success was attributed to his ability to

satisfy the strong moral sense of the American People. Father Ryan

considered the profound, sad aspects of life but always with

strength-giving faith and hope.[76] It could not be said of him, as

---

[69]Rev. Matthew Russel, op.cit., p.630.
[70]Painter, op.cit., p.112.
[71]Ibid., p.114.
[72]Ibid., p.113.
[73]Benjamin Francis Musser, op.cit., p.205.
[74]Ibid.
[75]Harris Taylor, "Abram J. Ryan," The Catholic Encyclopedia,
XIII (1912) 282.
[76]Painter, op.cit., p.117.

it was of others, that his poetry was as trifling in theme as it was
polished in workmanship. On the contrary, his was the ability to
handle some profound moment with real dignity. Likewise, his brief
lyrics, usually devoted to this single expression were easily understood by those reading them. Father Ryan's work for the most part
was simple, spontaneous, and clear.[77]

His selection of a poetic topic examplified this simplicity.
So, it was not unnatural for his theme to reflect the state of the
Union. In "The Land We Loved," he declaimed the indignities
committed under the guise of Reconstruction.[78] On the other hand,
this ardent Confederate praised the generous Northern aid given
during the South's yellow fever epidemic of 1878.[79] "Reunited" was
the very appropriate title of this poem. On another occasion he
wrote of his meeting with the saintly Pius IX.[80] Surely, interpretations varied as to the degree of Father Ryan's poetic greatness. Some were not impressed. One held he was a minor poet with
a flair for treating great subjects with simple dignity;[81] still,
another acclaimed him the South's greatest poetic genius since
Poe.[82] Above all, there was agreement that this popular priest made

---

[77] Ibid., p.115.
[78] Ibid., p.109.
[79] Ibid.
[80] Benjamin Francis Musser, op.cit., p.212.
[81] Edd Winfield Parks, op.cit., cxviii.
[82] Alderman, Harris, Kent, op.cit., X, 4623.

a considerable, positive contribution to the spiritual welfare of
Country, Church, and Confederacy. In him was fused patriot and
priest as he served his fellow men. To all, he was known as Father
Ryan. Not until the last five years of his short life, was he
relieved from his parish duties in order to devote more time for
writing. He was working on a prose Life of Christ when he died
April 22 or 23, 1886, at a Franciscan monastery in Louisville,
Kentucky.

It was a somewhat curious fact that the two recognized Catholic
poets of the South were contemporaries and priests. Seldom, did the
mention of Father Ryan fail to call to mind the equally frail,
clever convert John Bannister Tabb. This "unredeemed and un-
redeemable" rebel, who could claim the Washingtons and the Randolphs
for ancestors, was born March 22, 1845.[83] John, the third of four
children, grew up in the luxury of the slave economy on the family
estate near Richmond, Virginia. The Civil War saw his shipping out
in the capacity of a clerk on various blockade runners. (Even then,
his poor eyesight made combat service unfeasible.)[84] On one voyage,
he met Father John Bannon, a Confederate chaplain enroute to Rome,
supposedly, to enlist the sympathy of Pope Piux IX.[85] Perhaps, this

---

[83]M. S. Pine, John Bannister Tabb, the Priest-Poet, p.20.
[84]Francis E. Litz, Father Tabb. A Study of His Life and Works,
p.8.
[85]M. S. Pine, op.cit., p.16.

was his first prolonged contact with Catholicity. It had little to
do with his subsequent conversion, however, for in his own words,
"I was strange to say, not at all nearer the Church till I came to
live in Baltimore,"[86] an occasion taking place some time after the
war.

Following his capture, June 4, 1864, he spent eight months
captivity in the "bullpen," Point Lookout, Maryland. This dreary
circumstance was enlivened by his rich friendship with the acclaimed
poet Sidney Lanier, a fellow captive. Even after Lanier's death,
Tabb continued as friend and advisor to the family.

Tabb, released from prison in 1865, found his family estate a
casualty of the war. Forced to work, he turned to music and later
to teaching English. While attached to the Mt. Calvary Episcopal
Church School, Baltimore, he came under the influence of the pastor,
Rev. Alfred A. Curtis "whose face was already turned toward Rome."[87]
The teacher Tabb, after several months (April-Deptember, 1872),
followed Father Curtis into the Church. (Father Curtis, who
credited Cardinal John Henry Newman as a source for his conversion,
later became Bishop of Wilmington,[88] Delaware, 1886.) The other
convert entered St. Charles College, Ellicott City, Maryland, to
study for the priesthood. Yet, his ordination did not come forth

---

[86]Francis E. Litz, Letters: Grave and Gay and Other Prose of
John Bannister Tabb, p.249.

[87]M. S. Pine, op.cit., p.22.

[88]Francis E. Litz, Father Tabb, p.26.

immediately for he was pressed into service as a teacher, first at
St. Peter's Cathedral School, Richmond, and later at St. Charles.
Finally, in 1881, he entered St. Mary's Seminary and was ordained
by Archbishop James Gibbons,[89] December 20, 1884. Following
ordination he, naturally, continued to teach and for the rest of his
life he was a member of the faculty at St. Charles.

Father Tabb was one of those excellent, eccentric instructors,
too often called the "born teacher." For discipline, his caustic
tongue and his butting of students' heads sufficed. "If only one
student was to be punished, then Father Tabb would butt the
student's head against his own."[90] Some deemed him "vain, unreasonable, vindictive, hypercritical."[91] Balancing this was ready humor
plus enthusiastic and lucid explanations of grammar and poetry.
Although Father Tabb's book, Skeleton of English Grammar (the
familiarly known Bone Rules), branded him as a grammarian fundamen-
talist, he was able to instill in his boys a liking for literature.
Thus, Tabb the teacher often called upon Tabb the poet to garnish
rigid grammar with the joys of English literature. The dash of
actor in Father Tabb made his classroom interpretations of his
favorite Poe,[92] unique and highly interesting. He was interested
in the subject but also in the students and his influence over them

[89] Ibid., p.35.
[90] Francis E. Litz, Father Tabb, p.47.
[91] Francis E. Litz, The Poetry of Father Tabb, p.xli.
[92] Francis E. Litz, Father Tabb, p.48.

considerable.

> Boys who scarcely suspected their gifts, soon blossomed
> out as attractions or performers. They could do some-
> thing.[93]

Francis E. Litz declared that the "students of St. Charles never had

a more liberal or dependable friend among the faculty."[94] This no

doubt indicated a development in Tabb's personality, for William

McDevitt noted that the popular teacher in an earlier period, was

not a "favorite professor" for he had virtually no contact with the

main body of students.

> After he became a literary lion in the middle 90's when the
> reclame of his success as a poet was raging, his popularity
> took on the aura of fame and fortune: and the man who had
> so long been queer and odd of course became a 'remarkable
> character.'[95]

This remarkable character, nonetheless, carried the standard of

Catholic poetry in America.[96] To critic Gay Wilson Allen, he was a

minor Southern poet.[97] To a recent (1947) critic, he was one of the

few Catholics in America "to be distinguished in the field of

poetry."[98] A sincere but not a great poet. George Shuster, after

admitting the influence of Tabb was small, made the courageous

---

[93]William McDevitt, "Father Tabb at St. Charles College,"
Catholic World, CLVI (January, 1943) 413.
   [94]Francis E. Litz, Father Tabb, p.50.
   [95]William McDevitt, op.cit., p.415.
   [96]Emille Kessler, "Tabb and Wordsworth," Catholic World, CXLIII
(August, 1936) 572.
   [97]Gay Wilson Allen, American Prosody, p.304.
   [98]Sister Mary Humiliata, "Religion and Nature in Father Tabb's
Poetry," Catholic World, CLXV (July, 1947) 330.

statement that he was handicapped by the limited attention given to anyone not in the Puritan tradition.[99] The English poet, Alice Meynell, on the other hand, claimed him for one of the poets of America.[100] Oftentimes, the English published his verses after they had been rejected by American editors.

Although he had published in an important magazine such as Harper's in 1877, general acceptance evaded him until the '90's. For thirteen years he had "knocked almost in vain" at the doors of the great Triumviri,[101] The Century, Harper's, Scribner's. After 1894, and the publication of his bound volume, rejection ships came less frequently. Now the popular periodicals were quick to publish his work.[102] His biographer noted that he published little in Catholic magazines; a fact attributed to Tabb's dislike of publishing "without remuneration at all or without sufficient compensation."[103]

Father Tabb was a prolific, polished, precise technician with a preference for writing the shorter forms of poetry. Few of his

---

[99]George Shuster, "Father Tabb and the Romantic Tradition," The Month, CXLIV (December, 1924) 517.
[100]Alice Meynell, "Father Tabb," Catholic World, XC (February, 1910) 582.
[101]William McDevitt, op.cit., p.418.
[102]Francis E. Litz, Father Tabb, pp.94,95. The following periodicals printed Tabb pieces: Sunday School Times, p.53; Youth's Companion, p.53; Harper's Monthly, p.36; The Atlantic Monthly, p.35; Lippincott's, p.22; The Cosmopolitan, p.18; The Bookman, p.14; The Century, p.7; Harper's Weekly, p.8; Scribner's, p.2; The Era, p.2; The American Magazine, p.2; St. Nicholas, p.1; The Catholic World, p.1; English Illustrated, p.1; The Reader, p.1; Eclectic, p.1.
[103]Francis E. Litz, Father Tabb, p.95.

poems extended beyond the limits of the sonnet, while many were
still briefer, a favorite form being the quatrain. Allen, who
compared him with Emily Dickinson indicated that

> ... he used a greater variety of meters than Emily Dickinson,
> his rhythms are more regular, and his rimes correct. In
> fact his craftmanship is in every respect more finished.[104]

The Outlook (1897) reviewing "a dainty little volume," attested to
his originality.

> Father Tabb has not only a very delicate touch, but he had
> a very original fancy. He gives us the unobvious aspect of
> things; he makes us feel their hidden charm. His talent
> does not strike one as robust, virile, and creative on a
> great scale, but as gentle, penetrating, and searching.[105]

Primarily, he was a poet of nature expressing neatly the images
of gentle hills, "smooth-sliding streams," and the omnipresent
"little three" of birds, trees, and flowers. Observe this nature
was not a substitute for religion. In the ordered mind of Father
Tabb, nature served its place in the scheme of things when it
prompted men to "contemplate the Creator reflected in His
Creatures."[106]

> Niva, Child of Innocence
>   Dust to dust we go
> Thou; when winter wooed thee hence
>   Wentest snow to snow.[107]

When his eyesight finally failed completely, he wrote:

---

[104] Gay Wilson Allen, op.cit., p.305.
[105] The Outlook, LVI (May 8, 1897) 129,130.
[106] Sister Mary Humiliata, op.cit., p.336.
[107] William Hand Browne, "John Bannister Tabb," Library of
Southern Literature, XII, 5165.

> Back to the primal gloom
> Where life began
> As to my mother's womb
> Must I, a man,
>   Return:
> Not to be born again,
> But to remain;
> And in the School of Darkness learn
> What mean
>   "The things unseen."[108]

Contrasted with the preceding poem, the following, punning lines

were illuminating:

> There once were two brothers named Wright
> Who went up in aerial flight
>   But a poet I know
>   That much higher did go
> For he soared until "clean out of sight."[109]

In both instances he referred to his lost eyesight: the first, a

serious poem; the second, a quip. Yet, this was typical Tabb,

whose many moods expressed both the ridiculous and the sublime.

Accordingly, no attempt should be made to insert a mystical inter-

pretation where none was intended for almost half of his poetry was

merely fanciful.[110]

Further criticism scored his cliche's[111] and censored him for

being sometimes too elvish, too obscure, and too badly spotted with

wilful phrasing.[112] "He did not always succeed at expression; in-

deed he often resembles a boy striking matches in the wind."[113]

---

[108]Francis E. Litz, The Poetry of Father Tabb, p.257.
[109]Ibid., p.390.
[110]Alice Meynell, op.cit., p.580.
[111]Sister Mary Humiliata, op.cit., p.336.
[112]George Shuster, op.cit., p.524.
[113]Ibid., p.522.

One critic was unique in declaring him too static to be a lyric poet.[114] Another small debate existed over Tabb's "cameos", those single similes and metaphors "expressed in perfect phrase." Clement Wood believed that Father Charles L. O'Donnell of Notre Dame "was far superior."[115] Moreover, Lanier's biographer found him too original to show much influence."[116]

Tabb, original or not, also was influential. Overseas, the British wrote:

> Indeed all agree that no such workmanship has come out of America yet. As for the sentiment, we Catholics are particularly grateful for it: the literary trash in which religion has been heretofore offered to us having made all of us sick to death.[117]

Alice Meynell selected the poems for his English edition;[118] and, by 1922, only two Americans, Emerson and Tabb, had been included in the Oxford University Press: Epigrams[119] in the honored Garland Series. In addition to his periodical popularity, his Poems (1894) achieved at least seventeen printings.[120] His other verse publications included: An Octave to Mary, Lyrics, Child Verse, Two Lyrics, Later Lyrics, The Rosary in Rhyme, Quips and Quindits, A Selection

---

[114]D. J. Connor, "Father Tabb's Poetical Preferences," Catholic World, CXV (May, 1922) 427.
[115]Clement Wood, Poets of America, p.315.
[116]A. C. Clark, Sidney Lanier, A Biographical and Critical Survey, pp.357,358.
[117]William McDevitt, op.cit., p.419.
[118]Edd Winfield Parks, op.cit., p.202.
[119]Jennie M. Tabb, Father Tabb, His Life and Work, p.i.
[120]Willard Thorp, "Tabb, John Bannister," Dictionary of American Biography, XVIII (1936) 263.

of Verses, and Later Poems.[121] Who's Who in America accorded
Father Tabb a few lines (5) in its first edition.[122]

Most critics compared him quite favorably and often with Emily
Dickinson. One thought that the abundance[123] of his good poetry
was laudable and another was impressed not only with his short
lyrics but also with the "finish, ease, and grace" of his Italian
sonnets.[124] Father Tabb was a poet whose Romanticism was recon-
ciled to his Religion and many felt that he resembled the metaphysi-
cal poets of the 17th century.

> ... there was not a whit of the "highbrow" in his soul.
> What poetry he made was always purely human, the themes
> it took were everybody's. His speech, however, is
> illusive, intuitive, amatory.[125]

In my mind Father Tabb was a poet, a minor one to be sure, but
one of competence and genius. He was in his domain of the shorter
verse, a craftsman and a true poet. That other "unreconstructed
rebel," Father Ryan, probably had more popular appeal in their day
but it has been Father Tabb who received the critical acclaim of a
later period.

While the South had its poet of the "Lost Cause," the North
hailed the "Poet of Liberty,"[126] John Boyle O'Reilly. Here was no

---

[121] Francis E. Litz, Father Tabb, p.96.
[122] Who's Who in America, (1899) p.711.
[123] Alice Meynell, op.cit., p.582.
[124] Gay Wilson Allen, op.cit., p.305.
[125] George Shuster, op.cit., p.521.
[126] Katherine E. Conway, Watchwords from John Boyle O'Reilly,
p.xxvi.

native son, but an immigrant from Ireland by the way of the
Australian penal colonies. Yet, in Boston, that land of patriots,
he was the "chosen spokesman of the city of his home on several
historic occasions."[127] The early life of this patriot unfolded as
a melodramatic script.

John Boyle O'Reilly was born June 28, 1844, in Dowth Castle,
County Mead, just two and one half miles from the scene of the
Battle of the Boyne.[128] Young John, the son of a schoolmaster was
apprenticed to the Drogheda Argus, a newspaper. John was eleven at
the commencement of his literary career, which was interrupted by a
"hitch" in the British Army. This heir of powerful Irish princes,
unable to resist the siren appeal of Fenian conspiract, was court-
martialed and eventually shipped to Australia, arriving January,
1868. From there, aided by stout friends, sympathetic American
seamon, and several miraculous escapes, he made his way to
Philadelphia, November 23, 1869.[129] Within two months he reached
Boston just in time to embark as "a war correspondent" with a group
of Fenian adventurers determined to free Canada from the British
yoke. Returning from this ill-advised and fruitless expedition, he
resumed his literary career now as editor of the Boston Pilot. As

---

[127]A Memorial of John Boyle O'Reilly from the City of Boston,
p.65.
[128]James Jeffrey Roche, Life of John Boyle O'Reilly, p.1.
[129]Ibid., p.100.

in all true success stories, he soon bought an interest in The Pilot
and had for his partner the long-lived Archbishop John J.
Williams.[130] His life was far less hazardous after his return from
Canada and, in the role of the stable citizen, he married Mary
Murphy (1872). (Four daughters blessed this union.)

The twenty years of John Boyle O'Reilly's citizenship were
brimming full of services for his fellow Americans. The Chautauquan
acknowledged:

> Under his editorship The Pilot became the foremost exponent
> of Irish American thought, a powerful supporter of Catholic
> interests. But his identification with the higher life and
> literature of Boston gave him a still more enviable posi-
> tion. He was one of the founders of the Papyrus club of
> artists and men of letters and one of its most brilliant
> presidents.[131]

Nor were the lowly ignored. To newly arrived Irish he pleaded
to be good Americans in order to serve Ireland better. 'We can do
Ireland more good by our Americanism than by our Irishism.'[132] The
Negro American, "where his rights were at stake" found him a
vociferous ally to the extent that one Catholic paper rebuked, "It
if neither Catholic nor American to rouse the negroes of the South
to open and futile rebellion."[133] Nonetheless, it was an O'Reilly
poem which was read at the dedication services of a monument to a

[130] Robert H. Lord, John E. Sexton, Edward T. Harrington, History
of the Archdiocese of Boston, III, 393.
[131] Alexander Young, "John Boyle O'Reilly," The Chautauquan,
XII (December, 1890) 343.
[132] Lord, Seton, Harrington, op.cit., p.394.
[133] James J. Roche, op.cit., p.341.

Negro patriot. Later on request, the poet read this memorial,[134]
"Crispus Attucks, Negro Patriot Killed in Boston, March 5, 1770" to
an assembly of Boston's negro citizens.

> ... he hated tyranny and injustice in every form, and his
> heart and pen went out to negroes and Poles and Jews, and
> to every injured race, class, or individual.[135]

(One cause he did not favor was that of woman suffrage.)[136]

As a Catholic his prominence exceeded local circles for he was
the only layman, excepting the President and the Secretary of State
of the United States, to speak at the opening of the Catholic
University. Actually, his success "upon the platform" as lecturer,
orator, and poet won for him a national reputation. Moreover, the
poet could speak to all creeds.

> His poem at the dedication of the Pilgrim monument at
> Plymouth in August, 1899, was a wonderful illustration of
> his sympathetic insight into characters and conditions
> which as an Irish Catholic he was thought unfitted to
> appreciate.[137]

Keeping in mind that O'Reilly was a journalist, the judgment of
Oliver Wendell Holmes appeared attractive. "His poems show what he
might have been had he devoted himself to letters."[138] A similar
sentiment was that his early death (August 10, 1890) found his
poetic development in its earlier stages and given more leisure the

---

134 Ibid., p.326.
135 Lord, Seton, Harrington, op.cit., p.394.
136 James J. Roche, op.cit., p.227.
137 Alexander Young, op.cit., p.343.
138 Katherine E. Conway, op.cit., p.xix.

poet might have fulfilled his great promise.[139]

Little of his poetry was subjective. Narrative expressions of great causes and events were his favorites. Like Whitman's, his poetry forsook the misty traces of antiquity to sing the beauties of a new land and a new day. Circumstances in everyday life provided some of his inspiration. For instance, when Wendell Phillips died, O'Reilly wrote on the spur of the moment a memorial to his friend. Although he revised it but little, Whittier could comment, 'It is worthy of the great orator.'[140] At the reunion of the Army of the Potomac, Detroit, 1882, his "America" received this accolade from General Ulysses S. Grant, "That is the grandest poem I ever heard.'[141]

Songs from the Southern Seas published in 1878 established his literary reputation. This dramatic narrative portrayed the Australian character and scenery and featured adventure, pathos, and tenderness. The reviewer for The Catholic World,[142] however, noted its crudeness and harshness while another thought it lacked polish.[143] Generally, it was favorably received in America and the Dark Blue Magazine, a publication of Oxford University, was the first to print two of the "Songs." (When O'Reilly's political preferences

---

[139]Ibid., p.xi.
[140]John Boyle O'Reilly, Selected Poems (1913 edition), p.5.
[141]Ibid., p.37.
[142]Catholic World, XXXIII (September, 1881) 858.
[143]John Boyle O'Reilly, Songs, Legends, Ballads, "Opinions of the Press," p.10.

became known, the Dark Blue allegedly ceased to buy.)[144] Five years later, Songs, Legends, and Ballads was published containing the successful Southern Seas poems for ballast and adding various patriotic and religious verse. "Classic sweetness"[145] were two of the words used to describe his Statues in the Block, a volume of some twenty pieces devoted to love and philanthropy. Here, two styles appeared almost equally divided: one, graceful in form, "conveying some light fancy or suggestion; the other, careless to form, barren of rhyme, and irregular with the pulses of stern and passionate emotion."[146] Maintaining its judgment of his earlier poems, The Catholic World stated that the poet had not yet acquired that self-discipline that would enable him to write more technically perfect poetry. For O'Reilly, action and experience predominated over thought and meditation.[147] As for his moods, they varied from a religious one, earnest and tender, through the cynical to one of feverish patriotism.[148] Some of the poems from this collection, nonetheless were installed in the role of "favorites." "Jacque-minots" and "Her Refrain" enjoyed this particular distinction.[149]

[144]A Memorial ... op.cit., p.64.
[145]Catholic World, XL (November, 1886) 285.
[146]John Boyle O'Reilly, In Bohemia, "Opinions of the Press," p.6.
[147]Catholic World, XXXIII (September, 1881) 858,859.
[148]John Boyle O'Reilly, In Bohemia, "Opinions of the Press," p.1.
[149]Katherine E. Conway, op.cit., p.xxii.

My roses, tell her, pleading, all the fondness
    and the sighing,
All the longing of a heart that reaches thirsting
    for its bliss;
And tell her, tell her, roses, that my lips and
    eyes are dying
For the melting of her love-look and the rapture
    of her kiss.

      (Last stanza, "Jacqueminots.")[150]

In Bohemia, 1886, the last volume to be printed (although, not his

last poem), forced James Whitcomb Riley to burst in poetic praise:

I like the thrill of such poems as these,
    All spirit and fervor of splendid fact;
Pulse and muscle and arteries
    Of living, heroic though and act,
Where every line is a vein of red
    And rapturous blood, all unconfined,
As it leaps from a heart that has joyed and bled
    With the rights and the wrongs of all mankind.[151]

In Bohemia was an outpouring of his ethical tendencies featuring the

spirit of human brotherhood and an impatience with the existing

order. The Catholic World, steadfast in its line of criticism,[152]

cautioned that there was an occasional boldness of expression that

went beyond the "limits of phraseology within which writers careful

about their theology"[153] kept to themselves. Yet, even this critic

admitted that he was a true poet. A modern critic, Van Wyck Brooks,

thought that "A White Rose" from this collection was "a lovely and

---

[150]John Boyle O'Reilly, Selected Poems (1913 edition), p.34.
[151]James J. Roche, op.cit., p.300.
[152]Catholic World, XLIV (November, 1886) 284.
[153]Ibid.

lasting reminder of his delicate feeling."[154]

> The red rose whispers of passion
> And the white rose breathes of love
> Oh, the red rose is a falcon
> And the white rose is a dove.
>
> But I send you a cream-white rosebud
> With a flush on its petal tips;
> For the love that is purest and sweetest
> Has a kiss of desire on the lips.[155]

There was little doubt that "the O'Reilly" was appreciated by his contemporaries. Julia Ward Howe, H. Stoddard,[156] and John Greenlead Whittier[157] admired his poetry as did the editors[158] of The Atlantic Monthly, Scribner's, and Harper's. Horace Greeley[159] discovered him early and printed some of his best narrative poems in The New York Tribune. Catholic and Irish journals, especially his own Pilot, blazed often with a poem by John Boyle O'Reilly. Theodore Maynard noted that he was the only American Catholic poet represented in the Oxford Book of English Verse, but, added that O'Reilly was omitted from the revised edition.[160] This generous Irishman, for all his passion and patriotism, was not the great American poet envisaged by Emerson. To my mind, he was the

---

[154] Van Wyck Brooks, New England: Indian Summer, p.312.
[155] John Boyle O'Reilly, In Bohemia, p.24.
[156] Katherine E. Conway, op.cit., p.xxxviii.
[157] Ibid., p.xi.
[158] A Memorial ... op.cit., p.64.
[159] Ibid.
[160] Theodore Maynard, The Story of American Catholicism, p.565.

competent ballad-maker dramatically enlisting the sympathies of his readers. Today, his timely topics put into verse have suffered in appeal because later generations were immune to the causes he espoused. Yet, to the American of his day he proved that Catholicism was no bar to patriotism; and for his religion, he was the cultured layman whose mind and poetry appealed to all creeds.

The Mid-West, too, had its zealous Catholic layman in the person of the convert Eliza Allen Starr. This versatile woman, a New Englander by birth (August 29, 1824, Deerfield, Massachusetts) moved to Chicago in 1856 "where she was loved and admired as a teacher of drawing and painting." Miss Starr, an authority on art, was "preeminently a teacher and lecturer."[161] She, with that zeal peculiar to converts, deemed it her mission to familiarize Catholics with Christian Art.

> Miss Starr perceived that Catholics had far too slight an acquaintance with their great heritage, while non-Catholics displayed a greater appreciation of its artistic merits but were blind to its meaning.[162]

Furthermore, she keenly felt that Catholic indifference to Catholic literature.[163] To remedy these deficiencies, she taught, lectured, and wrote numerous articles and several books on Art, Liturgy, and the lives of the Saints. A sonnet dedicated to her testified that

---

[161]Annette S. Driscoll, _Convert Literary Women_, p.42.
[162]_Ibid._, p.40.
[163]Rev. James J. McGovern (editor) _The Life and Letters of Eliza Allen Starr_, p.275.

her generous exertions were appreciated. She

Striving thro' Art and Literature to move
The young-eyed souls to pure and high endeavor.[164]

From Pope Pius IX, she received a special blessing, 'Because' as he said, 'she writes for Catholic children.'[165] In the United States, Notre Dame University bestowed upon her its Laetare Medal[166] (1885) for her outstanding contributions as a Catholic laywoman.

Nevertheless, the busy Miss Starr still had time for writing poetry as she explained:

Prose always takes time, and I am apt to put it off... But poetry I can carry in my mind for a month and it comes to me anywhere.[167]

After reading some of her poetry, it became evident that Miss Starr broke into song on the slightest provocation. Religion, nature, and episodes from ordinary life supplied her inspiration. The putting to verse of bible history, dogma, and the lives of the saints provided her religious bent. Nature was served in pieces honoring the birds, the moths, the crickets, the leaves and flowers, the snow and rain.

I hear the soft low rain
Falling on the window pane
Feel it too upon my brain
Hardly pleasure, hardly pain,
Yet, I feel it upon my brain
As upon the window pane
Falls the dreary evening rain.[168]

---

[164]"Sonnet to E.A.S.," Ave Maria, XVII (October 15, 1881) 255.
[165]Ave Maria, XVII (March 26, 1881) 255.
[166]Annette S. Driscoll, op.cit., p.45.
[167]Rev. James J. McGovern, op.cit., p.274.
[168]Eliza Allen Starr, Poems by Eliza Allen Starr, p.62.

Poems dedicated to her father and brother, to Mary and Willie, to Fanny, to Fido, and to the family physician composed a portion of that poetry inspired by everyday life. Now was she blind to patriotism. "The Returned Regiment," "Colonel James A. Mulligan," and "Marian" indicated a love for our country sublimated to her love of God.

> Now the great rebellion 's over
> And the cruel war is done
> All the troops are gayly marching
> To the tune of "Home Sweet Home."
>
> Now, I cower before my anguish
> All this life-time left to me
> Only crying "God forgiving,
> Holy Mother, Comfort me!"[169]

The preceding, the first and last stanzas from "Marian," illustrated her great desire to express a feeling common to all and yet, dignify it with its proper relation to God. This and many of her other poems showed that a sincerity of belief could remove partially the effects of trite phrasing and too obvious rhymes. Miss Starr's poetry might never be considered important, nor even good; but, it would be difficult to assert that it hampered her desire to make Catholics more familiar with beauty and belief.

A much better poet who shared the same conviction was Joyce Kilmer. In a letter to his wife Aline, he wrote:

---

[169]Ibid., pp.78,79.

You see the Catholic Faith is such a thing that I'd rather
write moderately well about it than magnificently well about
anything else.[170]

Such an attitude was not permitted him until his conversion in
1913. Incidentally, in that same year, his most popular poem
"Trees" first appeared in Poetry magazine. By then adequately
launched in faith and poetry, Kilmer commenced working for the New
York Times Sunday Magazine and Book Review Section and the Literary
Digest. At one time, he was the poetry editor of Current Literature
and a faculty member at New York University (1916). He left these
promising situations to fight a war from which he never returned.

"Trees" and "The White Ships and the Red," won for him popular
acclaim. The latter displayed the anger and dismay experienced by
all over the sinking of the Lusitania.[171] Those more familiar with
his works recognized him as the poet of urban environment,[172] for
his writing "Delicatessen," "The Twelve Forty-Five, "Gates and
Doors," "Roofs," and "Alarm Clocks." Harriet Monroe noted, moreover, than his best poems were enriched with a deep religious
conviction. She realized that religion was the central motive of
his life and thought and credited him for creating some good
devotional poetry which "is of all kinds the rarest these days."[173]

---

[170]Joseph W. Dunne, "A Catholic Soldier Poet," The Month,
CLXXVIII (May-June, 1942) 220.
[171]"The Poems of Joyce Kilmer," Outlook, CXX (September 4,
1918) 12.
[172]Joseph W. Dunne, op.cit., p.218.
[173]Harriet Monroe, "Comment," Poetry, XIII (October, 1918)
33.

Miss Monroe was particularly attached to "Memorial Day," "The

Rosary," "In Memory of Rupert Brooke," "The Fourth Shepherd,"

"Prayer," and "Poets." This last named, she considered, perhaps,

his finest utterance burning "with the whitest heat of rapture."[174]

> Vain is that chiming of forgotten bells
>   That the wind sways above a ruined shrine
> Vainer his voice in whom no longer dwells
>   Hunger that craves immortal bread and wine.
>
> Light songs we breathe that perish with our breath
>   Out of our lips that have not kissed the rod
> They shall not live who have not tasted death
>   They only sing who are struck dumb by God.[175]

Harriet Monroe knew of course that he was an "enthusiastic convert

to Roman Catholicism."

The simplicity of Joyce Kilmer's poetry evoked various comments.

One found it simply exasperating[176] while another deemed it delight-

ful.[177] Simplicity to be effective had to be perfect.

> The air is like a butterfly
>   with frail blue wings
> The happy earth looks at the sky
>   and sings.[178]

The Outlook editorialized that Kilmer would admit the greater

part of his work to be mere verse, but verse of charm, tenderness,

---

174Ibid., p.34.
175Ibid.
176Salomon de Silva, "Main Street and Other Poems," Poetry, XI
(January, 1918) 282.
177Eunice Tietjens, "Trees and Other Poems," Poetry, V
(December, 1914) 140.
178Ibid.

now humorous, now devotional. Kilmer was always sane, sincere, vigorous, and courageous.[179] On the other hand, Ronald Bernard stated (1939) that "Joyce Kilmer wrote little that deserves the disproportionate fame it enjoys."[180] He agreed that it was the accepted thing to say that Kilmer showed great promise, but added that one cannot critically appraise unwritten poetry. There was more opinion, nevertheless, that Joyce Kilmer was a genuine poet, if not a great one.[181] He was the American poet invited by The London Spectator to write a poem commemorating the hundredth anniversary of Scott's Waverly novels.[182] His "Gates and Doors" reappeared in the 1950 issue of Collier's magazine. Kilmer, in my mind, was a Catholic poet capable of enlisting his reader's sympathy for things Christian and American. His ability to sing "the common experience of common men's eager souls' searching out for Christ"[183] should not be overlooked.

A totally different phase of Kilmer's career was the friendship and inspiration he offered his co-religionists. His correspondence with the young poet, Father Charles L. O'Donnell, C.S.C., revealed Kilmer as the dispenser of praise, criticism, and encouragement. As

---

[179]"The Poems of Joyce Kilmer," Outlook, CXX (September, 1918) 12.

[180]Ronald L. Bernard, "The Trend in Modern Catholic Poetry," Catholic World, CXLIX (July, 1939) 431.

[181]Joseph Landy, "Poet in Another War," America, LXXI (August 5, 1944) 456.

Marsden Hartley, "Tribute to Joyce Kilmer," Poetry, XIII (December, 1918) 152.

[182]Thomas Walsh, "Poems of Joyce Kilmer," Catholic World, C (December, 1914) 305.

[183]Outlook, op.cit.

a fellow craftsman, he criticized one of the young priest's poems for overly repeating the same sounds and the same rhyme scheme.[184] By way of encouragement in this same letter, he asked:

> Do you mind being called a Hoosier Francis Thompson? I think I'll call you that in The Literary Digest one of these days.[185]

On another occasion Kilmer asked to see more of O'Donnell's work "... for good Catholic poetry is rare in this generation."[186] The kindness of the convert poet expressed itself in other ways. At one time, he suggested a reliable publisher for the hoosier poet;[187] at another, he suggested Father O'Donnell as a future lecturer to the Catholic Summer School of America.[188] Possible, he detected some critical insight in Father O'Donnell as he wrote:

> Poetry is respected more and known more intimately at Notre Dame than at any secular university-- why not an article on this subject by the well-known author of "The Dead Museum" in the Poetry Review.[189]

His letters also revealed an awareness of the good fortunes of the people and things about him. He enjoyed reading the Ave Maria[190] and he rejoiced in the dialect poet, Thomas Daly's securing a new job on the Philadelphia Ledger at $7,500[191] a year! Thomas Walsh,

---

[184]Joyce Kilmer to Rev. Charles L. O'Donnell, C.S.C., (May 8, 1915) O'Donnell Papers. UNDA.
[185]Ibid.
[186]Ibid., (April 23, 1914)
[187]Ibid., (March 9, 1916)
[188]Ibid., (March 19, 1917)
[189]Joyce Kilmer to Rev. Charles L. O'Donnell, C.S.C., (June 14, 1916) O'Donnell Papers. UNDA.
[190]Ibid., (December 19, 1914)
[191]Ibid., (November 9, 1915)

in his mind, wrote excellent poetry.[192]   Among the fictionists,
Kilmer admired his friend Frank Spearman.[193]   Joyce Kilmer, even in
his letters, was an admirable Christian gentleman.

Joyce Kilmer had for a most worthy contemporary, Louise Imogen
Guiney, one of the several Americans who preferred to live abroad.
The versatile Miss Guiney turned her facile pen to the essay,
Scholarship, and criticism as well as to poetry.   Anne Fremantle,
in 1948, opined that although she was no mean poetess, "it is as an
essayist that she will be remembered."[194]   Louis Untermeyer held the
opinion: 'Her work is that of poeticizing rather than poetry.'[195]
Miss Guiney was a true, minor poet; but, one who failed either to be
exotic, popular, or sensational.   Perhaps, she was "too Catholic and
too English for New England."[196]   One appreciative critic, nonetheless, elected to compare her favorably with Emily Dickinson.

> Miss Guiney's work is warmer from the strain of the Celt,
> and richer from its seventeenth century background.   The
> one is of England in its chivalrous and romantic period,
> the other of New England in its yet bleak and repressed
> puritanism.[197]

An Irish Jesuit even went further in stating that she was one of the
four woman poets who would survive in time.   Therefore, she was

---

[192]Ibid., (May 21, 1915)
[193]Ibid., (April 10, 1916)
[194]Anne Fremantle, "Four American Catholic Essayists,"
Commonweal, XLIX (December 10, 1948) 228.
[195]Daniel J. Berigan, "Forgotten Splendor," America, LXX (March
4, 1944) 605.
[196]George O'Neill, S.J., "The Poetry of Louise Imogen Guiney,"
Studies, XX (December, 1931) 576.
[197]Jessie B. Rittenhouse, "Two Women Poets," Saturday Review of
Literature, IV (April 14, 1928) 758.

placed in the distinguished company of Elizabeth Browning, Christine
Rossetti, and Alice Meynell. The Irishman proclaimed her a good
technician who would not tolerate bad rhymes, bad grammar, and
forced constructions. She was equally opposed to the colloquial,
and to the stereotyped cacaphonies.[198]

Still on the positive side, several of her forcible and con-
densed expressions were noteworthy. For example, she described
Westminister Abbey as the 'storm-spent sea of ended kings', and an
old historian as 'the endless terraces of ended time.'[199] In her,
sense and spirit were found in rare balance and her gifts were
cultivated by intellectual and moral self-discipline.[200] She bore a
mystical passion, and, at times, the essence of her poetry was the
surrender of the temporal to the eternal.[201] Yet, it was a surrender devoid of dogmatic implication.

> Very little of her poetry deals directly with subjective
> religious experience, although there is always a profound
> spiritual background that gives breadth and vitality.[202]

Her poetry had a distinctive personal style, a style too fine
for popular appeal.[203] Her use of archaic phrases and her search

---

[198]George O'Neill, S.J., op.cit., p.577.
[199]Ibid., pp.577,578.
[200]Ibid., p.582.
[201]Jessie B. Rittenhouse, op.cit., p.758.
[202]Paula Kurth, "The Sonnets of Louise Imogen Guinet," America,
XLIII (August 9, 1930) 431.
[203]Jessie B. Rittenhouse, "The Charm of Louise Imogen Guiney,"
Bookman, LII (February, 1921) 519.

for the sources of beauty of yesterday evoked the comment that she
could not get her bearings in time. It might have been more appropriate to say that "she belonged to the age of the Stuarts"[204] and
felt no obligation to the twentieth century. In this manner, her
outlook was stunningly fresh and fearlessly detached. Her friend,
Bliss Carman, the Canadian poet, claimed for her:

> "The most undoubtedly genuine spark of genius in Auburndale,
> shall I say America? in Younger English today."[205]

Robert Louis Stevenson was another who liked her poetry. Included
among her better poems were: "The White Sail," "A Roadside Harp,"
"The Martyr's Ideal," "The Knight Errant," "Wild Ride, "The Three
Kings," "The Yew Tree," and "Astraea" which was included below:

> Since I avail no more, O men! with you,
> I will go back unto the gods content;
> For they recall me, long with earth unblent,
> Lest lack of faith divinity undo.
> I served you truly while I dreamed you true,
> And golden pains with sovereign pleasure spent:
> But now, farewell! I take my sad ascent,
> With failure over all I nursed and knew.
>
> Are ye unwise, who would not let me love you?
> Or must too bold desires be quieted?
> Only to ease you, never to reprove you,
> I will go back to heaven with heart unfed:
> Yet sisterly I turn, I bend above you,
> To kiss (ah, with what sorrow!) all my dead.[206]

---

[204]Jessie B. Rittenhouse, "Two Women Poets," op. cit., p.758.
[205]Jessie B. Rittenhouse, "The Charm of Louise Imogen Guiney,"
op.cit., p.516.
[206]Grace Guiney, ed., The Collected Lyrics of Louise Imogen
Guiney, p.35.

That Louise Imogen Guiney was an ardent Catholic was well
expressed by Father James Daly, the Jesuit poet. "It seemed to me
that all her energies and talents got their inspiration from her
faith." Like... "Joyce Kilmer she fused literature and her own life
in a Catholic spirituality of robust sacrifice and saintly sourte-
sies."[207] Obviously, to the discerning Catholic, Miss Guiney's
Catholicism was evident. Yet, this "intellectual aristocrat" would
not sacrifice poetic perfection for "remunerative popularity,"[208]
to the extent that only a few Catholics and non-Catholics alike were
aware of her excellence. This insight was given by her cousin,
Grace Guiney:

> It was natural to discount the force of Louise Guiney's
> sense of religion, for it was a subject of which she rarely
> spoke except in her poetry; and, much as she loved the
> multifarious symbolism of the Church, she had none of the
> external pieties so dear to our less perfect knowledge.[209]

If the mystic in Miss Guiney's poetry confused those with less
perfect knowledge, other indications existed revealing her love of
and interest in the Church. At one time, she wrote and asked her
friend Wilfrid Meynell to be one of the lecturers to a group of her
Oxford friends. She explained:

---

[207] James J. Daly, "Louise Imogen Guiney," _America_, XXIV
(November 20, 1920) 114.
[208] _Ibid._, p.113.
[209] Grace Guiney, "Louise Imogen Guiney," _Catholic World_, CXXI
(August, 1925) 598.

> We have been casting about...to see what we could do to
> increase the Community feeling among local Catholics, further
> intelligent interest in Catholic ideals and get a rather
> centrifugal congregation together, not indeed in a socialis-
> tic way, but in a human way.[210]

The solution was a lecture program, an informal one with coffee and

cakes, that brought not only the Meynell's but also Father Hugh

Benson, Father Joseph Rickaby, and Father Vincent J. McNabb, O.P.,

to Oxford. To Father Hudson, she advised the reprinting of some

"glorious old liturgical hymns" in order that "our American

Catholics" might contract some enthusiasm for their own neglected

inheritance.[211] To another friend, Father Daly, she wrote in praise

of Joyce Kilmer, 'He is the best kind of literary soldier of Christ:

I take an American pride in him and his clearness and cleanness.'[212]

This sincere American Catholic, Louise Imogen Guiney, was a true,

minor poet, highly regarded by a few poets and critics, given lip-

service by the editors of anthologies, and generally ignored by

Catholics and non-Catholics alike.

Whereas Miss Guiney, at times, rendered obscure her specific

religious preference; (Miss) Eleanor Cecilia Donnelly, (September 6,

1838 - April 30, 1917) repeatedly proclaimed her allegiance. This

'ultra Catholic' gave "nearly all her interest to the Church and its

---

[210]Grace Guiney, (ed.,) Letters of Louise Imogen Guiney, II,
120.
[211]Louise Imogen Guiney to Rev. Daniel E. Hudson, C.S.C.,
(March 4, 1910) Hudson Papers. UNDA.
[212]James J. Daly, op.cit., p.113.

welfare, writing at one moment odes and sonnets to celebrate its

festivals, and at another moment historical essays to interpret its

progress."[213] However, her fame rested chiefly on her poetry:

dramatic lyric.[214]

> It was her practice to turn into verse the life of one saint
> after another, and as soon, apparently as, there were enough
> of them, to group them together, dedicate them to a revered
> priest of her acquaintance and publish them.[215]

Of her fifty volumes written over a period of seventy years,

religious poetry constituted the bulk of her work, interspersed with

biography, fiction, juveniles, and essay. Happily, recognition was

not denied this admirable effort. Contemporary criticism did not

hesitate to place her poetry at the side of Henry Wadsworth

Longfellow's. Some credited her "Vision of the Monk Gabriel" as the

inspiration of Longfellow's "Legend Beautiful." Others hailed her

as the Adelaide Procter of America.[216] Father Daniel I. McDermott

wrote:

> Her muse ever tends to develop the better feelings of men,
> to excite pity for suffering and charitable consideration
> for erring humanity, and, in all and above, all, to promote
> the glory of God.[217]

The busy Miss Donnelly, in a letter to Father Hudson, dramati-

cally expressed this impelling mission of Catholics:

---

[213]John D. Wade, "Eleanor Cecilia Donnelly," Dictionary
American Biography, V (1930) 369.
 [214]Honor Walsh, "Eleanor Cecilia Donnelly," America, XVII
(May 19, 1917) 143.
 [215]John D. Wade, ibid.
 [216]Eleanor Cecilia Donnelly, Poems by Eleanor Donnelly with an
Introduction by the Very Rev. Daniel I. McDermott, p.6.
 [217]Ibid.

O, what beautiful sketches those of Mr. Stoddard are,
"With Staff and Script" Surely, his pen is the most elegant
of all your contributors and when he touches upon things of
the soul, his genius is so manly, yet tender, in its piety,
that it moves me powerfully. God speed his work!218

The modest Miss Donnelly did not hesitate to inform Father Hudson

that she was so occupied in literary work that she did not know what

to reply "to all these letters that come to me from Canada and the

States asking me why don't I write more for the Ave Maria and all

the other journals?" One of Miss Donnelly's fans had complained:

"I only took the Ave Maria on your account and I am so
often disappointed in looking for your poems."219

Obviously, the volume of her poetry was so great as to influence its

quality. The caustic leveller, Eliot Ryder, remarked of this:

If that strong-minded old maid only would spend more time
in polishing off her work, she would turn out more genuine
jewels and less "paste."220

Nonetheless, it was Eleanor Cecilia Donnelly, who paraded the

glories of the Church and its saints as well as the deeds of American

Catholic heroes like Commodore John Barry before the American

public. "Outside the Gates" exhibited her religious bent:

Open to me the low, low gate
    Of sweet Humility
That I may steal through the shadows late
    And walk alone with Thee.

218Eleanor C. Donnelly to Rev. Daniel E. Hudson, C.S.C.,
(January 13, 1886) Hudson Papers. UNDA.
219Ibid.
220Eliot Ryder to Rev. Daniel E. Hudson, C.S.C., (January 30,
1886) Hudson Papers. UNDA.

Weary am I of pomp and pride,
   Weary of self and sin,
Open the gate O Crucified,
   And let me in![221]

"The Cannon in the Convent Grounds" gloriously proclaimed the

charity patriotism of Catholics, specifically the seventy-five

Sisters of the Holy Cross from Notre Dame, Indiana; and elsewhere,

who worked in the floating hospitals caring for the casualties of

the Civil War.

Floating sweet saints, on the dark winding waters,
   Alone with the wounded, the dying, the dead,
Christ of the Holy Cross! bless Thy dear daughters,
   Brave help of our heroes who battled and bled![222]

If Eleanor Donnelly was voluminous in her verse-making, her

contemporary Agnes Tobin was the antithesis publishing hardly at

all. Fortunately, the distinguished convert scholar, Theodore

Maynard, rescued the latter from oblivion. Agnes Tobin also pre-

ferred to live abroad in London, "where she gained the enthusiastic

admiration of such exacting judges as Arthur Symons, Sir Edmund

Gosse, Alice Meynell, and Joseph Conrad."[223] Miss Tobin's forte was

translation, a skill she developed to an extremely high degree.

On the strength of her rendering of Petrarch,
the only one that brings to life in English the
passionate beauty of the original, Mr. Yeats pronounced her to be the finest poet America has
produced since Whitman.[224]

---

[221]Thomas Walsh, op.cit., p.144.
[222]Eleanor Donnelly, Crowned With Stars, p.130.
[223]Theodore Maynard (compiler) The Book of Modern Catholic
Verse, p.340.
[224]Ibid.

Prior to Maynard, other compilers of anthologies made similar exertions to bring more Catholic poetry before the public. Early in the period (1881), Eliot Ryder edited The Household Library of Catholic Poets, a collection heavily laden with selections written by American Catholics. The purpose of this volume was to inform "the children of the Church" what had been written by their co-religionists.

> ... 'Take the field of poetry for instance; how many persons can tell you the names of a dozen Catholic poets? They may know the poets and be familiar with their works, but they do not know them as Catholics.'[225]

In that same year, George F. Phelan also produced an anthology, one considering only American Catholic poets.

> Its object is to present one or more poems from Catholic American Poets. Although some three or four whose poems adorn this book have a reputation which is more than American, there are others who are not quite so well known, and whose true poetic feeling and charming power of expression deserve a wider field of expression.... We Catholic Americans should know our own strength. Surely we have among us those who write as strong prose in as graceful English and give expression to as true poetry as any in the republic of letters. If we as Catholics will not give our talented writers recognition, we may be sure that they will seek elsewhere that appreciation and reward we deny them.[226]

Eight years later Father Denis Oliver Crowley and Charles Anthony Doyle edited A Chaplet of Verse by California Catholic Writers. Father Crowley hoped the verse would have the

---

[225]Eliot Ryder, The Household Library of Catholic Poets from Chaucer to the Present Day, p.v.
[226]George F. Phelan, Gleanings From Our Own Fields Being Selections from American Catholic Poets, p.v.

the salutary effect of prompting us to practice the virtues
which they so fittingly extol while they teach us to love
more ardently still the semi-tropical beauty of our western
clime.[227]

This volume had for its most notable contributor, Charles Warren

Stoddard, the essayist and publicist of the South Seas. An intimate

of that California group of writers distinguished by Mark Twain and

Bret Harte, Stoddard, primarily, was an essayist. Nonetheless, like

his good friend Joaquin Miller, he wrote poetry. Religious feeling

did not always possess his various works. However, "Southern

Cross,"[228] one of his four poems published in this collection, once

again displayed strong religious fervor. In a collection of his

verse selected by Ina Coolbrith,[229] the convert Stoddard with such

poems as "Litany of the Shrines," "In a Cloister," "I AM THE WAY,"

gave evidence that he could sing not only of the romantic and exotic

but also praise God the Creator as well. Marion Muir, a contributor

to the Ave Maria, was another who combined religious sentiment with

local color. She believed prose inadequate to tell the full tale of

the bygone days of her childhood on the Colorado mining frontier.[230]

As a result, her religious verse, many times, contained distinct

western shades.

---

[227]Denis Oliver Crowley, Charles Anthony Doyle, A Chaplet of
Verse by California Catholic Writers, p.4.
[228]Ibid., p.136.
[229]Ina Coolbrith, (Collector), Poems of Charles Warren Stoddard
[230]Marion Muir Richardson Ryan, Shadows of the Sunset and
Other Poems, p.5.

It was the anthology, still, that carried the burden of making the poetry of Catholics better known. Joyce Kilmer (1917) and Theodore Maynard (1926) were among the good-intentioned whose anthologies brought this theme into more modern times. Often mentioned by various anthologists was Thomas Augustine Daly, the Philadelphia newspaperman whose forte was the "half-humorous, half-pathetic interpretations of the Irish and Italian immigrant."[231] His Canzoni (1906) and Carmina (1909), written in skillful dialect rhyming, indicate that he did not hold the immigrants in ridicule; instead, he presented them as human beings exposed by the change in environment.

> Seldom descending to caricature, Daly exhibits the foibles
> of his characters without exploiting them; even the lightest
> passages in McAroni Ballads (1919) are done with delicacy
> and a not too sentimental appreciation.[232]

Another journalist, James Ryder Randall, author of "Maryland, My, Maryland," a patriotic poem of lasting fame, achieved deep religious fervor with "Magdalen" and "Why the Robin's Breast is Red."[233]

That poetry and journalism were congenial was readily seen in the staff of the Boston Pilot, where not only O'Reilly but also his two capable assistants, (Miss) Katherine E. Conway and Jeffrey Roche, shared a strong love of poetry. Miss Conway, journalist,

---

[231]Louis Untermeyer, (editor), Modern American Poetry, A Critical Anthology, p.169.
[232]Ibid.
[233]William MacAteer, "James Ryder Randall," Mariale, p.161.

lecturer, and promoter of causes Catholic or otherwise, was considered an able poet. Her poetry, like her other zealous interests, gave "evidence many times repeated of a sincere and abiding belief in God."[234] Edmund Clarence Stedman, the eminent critic of this period, praised her "Outgrown" as a poem "so full of feeling and real lyrical quality."[235] In this same letter to Miss Conway, Stedman asked her opinion of certain literary figures. Her Pilot colleague James Jeffrey Roche in 1890.

> ...succeeded John Boyle O'Reilly as editor and as the idol of a Catholic intellectual group in Boston. A man of humor and generous social qualities, he became a leader in the St. Botolph and Papyrus Clubs, while the sons of old New England enjoyed his romances and cherished his friendship. While not a violent Irish partisan, he was, however an intense nationalist, keenly concerned with the uplifting of the Irish in America.[236]

His Ballads of Blue Water and Other Poems featuring "The Constitution's Last Fight," "Reuben James," "The Man of the Alamo," and "The Flag" was a manifestation of another Irishman's strong liking for the United States.

Boston, also, was the home of Mary Elizabeth Blake, an extremely active Catholic Reading Circle leader. Some of the Irish sociological difficulties in adapting themselves to American conditions plagued Mrs. Blake.

---

[234] Katherine E. Conway, The Color of Life, p.viii.
[235] Laura Stedman, George M. Gould, The Life and Letters of Edmund Clarence Stedman, II, 200.
[236] Richard J. Purcell, "Roche, James Jeffrey," Dictionary American Biography, XVI (1935) 63.

> So when a craven fain would hide the birthmark of his race,
> Or slightly speak of Erin's sons before her children's face
> Breathe no weak word of scorn or shame, but crush him where he
> stands,
> With Irish worth and Irish fame as won by Irish hands.[237]

Mrs. Blake deemed it necessary to remind her fellow countrymen of the brilliant record fashioned by the Irish in the American Civil War. The Irish, guardians of the soil, had kept the nation free.

Mrs. Blake, the active wife of Dr. John G. Blake, was typical of the many Catholics of various backgrounds, whose verses swelled the pages of various periodicals. Two Catholic Summer School favorites, Mrs. B. Ellen Burke (the teacher) and the scholarly Helena T. Goessmann; the mercurial George Parsons Lathrop and his wife, the former Rose Hawthorne; the mild "little giant" in the field of letters, Brother Azarias Mullany were such contributors. (Then, there were other Catholic poets breaking into print, poets destined to achieve their greatest fame in a later generation. Among these were Aline Kilmer (the widow of Joyce) and the poet-priests Charles O'Donnell, C.S.C., James J. Daly, S.J., and Hugh Fraser Blunt.) Returning now to the specific period, the religious intensity of Caroline D. Swan's The Unfading Light should be remembered.

Furthermore, the distinguished careers of two other Americans demonstrated the Catholic drive to profess pride in patriotic and

---

[237]James B. Cullen, The Story of the Irish in Boston, p.274.

intellectual achievements. The busy Conde B. Pallen, critic,
university professor, and an editor of the Catholic Encyclopaedia
wrote poetry. "Arise America" was a patriotic, almost jingoistic,
response to President Cleveland's Venezuelan message.[238] "Maria
Immaculata," "Death of Sir Launcelot," and "Ode for Georgetown
University" (Georgetown Centenary, February 21, 1889) showed the
variety of his interests he honored with poetry. Maurice Francis
Egan, in regard to Pallen's works, observed: "I can't help thinking
that Conde's poetry suffered from his devotion to scholastic
philosophy."[239] Egan, journalist, diplomat, critic, university
professor, said of his own work:

> At this time, I had written a little book of poems called
> Preludes and a series of stories, The Life Around Us. My
> ambition then was not to elevate the tone of the American
> literature written for Catholics, but to create a taste
> for a broader kind of literature.[240]

Perhaps, Mrs. Mary E. Mannix's poetic tribute to the versatile
Egan was the best example of this Catholic effort to employ poetry
for positive propagandizing.

> He was a loyal champion of the Faith
> Whose eager pen when malice sought to scathe
> Or scar, alert in every sense
> Sprang swift, unfaltering, to her defense.
> Who through the changing scenes of many ways
> The long and tortuous march of many days,
> Tasted and savored life's true joyousness,

---

[238]Conde B. Pallen, Collected Poems, p.81.
[239]Maurice Francis Egan, Recollections of a Happy Life, p.143.
[240]Ibid., p.144.

And dwelt not long on life's harsh bitterness.
Seeking the best of what in life he found,
His gentle chidings never left a wound.
Cheerful and hopeful, busy to the last,
Into the land immortal he has passed.

Be Thine own paths from earliest youth he trod,
To age, stretch wide Thine arms to him, O God![241]

Of the various poets mentioned here, contemporary critical
acclaim placed Father Tabb and Miss Guiney above the others. It was
odd that these two recluses, one bound to a college, the other to
England, should be the best of our poets. Both shared that spark of
genius to grasp a vision and to express it in a style not marred by
technical incompetence. Neither wore their Catholicity like a
badge, nor did they write a catechism in verse. Yet, they achieved
a poetry that won recognition from the expert and concluded the
search of those looking for good, religious poetry. It was a pity
that Agnes Tobin, who shared their muse, produced so little original
poetry.

Joyce Kilmer, had he lived, might have joined this exclusive
trio. In his enthusiasm for his religion and simplicity, he sometimes missed the poetic mark. His efforts, nonetheless, should not
be de-emphasized for he was the poet of militant Catholicism, highly
regarded both as a Catholic and as a poet. Equally militant was
Miss Donnelly whose good works were sometimes hidden by the mediocre
in her some fifty volumes of religiously inspired themes.

---

[241]Francis X. Talbot, S.J., The America Book of Verse, p.94.

Eliza Allen Starr, John Boyle O'Reilly, James Jeffrey Roche, Katherine E. Conway, Conde B. Pallen, and Maurice Francis Egan were among the cultured Catholics who felt it necessary to express their thoughts in verse. Admittedly, at times, their expression achieved more success in other mediums, yet, this poetry could never be dismissed completely. More important, these public figures demonstrated visibly that Catholicism was no bar to the appreciation of the beauty in art and poetry.

Father Abram Ryan's poetry was the first in a long line of patriotically inspired verse. He demonstrated that a Catholic could be patriotic and loyal even to a lost cause without disregarding his religion. O'Reilly and Pallen, Mrs. Blake and Miss Donnelly continued his crusade to reveal the Catholics' love for their country.

Equally hard to ignore was the volume produced by these Catholics. Active men and women from the various vocations and avocations parceled their time so they might write for the various periodicals. That these efforts were appreciated could be seen in the appearance of their poems in the anthologies edited by equally well-intentioned Christians. Charles Warren Stoddard, Thomas Augustine Daly, Marion Muir, Caroline Swan, James Ryder Randall, and many others wrote poetry of merit. All of these poets considered, constituted no organized Catholic poetry movement. Rather they existed as individuals who did much good and some

harm to the cause of poetry and who were a positive influence
in the supplying of religious and patriotic poetry to their co-
religionists in particular and to the world in general.

CHAPTER IV

SOUND COUNSEL FROM THE NON-FICTIONISTS
WITH SOME REGARD FOR
ART, DRAMA, LITERATURE, SCIENCE, EDUCATION, MEDICINE

During this thirty-five year period (1880-1915), Catholic
thought and opinion again found expression in the essays of talented
laymen and clerics. The essay lent itself readily to the task of
considering and evaluating life in these United States, and
Catholics did not hesitate to use this medium to reveal their hopes
and fears for their country and their faith. John Boyle O'Reilly,
for example, used his editorial pen to further "the cause of all
oppressed peoples: the Negroes, the Indians, the Jews," as well as
his beloved Irish.[1] The convert Charles Warren Stoddard wrote
"purely artistic" travel sketches of the South Seas, which won the
acclaim of no less an authority than William Dean Howells.[2]
Stoddard's South Sea Idyls (1873), a good example of the nature-
travel essay, sparkled with the charm of the Polynesians, much
similar to Lafcadio Hearn's enthusiastic portrayals of the Japanese.
Stoddard's lush descriptions, however, never achieved the recognition given to those of John Muir and John Burroughs, Teddy

_____

[1]Katherine Bregy, "American Catholic Essayists," Catholic
Builders of the Nation, IV, 146.
    [2]Ibid., p.149.

Roosevelt's naturalist friends. Louise Imogen Guiney, although essentially a poet, essayed criticism with authority and insight.[3] Miss Guiney, of course, dealt with her Seventeenth Century "favorites" Vaughan, Hazlitt, and Lady Danvers. That supposedly devastating dilemma, the conflict between science and evolution on the one hand and revealed religion on the other, found the Reverend John A. Zahm, C.S.C., leading the advanced thought of conciliation and integration.

> His earliest essays as a Catholic apologist were contributions to the Ave Maria and the American Catholic Quarterly and to The Catholic World, and had for their general thesis the harmony between that he called "the sciences of faith and the sciences of reason."[4]

Furthermore, the indices of these periodicals, Ave Maria, American Catholic Quarterly, and The Catholic World, disclosed a Catholic interest in varied subjects such as politics,[5] socialism,[6] the recent (1889) American Catholic Congress,[7] Freemasonry,[8]

---

[3]Ibid., p.150.

[4]John William Cavanaugh, C.S.C., Father Zahm, (Reprinted from The Catholic World, (February, 1922) p.6.

[5]John Gilmary Shea, "Anti-Catholic issue in the late election, the relation of Catholics to the political parties," American Catholic Quarterly, (hereafter abbreviated ACQR) VI (January, 1881) 36.

[6]William J. Kerby, "Catholicity and Socialism," ACQR, XXX (April, 1905) 225.

[7]John A. Mooney, "Our recent American Catholic Congress and its significance," ACQR, XV (January, 1890) 150.

[8]Augustus J. Thebaud, "Freemasonry," ACQR, VI (October, 1881) 577.

Tennyson,[9] Thackerary,[10] Francis Thompson,[11] Christian Science,[12]
the English Catholic Revival,[13] Mormonism,[14] alcoholism,[15] public
libraries,[16] women's rights,[17] and divorce.[18] The convert
Katherine Bregy, a capable writer in her own right,[19] named some of
the leading essayists of this pre-war era. Included were many
gifted but soon forgotten women: Madeline Vinton Dahlgren, Anne
Chambers Ketchum, Eleanor Donnelly, Eliza Allen Starr, Mary
Elizabeth Blake, Caroline D. Swan, Anna T. Sadlier, Virginia
Crawford, Helena Goessmann, Jeanie Drake, and Elizabeth Jordan.
Among their male contemporaries were Maurice Francis Egan, Joyce
Kilmer, Father John Talbot Smith, and William H. Thorne.

---

[9]George Parsons Lathrop, "Was Tennyson Consistent," ACQR,
XVIII (October, 1893) 101.
[10]A. J. Faust, "William M. Thackerary," ACQR, VIII (October,
1883) 597.
[11]Beryl, "The New Catholic Poet," Ave Maria, XXXVIII (April 28,
1894) 449.
[12]Rev. James Goggin, "Christian Science and Catholic Teaching,"
Ave Maria, LXXII (May 13, 1911) 577.
[13]Wilfrid J. Robinson, "England's Catholic Revival," Ave Maria,
III (New Series) (January, 1916) 7.
[14]"The Menace of Mormonism," Ave Maria, L (March 24, 1900) 370.
[15]M. D. J. Kelley, "Women and the Drink Problem," Catholic
World, LXIX (August, 1899) 678.
[16]William Stetson Merril, "Catholic Literature in Public
Libraries," Catholic World, LXXXIX (July, 1909) 500.
[17]F. C. Farinholt, Katherine F. Mullaney, Mary A. Dowd, "The
Public Rights of Women, A Second Round-Table Conference," Catholic
World, LIX (June, 1894) 299.
[18]W. H. Kent, "The English Royal Commission on Divorce,"
Catholic World, XCVII (April, 1913) 1.
[19]Katherine Bregy, op.cit., pp.148-153.

The scope of this effort was exhibited in the lives and essays of some of the prominent Catholics of this day. Indeed, the Church was fortunate in having for one of its enlightened champions, Miss Agnes Repplier, "America's best writer of the light essay."[20] Oddly enough, her literary career commenced in 1881, when The Catholic World paid her fifty dollars for "In Arcady," a sixteen-page love story with French, Catholic, and tragic overtones. At this time, the remarkable Paulist priest and editor of The Catholic World, Father Isaac Hecker, divined Miss Repplier's capacity for writing essays and advised her:

> 'I fancy that you know more about books than you do about life... Write me something about Ruskin and make it brief.'[21]

From then on, her primary interest was the essay.

That she ascended to a dominating position in the realm of the light, personal essay was seldom denied. Brevity-minded Newsweek was one of several periodicals labeling her at her death, "the dean of American essayists"[22] while Time cautiously added that:

> ...she had acquired an audience that remained fond of her well-bred talent for taking graceful potshots at varied targets.[23]

---

[20]Sr. M. Anastasia, C.S.C., The Catholic Essay, (Thesis, University of Notre Dame, Notre Dame, Indiana) p.15.
[21]George S. Stokes, Agnes Repplier, Lady of Letters, p.59.
[22]Newsweek, XXXVI (December 25, 1950) 45.
[23]Time, LVI (December 25, 1950) 55.

Much earlier during the first Cleveland administration, however, two
other magazines already valued the work of Agnes Repplier. In
addition to The Catholic World, which welcomed her contributions,
The Atlantic Monthly provided another steady outlet[24] for her
"barbed but gentle pen." The editor of this pillar of American
intellectual society, Thomas Bailey Aldrich, befriended her.
Through him and Agnes I. Irwin, Dean of Radcliffe College, she
became acquainted with all the proper New Englanders; Doctor Holmes,
Sara Orne Jewett, Mary E. Wilkins Freeman, James Russel Lowell and
Julia Ward Howe. Perhaps in these instances, "She met all the
important persons left."[25] Her work also appeared in Lippincott's
and, for thirty years, she contributed a weekly article to the old
Life,[26] the humorous journal, whose departure from the American
scene has been the occasion of nostalic lament. The author's
success with periodicals was duplicated by the appearances of
numerous bound volumes.[27]

----

[24]The New York Times, (December 16, 1950)
[25]Stokes, op.cit., p.86.
[26]Ibid., p.109.
[27]Books and Men, 1888; Points of View, 1891; A Book of Famous
Verse, 1892; Essays in Minature, 1892; Essays in Idleness, 1893;
In the Dozy Hours and Other Papers, 1894; Varia, 1897; Philadelphia,
the Place and the People, 1898; The Fireside Sphinx, 1902;
Compromises, 1904; In Our Convent Days, 1905; A Happy Half-Century
and Other Essays, 1908; Americans and Others, 1912; Germany and
Democracy, the Real Issue, the Views of Two Average Americans,
A Reply to Doctor Dernburg. (with J. W. White), 1914; Counter
Currents, 1916.

The bespectacled essayist, by the very nature of her craft,
shared her opinions with her fellow Americans.

> Her essays were a favorite jumping-off point for editorial
> writers for Miss Repplier could spot an American foible
> with insidious accuracy and do it to a superb though gentle
> crisp.[28]

For example, she wrote of a Los Angeles newspaper's account of a
young mother who had stolen clothes to replace the shabby garments
her daughter must wear to school. The newspaper set the public mind
aflame so that frocks by the "wagonload" were donated by generous
Americans. No court action, obviously, was taken against the hapless mother. Yet, the sharp Repplierian pen did not hesitate to
write:

> Now the interesting thing about this journalistic
> eloquence, and the public sentiment it represented, is
> that while shabbiness was admittedly too heavy a burden
> for a child to bear, theft carried with it no shadow of
> disgrace...Her mother's transgressions had covered her
> with glory not with shame.[29]

In another journalistic bout that year, the chain-smoking Miss
Repplier ripped into the advocates of teaching sex-hygiene to
children. She was against it, definitely. Such lectures were a
menacing, artificial stimulus rather than a safeguard. Her argument included the old saw, "If knowledge alone could save us from
sin, the salvation of the world would be easy work."[30] The Atlantic

---

[28]The New York Times, (December 16, 1950)
[29]Agnes Repplier, "Popular Education," The Atlantic Monthly,
CXIII (January, 1914) 7.
[30]Agnes Repplier, "The Repeal of Reticence," The Atlantic
Monthly, CXIII (March, 1914) 300.

Monthly also showed her defending New York City from its defamers, those who called it a 'city of the damned.' She indicated the city's friendship for the poor with its hospitals, day nurseries, swimming pools, libraries. Nor would the poor leave the city for they meant to live 'in the town, and on the town as well.'[31] Hospitable New York spent more than a million dollars on its hapless people and "It expended nearly four hundred thousand dollars for the care of aliens who had been in this country less than five years."[32] Furthermore, she defended the inclination of families, in need of the necessities of life, to attend moving-picture shows.

As a prejudiced observer (1915) of the first phase of the World War, the convent-educated Agnes Repplier gave this interesting diagnosis.

> The two amazing things about the attitudes of Americans toward the ruthless war which has been waged in Europe for the past four months are the flabbiness of our peace talk, the talk which starts from no premises and reaches no conclusions, and the mournful forebodings of pious Christians who lament the failure of Christianity to reconcile the irreconcilable, to preserve the long-threatened security of nations.[33]

She was so far from being neutral, that anti-German sentiment fairly boiled from her pen. A particular target was the apologetics of Professor Hans Delbruck.

---

[31]Agnes Repplier, "Our Lady Poverty," The Atlantic Monthly, CXIV (October, 1914) 458.
[32]Ibid.
[33]Agnes Repplier, "Christianity and the War," The Atlantic Monthly, CXV (January, 1915) 7.

> The amazing, and amusing statement made by this amazing
> and at all times amusing German is that Austria's ultimatum
> (the most bullying document of recorded history) was born of
> 'dire extremity' and was sent in the interests of peace.[34]

Some of her other opinions were interesting if not noteworthy.

While she admired "Gentlemen Jim" Corbett,[35] the fighter-actor; she

heartily disliked Jane Addams,[36] the "dogooder." Theodore Roosevelt,

she found 'blundering perhaps but as honest as the sun.'[37] As for

the cause of women's rights, she was not interested.[38]

> Neither did Agnes Repplier spare her fellow Catholics.

> The trouble is again that the average American Catholic
> lacks delicacy of taste, which is by no means nature's free
> gify to the well-intentioned.[39]

A cause for this Catholic want of literary background could be

traced, she felt, to the parochial school.

> When I was a little girl, Catholic schools placed in the hands
> of Catholic children a certain number of feeble and flavorless
> stories, which were so permeated with religious discussion
> that we skipped five pages out of seven. They were in effect
> light-armored controversies and not real stories at all,
> every incident and every conversation being so arranged and
> circumscribed as to lead up to the inevitable conversion of
> the particularly obdurate Protestant who was introduced to
> us in the first chapter.[40]

---

[34]Agnes Repplier, "A Commentary on Herr Delbruck," The Atlantic
Monthly, CXV (March, 1915) 427.
[35]George S. Stokes, op.cit., p.113.
[36]Ibid., p.159.
[37]Ibid., p.168.
[38]Ibid., p.167.
[39]Agnes Repplier, "The Choice of Books," The Catholic World,
LXXXIV (October, 1906) 54.
[40]Ibid.

This opinion, written in particular for the particular use of Catholics, was printed in The Catholic World. In regard to the controversial novel, she added the warning:

> A controversial novelist who should attempt to state his opponent's principles with candor, and to rebut them with fairness, would make scant progress. It is his part to set up the opposition arguments like nine-pins, and to bowl them over at short range with convincing ease.[41]

Furthermore, she noted that it was "generally a woman who handles fearlessly themes of which she is profoundly ignorant, who censures most where she has least authority."[42] However, all of Miss Repplier's critical force was not spent in pricking balloons. Her co-religionists found her voicing strong approval of Andrew Lang, a contemporary, English, Protestant, highly regarded man of letters. Lang held the personal conviction that Mary Stuart would make "eyes at every male saint in heaven."[43] Yet, his friend from Philadelphia noted carefully when Mr. Lang wrote:

> ... The Mystery of Mary Stuart, he did not do so in the spirit of a public prosecutor but of true historian, keen on the scent, and with a mind honorably opened to conviction.[44]

There was also an assurance that the picturesque ritual of the Church was the humanizing influence which sought "by exterior comeliness to

---

[41]Agnes Repplier, "The Birth of the Controversial Novel," The Catholic World, LXXXVII (April, 1908) 38.
[42]Ibid.
[43]Agnes Repplier, "Andrew Lang," The Catholic World, XCVI (December, 1912) 295.
[44]Ibid.

symbolize the sweetness of her spirit."[45] At another time, she
evaluated the limited advances of Catholic literature in the
world.[46]

Fortunately, Miss Repplier detected several flaws in Father John
Talbot Smith's protest that the Catholic publisher and the Catholic
reader were unduly indifferent to the efforts of the Catholic
writer. Her refutation included an account of her happy association
with The Catholic World. She also disagreed with Father Smith's
advice that the young Catholic writer should conceal his faith in
order to attain literary success; for, she was unable to trace any
of her failures to an editor's dislike for her religion.

> When I have failed, it was because my work was bad, a
> common cause of collapse, which the author for the most
> part discredits.[47]

This rebuttal forwarded the additional advice that Catholics should
not expect the secular press and the secular reading public to be
enthusiastically receptive to a book designed for Catholic reading
alone unless that book be a great literary masterpiece.[48]

Miss Repplier, for this ability to comment readily and
knowingly, if not always accurately, upon the pressing problems of

---

[45]Agnes Repplier, "Picturesqueness and Piety," The Catholic
World, XCII (March, 1911) 737.
[46]Agnes Repplier, "Catholic Letters and the Catholic World,"
The Catholic World, XI (April, 1915) 31-37.
[47]Agnes Repplier, "Catholicism and Authorship," The Catholic
World, XC (November, 1909) 173.
[48]Ibid., p.170.

the day, received many honors. The University of Pennsylvania in 1902 recognized a fellow citizen and awarded her a Doctor of Letters degree.[49] Eight years later, the University of Notre Dame presented her the Laetare Medal for 'distinguished achievement in letters and a noble exemplification of Catholic womanhood.'[50] In addition, Columbia, Marquette, Princeton, and Yale[51] also gave her honorary degrees. The National Institute of Arts and Letters[52] and the American Academy paid her tribute, and President Calvin Coolidge appointed her "to a commission for the Ibero-American International Exposition to be held in Seville in 1929."[53] The Catholic Poetry Society of America, at its inception in 1931 elected her vice-president[54] of the society.

Contemporary evaluation of Agnes Repplier's efforts varied. In her early period, a critic claimed that she was a specialist with competence in the roles of a booklover and a personal essayist. "One gets from her book, no echo of the world, only the echoes from the world of letters."[55] In this state, she depended upon vast quotations from various other authors to carry her attack by the force of numbers. By 1898, however, the Dial observed that she nr

[49]George S. Stokes, op.cit., p.143.
[50]Ibid., p.157.
[51]The New York Times, (December 16, 1950)
[52]Ibid.
[53]George S. Stokes, ibid., p.198.
[54]The New York Times, (December 16, 1950)
[55]Edward E. Hale, Jr., "Miss Repplier's 'Essays in Idleness,'" Dial, XV (October 16, 1893) 225.

longer placed such heavy reliance on the quotations and, now, included more of herself in the essay.[56] This same critic scored her want of original thinking; but, at the same time praised her powers of assimilation, discrimination, and appreciation. Seven years later, _Critic_ magazine proudly proclaimed that "countless Philadelphians shine proudly in the reflected glory of America's foremost essayist."[57] Even the _Literary Digest_ allowed she was distinguished.[58]

Agnes Repplier, the well-known essayist, impressed the literary world that here was a capable commentator who happened to be a Roman Catholic. She did not force her religion upon her public, nor did she conceal it. On one occasion, there was casual reference to her religious background.[59] At another time, her presentation of a particular aspect of Catholic life caused _The Critic_ to announce that she had so keenly awakened the interest of the reading youth that the appearance of _Our Convent Days_ was awaited only with "utmost patience."[60] A more modern critic, Howard Mumford Jones, felt that she was representative of an "intelligent and enlightened

---

[56]_Dial_, XXIV (March 1, 1898) 149.
[57]_Dial_, "The Lounger," _Critic_, XLVII (September, 1905) 204.
[58]_____, "A Plea for Reticence," _Literary Digest_, XLVIII (April 11, 1914) 827.
[59]Agnes Repplier, "Popular Education," _The Atlantic Monthly_, CXIII (January, 1914) 7.
[60]_____, "The Lounger," _Critic_, XLVII (September, 1905) 209.

Catholicism;"[61] to which The New York Times echoed: "Her life-long devotion to her Roman Catholic faith was apparent in much of her work."[62] So, in a small way, Miss Repplier projected some Catholic thought into the current of American literature.

An interesting contemporary of Agnes Repplier, Miss Katherine E. Conway, toiled diligently in the none too conspicuous field of Catholic journalism. Katherine Eleanor Conway was born in Rochester, New York, September 6, 1853, and was educated in convent academies in Buffalo and Rochester. While teaching in the latter city, she published "a modest little Catholic monthly"[63] and contributed to other Catholic periodicals. By 1880, she had moved to Buffalo where she was associated with the Catholic Union and Times; and, three years later she made the big step to Boston as she became an editorial assistant on the Pilot staff. O'Reilly thought she was not only a good newspaperwoman but also a 'gentle poetess.'[64] When the great editor, poet, and patriot died so suddenly, Miss Conway became an associate editor; and, in 1905, she assumed the editor-ship[65] of the Pilot, succeeding James Jeffrey Roche who resigned to accept a Theodore Roosevelt appointment. She, in addition to her

[61]Howard M. Jones, Book Review of Agnes Repplier: Lady of Letters by George Stewart Stokes (Philadelphia, Pa., 1949), The Saturday Review of Literature, XXXII (April 30, 1949) 32.

[62]The New York Times (December 16, 1950)

[63]Walter Lecky, Down at Caxton's, p.137.

[64]Ibid., p.127.

[65]Who's Who in America: 1906-1907, p.375.

editorial duties, wrote numerous poems, edited a volume of
O'Reilly's, and wrote several volumes of fiction and essay.

> Her influence in a literary way has been particularly
> exerted upon young women of the country, as her books were
> written especially for them.[66]

Here was a pioneer in the Catholic Reading Circle movement and
an ardent booster of the Catholic Summer School of America at Cliff
Haven, New York, where she appeared as a lecturer. In fact, it was
Miss Conway who read the paper, "The Catholic Summer School and the
Reading Circles,"[67] to the second Catholic Congress assembled in
Chicago, September 8, 1893. When the University of Notre Dame in
1907 named her the recipient of the Laetare Medal; William J.
Onahan, a prominent Chicagoan applauded the selection:

> She eminently deserves the distinction by her conspicuous
> services as a journalist and writer. Her pen has been ever
> employed in vindicating Catholic principles and pleading
> for all that is good, true and generous.[68]

In New York, Archbishop John M. Farley wrote that she was a loyal
Catholic and a capable writer.[69]

Some of her works indicated very clearly that she hoped to make
it easier for her readers to move politely through everyday life.
A Lady and Her Letters, for example, was a sound and fundamental

---

[66]The Notre Dame Scholastic, (March 16, 1907)
[67]Progress of the Catholic Church in America and the Great
Columbian Congress of 1893, (Two volumes in one binding published
by John S. Hyland, Chicago) II, 106.
[68]The Notre Dame Scholastic, (March 16, 1907)
[69]Katherine E. Conway, In the Footprints of the Good Shepherd,
ii.

book on the art of writing letters. Packed within its sixty-seven pages there was a frown for using postal cards for all occasions,[70] a warning against the writing of anonymous letters,[71] and an admonition for the warmhearted who "chill and stiffen the moment they put pen to paper."[72]

Advice from Miss Conway came, not as a scorching rebuke, but as a gentle reminder. For example, she wrote:

> The woman-suffragist, we must admit in the face of notable examples, is often a most admirable woman, whom we are compelled to like personally, however little our sympathy with her cause.[73]

As for women engrossed in club activities, she admitted the goodness of the club idea itself, while lamenting the development of the "professional" club member. The journalist-essayist anticipated Dale Carnegie by a number of years in publishing another little volume on manners, Making Friends and Keeping Them. In a style reminiscent of Dorothy Dix, the advice came forth:

> Certainly no loving and honorable wife will maintain openly or secretly any friendly intercourse with people with whom her husband is at variance.[74]

Reading the essays in Making Friends and Keeping Them some fifty years after they were written, this writer formed the opinion that

---

[70] Katherine E. Conway, A Lady and Her Letters, p.22.
[71] Ibid., p.64.
[72] Ibid., p.47.
[73] Katherine E. Conway, The Christian Gentlewoman and the Social Apostolate, pp.13,14.
[74] _____, Making Friends and Keeping Them, p.61.

Miss Conway treated the then modern woman's emergence into a changing world with a liberal dose of common sense tempered with regard and deep affection for her fellow men.

This same general regard was directed in a particular fashion to those who shared her faith. The weaknesses she spotted in the individual Catholic have been duplicated unfortunately in a later age. The frowsy appearance[75] of some Catholics at Mass and the "amazing bad habit of clambering over others getting in and out of a pew"[76] were minor, perhaps. However, the fondness for the "short" Low Mass[77] and an indifference toward the use of a missal[78] at Mass were practices meriting discouragement. There was a modern ring to the charge that:

> The pet fabrication that Catholics are not allowed to read the Bible... should not be encouraged by the indifference of Catholics to Sacred Scriptures.[79]

Of course, those Catholics, who desired to be so religiously inconspicuous as to be mistaken for Protestants,[80] were also victims of her polite indignation.

These "four little gems of manners and morals" previously mentioned: A Lady and Her Letters, Making Friends and Keeping Them, Questions of Honor in the Christian Life, and The Christian Gentle-

---

[75] Katherine E. Conway, Making Friends and Keeping Them, p.61.
[76] Ibid., p.41.
[77] Ibid., p.33.
[78] Ibid., p.51.
[79] Ibid.
[80] Ibid., p.37.

woman and the Social Apostolate were joined to another volume of
essays Bettering Ourselves to form the Family Sitting-Room Series.
By 1904, each of the volumes had accomplished at least two editions
while two of them had gone through five printings. Moreover, her
efforts did not end here, for at least two novels and two volumes of
selected poetry[81] could be credited to her pen as well as the very
readable history, In the Footprints of the Good Shepherd. (This was
a tribute to the cloistered nuns of the Good Shepherd in New York.)
In the role of editor, she helped bring forth a volume of O'Reilly's
poems and A Handbook of Christian Symbols and Stories of the Saints.
Indeed, she was a busy woman.

Happily, her contemporaries recognized and appreciated her work.
A reviewer for The Catholic World noted that the lines of conduct
and modes of thought suggested by A Lady and Her Letters "cannot
fail to be of lasting benefit to all those who lay them seriously
to heart and are influenced by them in their actions."[82] The
following year The Catholic World reiterated its praise, but this
time it was for Making Friends and Keeping Them.

---

[81]Lalor's Maples, (Novel. Third edition by 1904)
  The Way of the World and Other Ways, (Novel. Section edition
by 1904)
  A Dream of Lillies, (Poetry. Third edition by 1904)
  On the Sunrise Slope, (Poetry)
  Katherine E. Conway, (editor) Watchwords from John Boyle
O'Reilly, (Poetry)
  [82]"Talk About New Books," The Catholic World, LXI (July, 1925)
565.

> There are thousands of women to whom it ought to prove
> invaluable in cases where want of good advice might prove
> to be a lamentable circumstance.[83]

Of this same volume, the Boston Herald wrote: "If Miss Conway's

suggestions were faithfully followed, a great many people would find

life far sweeter and more beautiful."[84] The Boston Gazette opined

that "Every girl should own this little book"[85] in its review of

A Lady and Her Letters.

As for matters particularly Catholic as portrayed in Questions

of Honor in the Christian Life, Eliza Allen Starr praised the author

for touching "sacred things so safely and with such a trained

hand."[86] Relative to this same book, perhaps the greatest praise of

all came from the convert, Charles Warren Stoddard, "You have done

the very thing that was most needed in Catholic literature and you

have done it perfectly well."[87] Of course, volumes by more recent

authors have superseded some of those of Miss Conway; yet the

judgment persisted that here was a capable writer interested in

bringing grace and comfort to her fellow Americans.

So far, attention has been focused upon the literary efforts of

two talented women: Agnes Repplier and Katherine Conway.

---

[83]"Talk About New Books," The Catholic World, LXII (January, 1896) 560.
[84]Katherine E. Conway, The Christian Gentlewoman and the Social Apostolate, (1)
[85]Ibid., (2)
[86]Ibid., (5)
[87]Ibid.

Consequently, the career of Conde B. Pallen would discourage the
notion that the essay on matters Catholic was exclusively a feminine
affair.

Conde Bencist Pallen, a most distinguished alumnus of Georgetown
and St. Louis universities was born in St. Louis, December 5, 1858;
and, for the greater part of his seventy years, he, in so many ways,
worked for the benefit of his country and his church. The President
of the United States, Herbert Hoover, publicly acknowledged his
worth, while papal honors were bestowed both by Pope Leo XIII and
Pope Pius XI.[88] Versatility was the keynote of his career as he
ably acted as literary critic, lecturer, poet, editor, encyclopedia
promoter, and contributor to literary and philosophical journals.
At the first Catholic Congress of Laymen in America, held in
Baltimore, November 11, 12, 1889, Pallen addressed the gathering and
charged that the Catholic writer must enter the popular arena.[89]
Then, he spent the rest of his life living up to this speech,
fulfilling the obligation of advancing a Catholic viewpoint in
American affairs.

To achieve this, he accepted the positions of the "Catholic
revisory editor" for the Encyclopedia Americana and the New

---

[88]The New York Times, (May 27, 1929)
[89]Official Report of the Proceedings of the Catholic Congress,
pp.130-142.

International Encyclopedia.[90] It was not enough. In order to
correct the errors pertaining to the Church in other encyclopedias
errors regarded as sources of flagrant misinformation, he became a
key figure in the publishing of the Catholic Encyclopedia. (As its
managing editor (1904-1920), he used his own money in meeting the
early financial emergencies.)[91] "Of all the causes he defended,
that of Catholic education was probably nearest his heart."[92] In
the religion-in-the-school controversy, Doctor Pallen maintained
that the papal bull, Tolerari Potest, could not be interpreted to
mean "that the state has in itself the right to educate;"[93] and,
that bishops, pastors, and congregations were excused from building
schools only where poverty or some other sufficient reason existed.
Serving the popular front of Catholic education, he was a frequent
lecturer at the Champlain and Western Catholic Summer Schools and
the New Orleans Winter School. He reasoned:

> As long as Catholics are surrounded by adverse intellectual
> influences that make against the integrity of their faith,
> so long will institutions like the summer school be needed
> to instruct and educate them in the stability of Catholic
> thought.[94]

---

[90]The New York Times, (May 27, 1929)
[91]James J. Walsh, "In Memoriam: Conde Benoist Pallen,"
Commonweal, X (June 26, 1929) 214.
[92]"Conde Benoist Pallen," Commonweal, X (June 12, 1929) 144.
[93]Conde Pallen, "The Catholics and the Public Schools, The
True Significance of 'Tolerari Potest,'" Educational Review, IV
(December, 1892) 462.
[94]Conde Pallen, "The Catholic Idea of Popular Summer Schools,"
Ecclesiastical Review, XV (July, 1896) 70.

The topics of his lectures bespoke his varied interests.
"Savonarola," "The Church and Socialism," "The Philosophy of
Literature," "The Epochs of Literature," revealed that his concern
for such things as Church and literature enveloped both past and
present. A reviewer for The Catholic World did not take too kindly
to The Philosophy of Literature when it appeared as a bound volume;
saying that no new truths were stated, the style was too ornate and
serious, and that the author erred in assuming that his audience was
equally erudite.[95] A year later, Epochs of Literature was deemed a
good synthesis by this same journal.[96] Still more successful was
The Meaning of the Idylls of the King (1904). This critical volume
received world-wide attention and Tennyson himself sent a letter of
praise acknowledging that Pallen had 'seen further into the real
meaning of the Idylls of the King than any of my commentators.'[97]

His relations with the English literary set had not always been
this cordial. An English magazine was taken to task for its wholesale condemnation of American manners as Pallen pointed out the
inability of this particular English author to recognize the
difference of American customs.

It is a radical mistake on the part of a foreigner to
expect to impress upon the American mind the notion of
his transatlantic superiority, or to overwhelm it with

---

[95]"Talk About New Books," Catholic World, LXIV (March, 1897)
833.
[96]"Talk About New Books," Catholic World, LXVII (August, 1898)
706.
[97]James J. Walsh, op.cit., p.215.

the magnitude of his social distinction....While we have
social distinctions and classes well marked off, yet it is
within the power of every individual to life himself by
ability to positions to which his worth entitles him.[98]

Americans, however, were far from perfect. Doctor Pallen hoped

that his fellow nationalists would become better conversationalists,

particularly among chance acquaintances. Too often, a potentially

stimulating conversation had been ruined by those taking refuge in

the "weather."[99] For his co-religionists, this editor of Church

Progress and Catholic World (1887-1897) and president of the

Catholic Press Association (1891), hoped to limit the number of

Catholic journals since Catholic patronage was being wasted "in

supporting journals that fulfill their functions but in-

differently."[100] As for Father John A. Ryan, the brilliant,

courageous advocate of enlightened Christian Social doctrine, Pallen

thought Father Ryan much too radical and the recipient of much un-

warranted press coverage.[101] (As he lived into another age, Conde

Pallen continued to criticize. "Feminism," he said, cheated women

out of their real destiny. Restricted immigration was not desirable.

He was critical of President Woodrow Wilson and the League of

Nations. Moreover, there was to be no diplomatoc recognition of

---

[98]Conde Pallen, "American Manners," The Month, LVIII
(September, 1886) 62-64.
[99] _____, "A Chat by the Way," The Catholic World, XLII
(November, 1885) 270.
[100] _____, "The Independence of the Catholic Press,"
Ecclesiastical Review, X (May, 1894) 342.
[101]The New York Times, (May 27, 1929)

Russia.)[102]

Throughout his career Conde Pallen remained a critic.

> There was in Mr. Pallen the gift of criticism in the best
> sense of the word, the power of seeing what is good as well
> as what is defective.[103]

As a critic, Conde Pallen surveyed the American scene and inter-

preted it with the keen, kindly eyes of an American Catholic. Some,

naturally, differed with his views, both national and religious;

yet, few Americans failed to recognize the intentions of this

earnest man.

> The dedicated devotion which Dr. Pallen gave to Church and
> country throughout his seventy years of full and ardent
> living is in itself the mark of a generosity heroic and
> hence exceptional; and it was fused, in him, with other
> factors which made him a symbol unique in the history of
> American Catholicism.[104]

Unique or not, Conde Pallen would have admitted that his

physician friend, Doctor James J. Walsh, was worthy of standing by

his side as a Catholic champion. Archbald, Pennsylvania, in the

heart of the anthracite coal regions, was the future doctor's birth-

place April 12, 1865. Leaving the Jesuit novitiate to study

medicine, the young Walsh never abandoned the militant zeal and love

for the Church characteristic of Loyola's followers. After

graduating from the University of Pennsylvania, he went abroad to

study in Vienna, Paris, and Berlin (1895-1898). His career as a

---

[102] Ibid.
[103] The New York Times, (May 29, 1929)
[104] "Conde Benoist Pallen," Commonweal, X (June 12, 1929)
144.

medical writer commenced during this European sojourn.[105]

Writing from then on became an important avocation of his career, since, officially he was the Dean of the Fordham Medical School and its professor of neurology. He wrote for many of the medical journals, was a contributing editor to the Journal of the American Medical Association, and the medical editor of the New York Herald and the Independent. An article, "The Popes and the History of Anatomy" published in the Medical Library and Historical Journal[106] indicated the direction of his writings and his aim of removing the cancerous idea that the Church was the enemy of science. Since some fifty books, in addition to his lectures and articles, came from this writer, it was true to say that Doctor Walsh "hit hard, repeatedly and with authority at religious, moral, historical errors which attacked the Catholic Church."[107] Thus, his The Popes and Science (1908) was a reply to Dr. Andrew D. White's On the History of the Warfare of Science with Theology in Christendom.[108]

Books and articles such as Old Time Makers of Medicine (1911), Medieval Medicine (1920), The Century of Columbus (1914), "Basil Valentine, a Great pre-Reformation Chemist,"[109] "Michael Servetus

[105]Archbald Malloch, "James J. Walsh," Science, XCV (May 22, 1942) 522.

[106]Ibid.

[107]Commonweal, XXXV (March 13, 1942) 501.

[108]"Dr. James J. Walsh," The Catholic World, CLX (April, 1942) 110.

[109]James J. Walsh, "Basil Valentine, a Great pre-Reformation Chemist," American Catholic Quarterly Review, XXXI (April, 1906) 342-358.

and Some Sixteenth Century Educational Notes,"[110] and "Geography and
the Church in the Middle Ages,"[111] were a part of his process of
integrating science with Christianity. The popular writer, wrote
Walsh, was guilty of creating the fiction that scientists

> have either lost their beliefs or have had their faith in
> a Creator, in Providence and in a hereafter of reward and
> punishment seriously impaired.[112]

On the contrary, most scientists were firm believers, while some
were devout. Doctor Walsh had visited Jules Verne and was delighted
to report that the astonishing French author was a fervent Catholic
and "by no means the indifferentist one might suppose him by judging
only from his works."[113] The aim of Verne's books, observed Walsh,
was not to teach religion; "but rather to interest in science and to
instruct by amusing."[114] More in keeping with Walsh's theme of
positive propagandizing was the piece regarding John Gilmary Shea.
The writing of history, Shea's avocation, "proved of a great value
to his countrymen and especially to his fellow Catholics."[115] While
acknowledging the History of the Catholic Church in the United
States to be monumental, he also praised Shea the pamphleteer, who

---

[110]James J. Walsh, "Michael Servetus and Some Sixteenth Century
Educational Notes," American Catholic Quarterly Review, XXVI (1901)
714-732.
[111]_____, "Geography and the Church in the Middle Ages,"
American Catholic Quarterly Review.
[112]_____, "Scientists and Faith," American Catholic Quarterly
Review, XXXV (April, 1910) 217.
[113]James J. Walsh, "Jules Verne and the French Religious
Situation," The Dolphin, VII (May, 1905) 554.
[114]Ibid.
[115]James J. Walsh, "John Gilmary Shea," American Catholic
Quarterly Review, XXXVIII (April, 1913) 203.

many times represented the Catholic point of view on certain important subjects.

The erudite physician not only believed that a pamphlet or book could adequately present the Catholic aspect of things but held that to be agents of conversion.

> Of course there is no question that it is extremely dangerous for Protestants to consult Catholic books.... Nothing will so soon make Catholics out of Protestants as the reading of Catholic books ... Our good Protestant friends need to come out of the "dark ages" here in America and let themselves learn something about the only Christianity which has a history that goes back to Christ Himself.[116]

The "dark ages" in America referred to that era beginning at mid-nineteenth century with its multi-shaped, styleless architecture and its calumnies against the Church such as "Peter Parley's" Universal History for Children.[117] Naturally, the statement that "Ireland being now happily united with England" did not pass this Fordham Irishman unchallenged.[118] The Protestants' relations with their Catholic brethren in the northern United States had shown "great improvement;" but, the West and South were still bigoted because the people in those areas were not acquainted with Catholics and their good works.

---

[116]James J. Walsh, "The Dark Ages in America," American Catholic Quarterly Review, XLIII (January, 1918) 19.

[117]Ibid.

[118]Ibid., p.3.

Northern Protestants have passed through this phase, but
now they need to pass through the other stage of learning
about Catholicity from Catholic books and educated
Catholics.[119]

To produce more Catholic books, he founded the Fordham

University Press in 1907.[120] For Doctor Walsh, a Catholic book had

all the powers claimed for patent medicines. That same year, for

example, he sent a copy of his latest, The Thirteenth, Greatest of

Centuries, to Father Hudson with the notation that he hoped it would

attract the attention of the Catholic press. The principal reason

for wanting a good press coverage, wrote Walsh, was for the sake of

Catholic Summer School of America, the (original) publishers of the

book.

There has been an idea that we are not doing serious work
up there and this I think will serve to show one phase of
that work from an interesting standpoint and demonstrate
its intellectual value for Catholics and Catholicity.[121]

He, as a trustees of the Summer School, hoped that institution

would continue to serve Catholics with intellectual stimulation

amidst the pleasant recreational atmosphere of Lake Champlain. His

contributions to The Catholic Encyclopedia was another phase of

manifesting his religious preference before the nation. As copious

and brilliant as his writings were, Father Wilfrid Parsons thought

[119]Ibid., p.20.
[120]Commonweal, XXXV (April 10, 1942) 618.
[121]James J. Walsh to the Rev. Daniel E. Hudson, C.S.C.,
(September 3, 1907) Hudson Papers. UNDA.

that Doctor Walsh was at his best as a lecturer.[122] Furthermore,
he was an original member of the Calvert Associates, the founders
of The Commonweal. He also participated in the organization of the
Catholic Writers' Guild.

There was reward on earth for these magnificent efforts. While
Georgetown and Catholic University gave him honorary degrees; Notre
Dame, in addition to an honorary degree, named him the recipient of
the Laetare Medal, 1916. Rome appointed him a Commander of the Order
of Saint Gregory. Although Catholic critics have assailed Doctor
Walsh for being too partial to The Thirteenth, Greatest of Centuries,
he estimated in 1933 that the book had netted him $40,000.[123] All
in all, James Joseph Walsh was an able man.

> ... he opened new ways of thought to his countrymen, and
> helped them to understand a body of philosophy, art, and
> history, of which many of them had never heard. In his
> lectures and writings upon Catholic culture, Doctor Walsh
> was distinctly a pathfinder... he is worthy of grateful
> remembrance for his incessant effort to give to his country-
> men a wider and more accurate appreciation of the work of
> the Catholic Church in creating and sustaining our Christian
> civilization.[124]

Better known internationally than either Doctor Walsh or Conde
Pallen was Theodore Roosevelt's friend, Maurice Francis Egan (1852-
1924). The bushy-bearded Philadelphian shuffling back and forth

---

[122]Wilfrid Parsons, "Dr. James J. Walsh," Commonweal, XXXV
(March 27, 1942) 551.
[123]Ella Marie Flick, "Dr. James J. Walsh, 1865-1942," The
Catholic World, CLV (May, 1942) 162.
[124]America, LXVI (March 14, 1942) 631.

between the college campus and journalism's offices ultimately came
to rest as the United States minister to Denmark in 1907. As a
teacher, he taught at Georgetown, Notre Dame, and Catholic University;
while his lectures took him to Johns Hopkins, Harvard, and Yale. As
a writer, he contributed to most of the Catholic periodicals and to
such secular journals as Lippincott's, Scribner's, St. Nicholas, and
the Independent. As a journalist, Magee's Illustrated Weekly, The
New York Freeman's Journal, and the Catholic Review employed him in
an editorial capacity; moreover, the publishers of the Century
Magazine treasured his friendship as well as his work.

Whether professor, journalist, or diplomat, Egan's prolific pen
seldom was still as it wrote poetry, fiction, essays, juvenile
novels, literary criticism, and translations. At the "listening-
post" of the Copenhagen ministry during the exceedingly tense years
(1907-1917), the diplomat would write to his friend Father Hudson
telling him not only the trends of European war and intrigue but
also the progress of his next article for the Ave Maria. In one
letter, he wrote:

> I met Monsignor Benson in London. He is very interesting
> and unpretentious. I like his historical novels, but as I
> told him very frankly I think books like "The Conventionalist"
> and "The End of All" gave people a very mistaken idea of the
> Catholic Church.[125]

---

[125]Maurice Francis Egan to the Rev. Daniel E. Hudson, C.S.C.,
(September 30, 1913) Hudson Papers. UNDA.

Egan, whose "services in Denmark was of far greater value to his country than could ever be repaid,"[126] justifiably, could have placed the welfare of his co-religionists into the shadowed background. But, this was not the case.

> He held strictly to the self-imposed task of promoting Catholic literary expression in the fields of journalism, fiction, and poetry, at a time when we had great need of the things he did and when there were few to do them. His practical loyalty to his faith, and the conviction that he could do nothing nobler than to commend his faith and his Church to the American people, surveyed his path through life, and he followed it rejoicingly.[127]

As with these other Catholics, the power of the written word was not lost upon Maurice Francis Egan. He feared bad novels. If a good novel was a gift of God, "a bad one was perhaps one of the most insidious gifts" of Mephistopheles. Thus, a bad course in reading influenced one's "honor and honesty, purity of intention, and energy of action."[128] Too many newly emancipated, young girls on the street car passed over literature to devour the latest paper-covered novel. (The trashiest of all the paperbound novelists, wrote Egan, was Miss Mary Jane Libby).[129] Constant novel reading, even of the good novels, was bad for every faculty. The "lower books," whose supply, unfortunately, was amplified with cheap English reprints,

---

[126]Outlook, CXXXVI (January 30, 1924) 170.
[127]William J. Kerby, "Maurice Francis Egan," The Catholic World, CXVIII (March, 1924) 679.
[128]Maurice Francis Egan, Lectures on English Literature, p.164.
[129]Ibid., p.13.

gave a false idea of life. Young women, he feared, "looked on Literature as only an ornament of life, a polite accomplishment or the amusement of an idle hour."[130] Still another false notion did not escape his rebuke:

Among Catholics there sometimes crops out a kind of in-sincerity which almost amounts to snobbishness. It is the tendency to praise no book until it has had a non-Catholic approbation.[131]

On the positive side he praised the Reading Circles of Catholic Americans for studying the worthwhile books, Catholic or otherwise, and thereby escaping the stigma that reading was only a "polite accomplishment."[132] His co-religionists were informed that there were literary masterpieces other than those supplied by the English Protestant tradition. Shakespeare's Spanish contemporary, Calderon,[133] the poet and dramatist, should never be ignored; nor should the other Catholics, Robert Southwell, Richard Crashaw, and William Habington; all writing in the "great shade of Avon's bard."[134] Chaucer, in an earlier age, and artists of a later age such as Aubrey de Vere, Adélaide Procter, Lady Georgiana Fullerton, and Alice Meynell were accomplished writers professing Catholicism.[135] As for novels reflecting convent life, Kathleen

---

[130] Ibid., p.7.
[131] Maurice Francis Egan, A Gentleman, p.128.
[132] Ibid., p.131.
[133] Maurice Francis Egan, The Ghose in Hamlet and Other Essays in Comparative Literature, p.174.
[134] Maurice Francis Egan, Lectures on English Literature, p.87.
[135] Ibid., pp. 22,110,142,143.

O'Meara's <u>Narka</u> gave a true picture while Admiral Porter's character "Louise Norton" seemed absurd in relinquishing piracy and murder for the convent where she became its prioress, all before she was twenty-eight years old.[136] Obviously, Egan disliked seeing Catholicism treated in a frivolous fashion.

In one circumstance, Catholic homes frequently displayed the "gaudiest religious" prints with crudely drawn figures and splashy colors that bordered on the sacriligeous. "And this in spite of the fact that we possess a thousand exquisite and poetical conceptions."[137] In the past, some Catholic publishers had violated what was considered "good taste."

> There was a time when a great deal of the output from certain Catholic publishing firms was dear and nasty. It was veritable junk, horrible stuff, glittering to the eye, but worse than dead sea fruit to the cultivated taste. And this helped to give us all, authors and publishers, a bad reputation. But, that time is gone, and ought not to be recalled except as a part of history which has an evil effect on present conditions; and one of its results is that no Catholic author who appeals to a Catholic public can live, even frugally by his work...
> What, then ought to be the duty of people who need decent literature, which does not insinuate cynical unbelief, palliate free love, plead for sexual lawlesness, or, in a word, debase the moral currency? To support the efforts of the Catholic publisher, to enable authors to be free of anxiety, and to better literary conditions, that are beginning, thank God! to improve.[138]

---

[136]Ibid., p.178.
[137]Ibid., p.55.
[138]Benziger Brothers, The Best Stories by the Foremost Catholic Authors with an Introduction by Maurice Francis Egan, I, ix, x.

Other improvements previously had suggested themselves. Young
men from fifteen to twenty years of age could profit from a thorough
understanding and practice of a gentleman's manners. Egan's handbook emphasized that it was the "small things of our daily inter-
course with our fellow-beings which make the difference between
success and failure."[139] Thank goodness, swearing and spitting had
declined since Dickens' memorial visit to the United States.[140] For
the most part of this book, Egan was on the solid ground of common
sense with worthwhile suggestions regarding how to dress and what to
do with olives and finger bowls at the dining table. His readers,
though, must have balked at the anecdote illustrating the virtue of
eating a lettuce-caterpillar to save one's dinner hostess from
embarassment.[141] Once more the scholarly diplomat cauterized the
trashy novels and hoped there were no bookless homes in all the land,
"least among us Catholics."[142] (Two years prior to Egan's guide of
1893, Lelia Hardin Bugg had written The Correct Thing for Catholics
which was a suggested model

> ... for the exterior conduct of Catholics on some of the
> occasions where there is a liability of annoying mistakes,
> and a reminder of obligations understood but often for-
> gotten.[143]

---

[139]Maurice Francis Egan, A Gentleman, p.5.
[140]Ibid., p.67.
[141]Ibid., p.13.
[142]Ibid., p.206.
[143]Lelia Hardin Bugg, The Correct Thing for Catholics,
p.5.

Another Catholic, Madeline Vinton Dahlgren, had written the
specialized The Social-Official Etiquette of the United States
(1894).[144]

Maurice Francis Egan exhibited his interest in the Church's
progress in other ways. He edited and extended Monseigneur Charles
de T 'Serclaes' The Life and Labors of Pope Leo XIII because he
thought such a book must especially appeal to Catholic Americans.

> ... there is no personage in recent history for whom the
> intelligent people of the United States of all creeds and
> opinions, have a more devout admiration than for this Leo
> XIII.[145]

His admission that his friend and associate, James A. McMaster,
originally a Presbyterian, had so much zeal for Catholicism that it
bordered on the excessive, was an understatement. (Egan the
diplomat was a good foil for the pugnacious McMaster). Yet,
McMaster who, against his own inclinations,[146] became a journalist
to satisfy the need for a Catholic paper; succeeded in making the
New-York Freeman's Journal into an influence upon metropolitan life
and the "recognized representative organ, as it is today, of
Catholicity in America."[147] The Glories of the Catholic Church in

---

[144]Madeline Vinton Dahlgren, The Social-Official Etiquette of
the United States.

[145]Monseigneur Charles de T 'Serclaes,' The Life and Labors of
Pope Leo XIII with a Summary of His Important Letters, Addresses, and
Encyclicals edited and extended by Maurice Francis Egan,   x.

[146]Maurice Francis Egan, "James A. McMaster," Illustrated
Catholic Family Annual, xx (December, 1888) 44.

[147]Ibid.

Art, Architecture, and History, which Egan edited, also contributed
in making American Catholics aware and proud of their vast inheritance. Egan held the ideal:

> ... I do not ask you to follow me blindly; but I insist we
> Catholics, we Christians, shall in literature, as in all
> other sciences and arts, lead not follow.[148]

He himself contributed to that ideal; and Notre Dame University,
in behalf of his fellow Catholics, presented him with the Laetare
Medal (1911). Maurice Francis Egan, moreover, served Catholicism in
another way. This exceedingly competent diplomat and scholar
demonstrated to Theodore Roosevelt and to the other men in public
life that an exemplary Catholic made a first-rate American citizen
and servant.

Egan, who promoted the Catholic concern in the faith-inspired
beauties of art and literature, wrote that Eliza Allen Starr (1824-
1901) was the

> one woman in all this land who has, in spite of the
> vulgarity and ignorance around her, preached the aesthetics
> of religion.[149]

New England born but ultimately a revered resident of Chicago, Miss
Starr developed her girlhood fondness for art into a missionary
career. After her conversion in 1854, she attacked the glaring
weakness, the unfamiliarity of Catholics with their own Christian
art. Primarily, she was a lecturer and collector; and her Chicago

---

[148]Maurice Francis Egan, Lectures on English Literature, p.23.
[149]Ibid., p.55.

home, a two-storied brick flat with a full basement, proudly named
"Saint Joseph's Cottage," was a veritable museum housing the finest
reprints and reproductions. In 1875 she traveled extensively in
Europe visiting the galleries and shrines. When she returned, she
felt impelled to share her enthusiasm and knowledge. Consequently,
"St. Joseph's Cottage" and other fashionable Chicago homes were the
sites of many lectures. Her fame spread as she lectures in other
cities as well. These lectures, of course, furnished Miss Starr with
the basis of a book or two. Of these books, the eminent scholar,
Brother Azarias Mullany wrote:

> Etchings and engravings by various admirable processes have
> brought the great masterpieces within the reach of all, and
> it were not to our credit to neglect their study. Under
> the guidance of the charming volumes of Miss Eliza Allen
> Starr you find much to admire. Their full meaning will be
> unrolled before you. She has made art a life-study; and I
> may safely say that there is not a great painting of Europe
> of which she has not the key, and which she cannot describe
> in apt and clear-cut phrase.[150]

Miss Starr loved fine art and she loved her fellow men. Yet, in
the role of the critic, she wrote to her friend Father Hudson:

> Our people are sorrowfully in want of culture and the way to
> cure this is to familiarize their minds with the subject,
> put a higher standard of culture before them and wean them
> from the love of riches.[151]

To make this higher standard accessible to Catholics was the
object of her life. Reading her volumes some seventy years after

---

[150]Brother Azarias Mullany, Books and Reading, p.58.
[151]Eliza Allen Starr to Rev. Daniel E. Hudson, C.S.C., (March.6,
1879) Hudson Papers. UNDA.

their initial appearance and aware of the excellent color photographs of art objects, Miss Starr's modern reader still was impressed with her enthusiasm, her fine descriptions, and her own illustrations. Whether she realized it or not, Miss Starr anticipated the audio-visual techniques of contemporary education. She, like the educationists, hoped that pictures would prove to be "catechisms of instruction."

> Whatever helps the Catholic parent to preserve Catholic traditions, Catholic customs, and a Catholic sentiment, in his family will bring a blessing on any house; and for this reason I beg of you Catholic fathers and Catholic mothers to keep on your walls such pictures, such representations of the Divine mysteries of the sacraments and of the saints, as will encourage a truly Christian spirit of devotion in your families.[152]

Furthermore, she projected the visionary attitude that an adequate acquaintance with Christian art on the part of Catholics would produce several worthwhile results. Not only would culture be served; but, the Catholic also would have a more penetrating and appreciative insight of his religious beliefs. For example, she wrote of the reproductions of the great masterpieces depicting the archangels and guardian angels, that they were more than mere ebellishments, they were a device to instill the "images of these celectial friends in the memories and imaginations of all who become familiar with them."[153] Still another benefit to be acquired was

---

[152]Eliza Allen Starr, Patron Saints, p.33.
[153]Eliza Allen Starr, The Archangels and the Guardian Angels in Art, p.14.

that the printed page and picture might prove the incentive for
thousands of "youths and maidens in these United States to visit
Europe, Italy, Rome, with the intentions of pilgrims rather than of
tourists."[154] Most visionary of all was her hope that a worthwhile
religious art would develop and install a change in these United
States.

> The time may not be far distant when America may be called
> "Land of Saints;" and we may see companies of pious pil-
> grims to some shrine, or spot of extraordinary interest,
> taking the place of those pleasure parties which now set
> no limit to their ambition save such as the oceans on
> either side of this vast continent may compel.[155]

Miss Starr realized that the immediate need was to circulate the
idea that true Christian teaching did not imply a rejection of
science nor the arts. Her approach was historical. For example, she
gave "thirteenth century Siena," the Italian city of artists, saints,
and scientists, as a center of a highly developed culture where the
arts and scientists were so carefully ingrafted with "the supernatural virtues born of faith."[156] Nor should the Catholic influence
in England be underplayed for the glories of her best history and
literature and her "noble, Christian, Catholic laws"[157] were not
obliterated by the Tudors' religious innovations. This similar
thought appeared in a letter to the Notre Dame archivist, James F.
Edwards, when she proposed to lecture about the scientist Isaac

---

[154]Eliza Allen Starr, _Pilgrims and Shrines_, I, vii.
[155]Eliza Allen Starr, _Patron Saints_, p.33.
[156]Eliza Allen Starr, _Pilgrims and Shrines_, II, 199.
[157]_Ibid._, p.35.

Newton, for few knew that he was a Catholic.[158] (In this same letter, Miss Starr, the recipient of the Laetare Medal in 1885, also informed Edwards that she wore the medal at her lectures). Other immediate activities in promoting the faith were revealed in her correspondence with Father Hudson. For a Protestant group, the Chicago Fortnightly, she read a paper on St. Benedict.[159] Quite different was her asking Father Hudson whether or not he would like to print an article on the approaching tri-cetennial of the Carmelites of New Orleans, which the sisters had asked her to write.[160] At the World's Columbian Exhibition in Chicago, 1893, she received the "only gold medal bestowed on any art exhibitor."[161]

Lecturer, exhibitor, writer, Eliza Allan Starr fervently paraded the glory and beauty of religious art before the American public. Whether at "St. Joseph's Cottage" or at a Catholic Summer School platform, or some other appropriate location, her lectures testified that a strong religious faith was no bar to the cultured study of art, literature, and history. Instead of remaining in her comfortable home and criticizing her co-religionists, she went to their aid. Success, apparently, attended this effort. Abroad, Pope Leo XIII honored her, whereas the Catholic Congress of Laymen in

---

[158]Eliza Allen Starr to James F. Edwards (April 6, 1886) UNDA.
[159]Eliza Allen Starr to Rev. Daniel E. Hudson, C.S.C., (March 23, 1881) Hudson Papers. UNDA.
[160]Eliza Allen Starr to Rev. Daniel E. Hudson, C.S.C., (July 16, 1882) Hudson Papers. UNDA.
[161]William Stetson Merrill, "Eliza Allen Starr," The Catholic World, LXXIV (February, 1902) 609.

Baltimore hailed her as "the most accomplished lecturer in America
on Christian art."[162] The American Catholic Quarterly Review
praised her Patron Saints for satisfying "the great want of today's
literature, sound, practical pleasing reading for the young."[163]
One of the more appreciative opinions respecting Miss Starr's work
in behalf of Christian art appeared in The Catholic World (1902).
In this article, the key to Miss Starr's intense interest in art was
revealed.

> But the mission of Christian art is to present the beauty
> of a character made like unto God's, as exemplified in the
> saints, in the Blessed Virgin, in the human nature of the
> Incarnate Word. It has thus a religious mission in the
> world which raises it above the sphere of art for art's
> sake.[164]

Whereas Eliza Allen Starr sought to give Catholics some knowledge of Christian art and literature, the Reverend John Talbot
Smith imposed upon himself the equally herculean task of making the
stage serve Catholicism. True, many of the famous American actors
were Catholics; but they were recognized more for their entertainment
value than for religious activities. (At that time, actors like
professional ball players, often were regarded as second-class
citizens). Father Smith's design to help the stage help itself was

---

162Richard H. Clarke, "What Catholics Have Done in the Last
Hundred Years," Official Report of the Proceedings of the Catholic
Congress Held at Baltimore, Md., November 11,12, 1889. p.176.
    163Eliza Allen Starr, Pilgrims and Shrines, I, 329.
    164William Stetson Merrill, "Eliza Allen Starr," Catholic World,
LXXIV (February, 1902) 608.

the more remarkable for it was but one of his activities in behalf
of the Church.

> No American priest of his period understood so well as
> he that all great engines of current life are employed in
> working against Christ, the press, literature, drama,
> education, money. I cannot recall any modern priest who
> more incessantly preached the need of converting these
> enormous resources to Christianity, nor any who so bravely
> and perseveringly labored to convert them.[165]

John Talbot Smith (1855-1923) deserved this praise. As sucessor
to the venerable Patrick Valentine Hickey as editor of The Catholic
Review, Father Smith (1889-1892) strove to make "that paper a power
for the welfare and advancement of the Church in the United
States."[166] The Catholic Summer School of America, knew him as a
supporter from its inception, as founder of the tent city known as
the College Camp, and as its fourth president (1905-1909). Father
Smith, as a writer, wrote history, biography, fiction, essays. At
least six novels, the histories of the Dioceses of New York (1905)
and of Ogdensburg (1885), the biography of Brother Azarias (1897),
and a volume ultimately entitled The Training of A Priest (1896) came
from his pen.

The last named work, originally labeled Our Seminaries, an Essay
on Clerical Training, was "such a Firpo-Dempsey entertainment as to
offend and dismay certain ecclesiastical authorities at first."[167]

[165]The Catholic Summer School, Rev. John Cavanaugh, C.S.C.,
"An Appreciation of Dr. John Talbot Smith." p.5.
[166]The Catholic Summer School, "Monsignor Lavelle's Eulogy,"
p.17.
[167]The Catholic Summer School, Rev. John Cavanaugh, C.S.C.,
"An Appreciation of Dr. John Talbot Smith." p.4.

In this case, Father Smith, in trying to help his Church, hit with the power of a heavyweight. The seminaries, he charged, were "aiming to turn out a clerical tradesman rather than a man of culture."[168] It was lamentable that some priests were poor physical specimens "in consequence of the poor physical training provided in our seminaries."[169] (Father Smith, due to an early joust with tuberculosis, was, like Theodore Roosevelt, an advocate of the "Great Outdoors.") Furthermore, priests who were to have the "fullest influence over all classes of citizens must have the manners, habits, and appearances of gentlemen."[170] The Catholic college received this criticism:

> It is not the best commentary that the graduate of the average Catholic college must spend two or more years in non-Catholic institutions to make up for the gaps in his knowledge.[171]

Our Seminaries suggested several reforms. Since the American boy was not a European, it advised, "He must be taken as he is, armor and impudence together and trained from his own starting point."[172] Text-books were to be adapted to the American situation, political and social, so that the "merits and defects, the strengths and needs of his nation"[173] would not escape the young priest. A

---

[168]John Talbot Smith, Our Seminaries, an Essay on Clerical Training, p.167.
[169]Ibid., p.85.
[170]Ibid., p.16.
[171]Ibid., p.32.
[172]Ibid., p.6.
[173]Ibid., p.21.

curriculum change was included.

> The conclusion is irresistable that literature ought to
> take its place in our seminaries. It should never have
> been thrust from that place to make way for any other
> science or art, and its absence from the curriculum is a
> blot upon all our institutions.[174]

In another equally critical article, Father Smith strenuously

objected to the indifference shown by Catholics to their champions

such as Orestes Brownson, John Gilmary, Shea and Father Louis

Lambert. "Youth must have models," he wrote; yet, Brownson, Shea,

and Lambert were unknown to them for the three departed "amid the

oppressive silence and indifference of those whom they had most

nobly served."[175] Of all the causes espoused by the versatile priest

and author, none seemed to cause him more alarm and pleasure than the

condition of the American Theatre.

Hardly any aspect pertaining to the stage escaped his scrutiny.

After acknowledging the creative ability of both Ibsen and Shaw,

Father Smith judged that their plays were void of religious in-

spiration and better not produced. 'Ibsen could write "more deftly

than any living playwright, a drama in which there will be no God,

no religion, no humanity, no morality, no love, no thought of

eternity..."[176] When Ellen Terry came back for a few weeks to play

---

[174]Ibid., p.299.
[175]John Talbot Smith, "Father Lambert and Robert Ingersoll,"
Ave Maria, LXXI (December 3, 1910) 709.
[176]John Talbot Smith, "The Popular Play," American Catholic
Quarterly Review, XXVIII (April, 1903) 349.

in Captain Brassbound's Conversion, the priest-critic wrote that the playgoers came to see the aged actress for Shaw's play did not "amount to much, being an earlier effort of the Irish humorist and wit."[177] The celebrated Mrs. Patrick Campbell's appearance in The Sorceress brought the comment regarding the playwright: "In his old age, Sardon has gone daft on religion, and seems to think it his mission to denounce the Catholic Church."[178] If the theatrical season of 1904 was any indication of his judgment, the patriotic priest preferred to see American rather than foreign plays presented if the subject treated was contemporary.

> Out of the seven European plays one only displays artistic power, the creative faculty, rising above the level of the inane. The other six are booked for the dust heap or the stock-companies. As a pleasant contrast to this condition four American plays on American life have won the only success worth winning in life: let us call it heart-success, which means fame for artistic work, and gold for the power to touch the hearts of the multitude.[179]

Mrs. Minnie Maddern Fiske, he believed, was the cleverest actress of her time and her performance in The New York Idea, a satire on divorce and the divorce crowd, was just the right mixture of gentility and wit.[180] In her producer-husband, Harrison Grey

---

[177]John Talbot Smith, "The Poetic Drama," Donahoe's Magazine, LVII (March, 1907) 288.
[178]John Talbot Smith, "Foreign Plays on the American Stage," Donahoe's Magazine, LII (November, 1904) 479.
[179]Ibid., p.484.
[180]John Talbot Smith, "A Chance for the Religious Drama," Donahoe's Magazine, LVII (February, 1907) 155.

Fiske, he visualized the successor to the "brilliant Augustine"
Daly.[181] Maxine Elliott was "seen to advantage" in Clyde Fitch's
Her Great Match, a comedy treatment of the timely topic, the
American girls' romantic caprices with impoverished European
royalty.[182] During the age of the great trust-buster, the outraged
drama critic attacked the "theatrical trust" composed by Joseph
Brooks, Mark Klaw "and his partner Erlanger."

> Their methods consists chiefly in getting hold of all the
> leading theatres along the main routes and then charging
> the dramatic companies for the use of the theatre, for the
> privilege of booking, and a fine percentage of their
> general profits. The first two charges are legitimate, the
> third is the tax of the pirate.[183]

Arranged against these pirates were such noble gentlemen as David
Belasco, Harrison Grey Fiske, and the Schuberts. His opinion of
Oscar Hammerstein ran hot and cold. On one occasion he accused
Hammerstein of being a mere moneymaker, offering the public anything
that would sell.[184] Nearly eleven years later he applauded
Mr. Oscar Hammerstein for giving Grand Opera to the people by
building the Manhattan Opera House in competition with the
Metropolitan. The Manhattan Opera House he built unaided with no
Society, no capitalists, no Theatrical Syndicate as partners.[185]

---

[181]John Talbot Smith, "The Fiske Season in New York," Donahoe's
Magazine, LII (October, 1904) 356.

[182]John Talbot Smith, "An Australian Singer," Donahoe's
Magazine, LIV (October, 1905) 425.

[183]Ibid., p.424.

[184]John Talbot Smith, "Augustin Daly," Donahoe's Magazine,
XXXVI (July, 1896) 54.

[185]John Talbot Smith, "Grand Opera for the People," Donahoe's
Magazine, LVII (January, 1907) 56.

Over this obvious concern with things theatrical, Father Smith transposed his love for Catholicism. The harm that some of his co-religionists did the stage and stage people, he tolerated; yet, he hoped that their attitude could be changed. The priesthood was a divided body on the question, "with an official majority, however, against the stage."[186] Catholic journals, for the most part, either coldly mentioned the stage in passing criticism or ignored it entirely. Editorially, the tone was denunciatory. Curiously enough, this official opinion of the stage was "at variance with popular and individual sentiment."[187] There was no mistaking Father Smith's stand:

> Convinced years ago that the leaders had no call to neglect so important a social force as the theatre, which the clergymen themselves had revived in the early centuries, I gave place to criticism of current drama and notices of Catholic actors in a Catholic journal then under my charge. The usual hue and cry arose from the scandalized, and authority was asked to use its gracious influence in suppressing the scandal. I pointed out to the authorities the significant facts in the case as a vindication of my course: that the play was more moral than the press, that American actors were at least one third Catholics, that it would not do to ignore them and their plays; that if Christian sentiment was to have any influence on the play Christians must take an interest in it other than that of the watchdog; that in Paris such Catholic journals as Le Correspondant reviewed plays both good and bad, while I noticed only the good; that no public paper in Europe presumed to ignore the theatre,

---

[186]John Talbot Smith, "The Popular Play," American Catholic Quarterly Review, XXVIII (April, 1903) 339.
[187]Ibid.

and that even so conservative, a journal as the London
Tablet often reviewed the current drama.[188]

Father Smith continued to act according to this 1896 observation. The stage was not a wicked place and actors as a class would
be compared favorably with any other class of professional people.
Good people, misinformed and inexperienced, too often were led into
false impressions by the popular confessions of retired actresses
erupting into pious journals, and the legens continued. Combatting
this, Frank Keenan, a leading player in The Girl of the Golden West,
was quoted:

> I never could see why a bar should be placed between me and
> the Church in which I was born and baptized, simple because
> I have taken up the acting profession. There is no actual
> bar of course. I refer to the general sentiment of the
> pious and decent, that the life of an actor must necessarily
> be more or less wicked owing to the association of the
> stage. My experience is all to the contrary.[189]

Catholics were not aware of the various achievements of their own
brethern in the various departments, let alone the considerable
Catholic contribution to the theatre. They needed reminding that
many talented stage people were practicing co-religionists. From
time to time, the thoughtful priest advanced the names of Catholic
actresses and actors such as: Margaret Anglin, Grace George, Marie
Cahill, Edmund Breese, Frank Keenan, the Four Cohans,[190] James

---

[188]John Talbot Smith, "Augustin Daly," Donahoe's Magazine,
XXXVI (July, 1896) 55.
[189]John Talbot Smith, "The Morality of the Players," Donahoe's
Magazine, LV (March, 1906) 251.
[190]John Talbot Smith, "The Catholic Actor in New York,"
Donahoe's Magazine, LV (January, 1906) 58,59.

Young, Fritz Williams, and Leo Ditrichstein.[191] Variety was served
in this listing, the diversification including: Elsie Janis,
destined to be "The Sweetheart of the A.E.F.," and Paula Edwards of
the comic opera;[192] for Great Ladies of the legitimate stage, Mary
Anderson and Helen Modjeska[193] easily topped the standard. Frank
Keenan was a particular favorite of Father Smith who used his life
to illustrate the value of the acting profession to the Church.

> Yet Frank Keenan diffuses among all his acquaintances love
> and respect for the Church, is a real missionary of Christ,
> while the humble Catholics who read Lord Acton suffer
> tremendous temptations against the faith.[194]

Even more important than establishing the actor as a respected
citizen, was the hopeful priest's desire to see the ascendancy of
the religious drama. He deplored Ibsen's plays with all their pagan
banalities being produced while "the stirring problems of the
Christian life uplifting and consoling, are left in obscurity."[195]
Although it was gratifying to see religious scenes and emotions as
displayed in ordinary life naturally introduced in David Belasco's
The Rose of the Rancho, he despaired of the revival of religious
drama for the managers were interested only in profit-taking and

---

[191]John Talbot Smith, "The Morality of the Players," Donahoe's
Magazine, LV (March, 1906) 248-251.
[192]John Talbot Smith, "A Chance for the Religious Drama,"
Donahoe's Magazine, LVII (February, 1907) 154.
[193]John Talbor Smith, "The Catholic Actor," Donahoe's Magazine,
L (October, 1903) 384.
[194]John Talbor Smith, "Catholic Plays and Players," Donahoe's
Magazine, LV (June, 1906) 636.
[195]John Talbot Smith, "Hades and Ibsen," Donahoe's Magazine, L
(November, 1903) 508.

because the religious class, "who are not playgoers, object to the supposed irreverence."[196] There were other things. The Catholic playwright Augustine Daly, true to his own ideals, made positive contributions toward uplifting the theatre "without bothering himself, I suspect, about the religious side of the drama."[197] The old-time efforts of the amateurs to produce religious drama were so disastrous as to deter the skillful from attempting it. And for a splendid effort such as David Belasco's (a non-Catholic), the counteracting dud appeared in the guise of The Straight Road which was unconvincing because "Clyde Fitch has no more understanding of the saving of a soul than of the question of Chinese labor."[198]

On the other hand, the cause of the religious drama received support from Madama Selma Kernold's Oratoric Society which aimed

'to produce dramatic representations of celebrated events and personnages, chosen from Bible narratives and the history of the Christian era; and to give opportunity to Catholic men and women to develop their musical and dramatic talents under influences in keeping with these sacred subjects.'[199]

The Society in turn received approval in high places. When the celebrated novelist Mrs. Pearl Craigie, "John Oliver Hobbes,"

---

[196]John Talbot Smith, "A Chance for the Religious Drama," Donahoe's Magazine, LVIII (February, 1907) 146.
[197]John Talbot Smith, "Augustine Daly," Donahoe's Magazine, XXXVI (July, 1896) 56.
[198]John Talbot Smith, "A Chance for the Religious Drama," Donahoe's Magazine, LVII (February, 1907) 154.
[199]John Talbot Smith, "A Few Catholic Playwrights," Donahoe's Magazine, LV (February, 1906) 134.

volunteered to lecture to the group, the Archbishop of New York,
John M. Farley was on the platform. Some of the colleges had produced creditable religious plays. As for individual playwrights of
this nature, John D. McCarthy, author of Telemachus and In the
Fool's Bauble, and Father Francis L. Kenzel, The Mystic Rose,[200] had
created plays worthy of their subjects. Unfortunately, the
religious drama did not expend in these channels.

So, in time, Father Smith conceived the plan of making the
parish theatre its citadel. Commercialism was ruining the drama and
the photo-drama leaving the demand upon the Parish Theatre to portray
local and historical Christian life. Catholicism had not been
treated fairly by the historians, "It is a sorrowful fact that the
beautiful Catholic life on American soil has only a slight record
in history, and none at all in the arts..."[201] An active parish
dramatic society could correct some of these oversights.

> But the very fact that you have a parish theatre postulates
> Catholic plays, Catholic playwrights, as it does Catholic
> actors and audiences. The great Catholic leaders of the
> past should not be enclosed in handsome tombs, or merely
> described in tomes of history; they should live again their
> noble lives and splendid deeds on their own people's stage.[202]

The beneficiaries of this proposed Catholic activity would include
not only the actors and playwrights but the audience as well.

[200] Ibid., pp.137,142.
[201] John Talbot Smith, The Parish Theatre, p.44.
[202] Ibid., p.43.

Perhaps, the last named were to benefit most of all.

> The common crowd, it must be admitted, do not reflect much,
> and, when they do, reach regrettable conclusions only two
> often. They do need steady instructions, advice and re-
> straint from wise friends. The drama can be used to teach
> them. Now, the Parish Theatre from this point of view, has
> a splendid field to itself.[203]

Father Smith did more than write about the stage and its

possibilities. At Summer School exhibits, the photographs of actors

and actresses professing Catholicism were displayed side by side

with the images of other Catholics prominent on the American scene.

He composed The Wayfarers Prayerbook especially for actors, and

although 5,000 copies were sold, he did not regard it as too

successful.[204] It was natural for him to be a prime mover in the

organization of the Catholic Actor's Guild in 1914. At this time,

the organization of actors was not original with Catholics for the

Actors Church Alliance under Episcopalian sponsorship already was

doing its good work. The Episcopalians urged the Hebrews and the

Catholics to form branches of the Alliance; and the latter responded

ultimately by establishing their own independent organization. By

now, the motivation should be familiar. To stimulate interest in

the stage by bringing actor and playgoer together, to assist the

Catholic actor, and to prepare the way for the Catholic drama of the

future.[205] One appreciative critic called the Guild "a wedge

---

[203]Ibid., p.26.
[204]John Talbot Smith, "Catholics and the Stage," Catholic
Builders of the Nation, IV, 264.
[205]Ibid., 261.

opening the way to a broader and more charitable interpretation of stage life."[206] In my opinion, Father Smith was the worthy mallet driving this wedge.

John Talbot Smith's biography Brother Azarias was a gracious tribute to the Christian brother, Patrick Francis Mullany (1847-1893). Education, his own and that of others occupied much of his time. As an educator, author, literary critic, and philosopher, his reputation extended into the secular world. While he was president of Rock Hill College, Ellicott City, Maryland, he won the admiration and friendship of Daniel Coit Gilman, president of John Hopkins.[207] Another admirer was Herbert Baxter Adams.[208] The Honorable Andrew D. White, while minister to Germany wrote:

> The breadth and depth of Brother Azarias' view of literature is a revelation to me, and had I known he was giving such lectures I would have urged him during my presidency to Cornell, to present them to our students.[209]

Brother Azarias lectured before the Concord School of Philosophy and the International Congress of Education. The United States Commissioner of Education had invited him to write a volume concerning the History of Education from its origin.[210] After his return from Europe (1888), "the non-Catholic world found him and made earnest demands on his talents,"[211] according to Father Smith. His

---

[206]The Catholic Summer School, Rev. Martin E. Fahy, "Father Smith and the Catholic Actors Guils of America." p.8.
[207]John Talbot Smith, Brother Azarias, the Life Story of an American Monk. p.97.
[208]Champlain Educator, XXIV (April-June, 1905) 115.
[209]John Talbot Smith, Brother Azarias. p.256.
[210]Ibid., p.177.
[211]Ibid., p.256.

friendships with Cardinal Gibbons and Archbishop John J. Keane, his appearances before non-Catholic groups, his articles in the Educational Review of New York, the International Review, the International Journal of Ethics, the American Ecclesiastical Review, the American Catholic Quarterly Review, The Catholic World, and the Ave Maria, probably made him the best known Catholic religious in America at that time.[212] Like Father Smith, he was a benefactor and lecturer of the Summer School.

Brother Azarias resented the fiction of the "new educator" and its divided training; "the mental in the school and the spiritual in the household or temple."[213] He preferred to retain the tradition of developing the youth's entire nature, spiritual and mental. Naturally, in accordance with this view, he favored church-sponsored schools. He revealed that the noted educator, Doctor Henry Bernard, was fair to Catholics and familiar with the teaching methods of the Jesuits and the Christian brothers. Brother Azarias wrote of Bernard:

> He went back to the educational traditions of the early
> Christian schools, and feared not to speak the truth, so
> far as he knew it, concerning the efforts of the Catholic
> Church to preserve learning and maintain schools during
> the ages of violence, through which she was striving to
> civilize the barbarous who overran Europe.[214]

---

[212] Catholic Reading Circle Review, II (September, 1802) p.713.
[213] John Talbot Smith, Brother Azarias, p.177.
[214] Ibid., p.185.

Brother Azarias' refutations of secular slander sometimes assumed
the shape of scholarly historical essays. "Time was," he wrote, "and
that not very long ago, when men were convinced that in France
primary education began after the Revolution."[215] However, the
great archival activity in France between 1857-1868 produced documentary evidence, which Abbe Alain and others used to show many
instances of Church-inspired primary education centuries prior to
1789.

In Cloistral Schools Brother Azarias printed the accusations of
one James Johonnot, presumably an authority on education since he
wrote a book, Principles and Practice of Teaching.

> The effort of the monkish teachers was as much directed to
> the exclusion of such knowledge as did not directly suggest
> their views and authority, as it was to promulgate that of
> the opposite kind. The school did little or nothing to
> banish ignorance from the people. Science was interdicted
> by the Church as opposed to religion. 'For centuries,'
> says Hallam, 'to sum up the account of ignorance in a word,
> it was rare for a layman of whatever rank to know how to
> sign his name.[216]

The public-school teachers, noted the Christian brother, had been
"chewing on this tid-bit for the past ten years."[217] Indeed, it was
reckless writing and Mr. Johonnot was unaware apparently that
Hallam's assertion was thoroughly refuted by Maitland's Dark Ages.
Brother Azarias continued by stating that the curriculum from the

---

[215]Brother Azarias, The Primary School in the Middle Ages,
p.3.
[216]Brother Azarias, Cloistral Schools, pp.3,4.
[217]Ibid., p.3.

fifth to the twelfth centuries could be reconstructed by reading the lives of the saints;[218] that Gerbert (d.1003), Fulbert (d.1028), Lanfrance (1005-1089), and Anselm (1034-1109) were able scholars;[219] that, after the crusades helped to break down the barrier of caste in the twelfth century, the schools became secularized so great was the demand for knowledge; and, in this promising atmosphere, scholasticism took root.[220] F.V.N. Painter's A History of Education he criticized as too full of bile and bitters to do justice "to the grand role played by the Church and by great Catholic educators in the work of education."[221] He thought it a shame that Professor Payne had not translated for his students some work other than M. Gabriel Compayre's, which shamefully mislead the uniniated with misrepresentations contrary to historical fact.[222]

Admittedly, the articles just described were of a scholarly nature and, perhaps, appealed only to a limited number of Catholics. Yet, in addition to his erudite defense of the Christian educational system, he gave all Catholics the benefit of his wisdom and experience in a small, popular volume entitled Books and Reading. Probably, even parts of these essays escaped some readers; but, his

---

[218]Ibid., p.27.
[219]Ibid., pp.33-35.
[220]Ibid.
[221]Brother Azarias, "The Simultaneous Method in Teaching," Essays Educational, p.207.
[222]Brother Azarias, "M. Gabriel Compayre as an Historian of Pedagogy," Essays Educational, p.264.

plea to read with a purpose should not have escaped anyone. Anti-
cipating Mortimer Adler by a number of years, Books and Reading was
a guide-book on how to read and what to read. Brother Azarias indicated the value of taking notes and consulting a dictionary.
Honesty in research demanded the reading of both sides of every
question "under proper guidance."[223] Books had, he maintained, both
a positive and a negative side. To get the positive side, "place
yourself in sympathy with the author;" for the negative:

> Note how far the author has gone over the ground of his
> subject-matter, and wherein he falls short in his treat-
> ment. There are times when what an author does not say is
> as expressive as that which he says. His omissions are an
> important clue to his fame of mind. They reveal his likes
> and dislikes, his aptitudes, his tastes and tendencies.[224]

The good old custom of reading aloud in the family circle and dis-
cussing the books and their authors was worth reviving.

After outlining the proper technique for reading, Brother
Azarias, then, named some of his favorite reading material. Since
"much good is done by every well-edited Catholic journal," such
periodicals as the Ave Maria, The Catholic World, the American
Catholic Quarterly Review, The Messenger of the Sacred Heart, and
Donahoe's Magazine did much in determining "our bearings as Catholics
upon the issues of the day."[225] Although Boswell's Life of Johnson
was the only biography unrivaled in our language, Kathleen O'Meara's

---

[223]Brother Azarias, Books and Reading, p.34.
[224]Brother Azarias, Books and Reading, p.38.
[225]Ibid., p.45.

Frederic Czanam was a biography "strong enough to mark an epoch in the life of any thoughtful Catholic young man."[226] Placed in the hands of young men, the book would quicken "their sympathies in behalf of misery and suffering, and aid the good that is in them to bloom out and bear fruit."[227] Cardinal Newman's Apologia was the one exception to the generality that "autobiography has been recently most disastrous to the writers thereof."[228]

Though America and England had no single great national novel as Cervantes' Don Quixote or Tolstoi's Anna Karenina; still Dickens, Hawthorne, Bulwer Lytton, and Thackeray, "in all these and many others we can find amusement, instruction, and improvement."[229] Evidently, Brother Azarias believed that novels should bring "home to us many a beautiful lesson"; and he approvingly wrote that William Dean Howells "once remarked to me that he could no more conceive a novel without a purpose than an arch without a keystone."[230] Among the critics he favored were: Walter Pater was wordy but thought-provoking; W. E. Henley's works were models of good taste and sound literary judgment; Matthew Arnold preferred "estimates carefully made;" James Russell Lowell was "occasionally too long drawn out;" Edmund Clarence Stedman was the most "fair-minded, genial, and sympathetic of critics;" Aubrey de Vere, gave

[226] Ibid., p.47.
[227] Brother Azarias, Books and Reading, p.47.
[228] Ibid.
[229] Ibid., p.52.
[230] Ibid., p.53.

one a majestic view of his master Wordsworth; Richard Holt Hutton's
"theological opinions have no value for Catholics" but his literary
essays were valued "for their thoughtfulness, breadth of view, and
grasp of subject."[231]

For Catholics in particular, the scholarly brother had some
advice. In the past, Catholic reviewers had felt obliged to encourage all the efforts of Catholic authors, and, in the process,
works varying from mediocre to poor were forced upon the reader.
There might have been a slight justification for this practice when
the Catholic literary output was small. However, with the increased
volume of fiction, poetry, history, and biography, the "range and
scope of Catholic literature are now sufficiently large for our
critics to recommend nothing but the best."[232] Catholics, on other
occasions, were guilty of being apathetic toward some of their own
writers of merit; thus, disservice was done to Coventry Patmore,
George H. Miles, and Aubrey de Vere.[233]

Still another of his observations proved most interesting. "I
am not unmindful of the distinctively Catholic novel. It is of
recent growth on English soil."[234] The English prelate, Nicholas
Cardinal Wiseman, with Fabiola and Callista successfully brought before the minds of the people, "a vivid picture of the Christian

---

231Ibid., pp.56,57.
232Brother Azarias, Books and Reading, p.204.
233Ibid., pp.203,204.
234Ibid., p.54.

Church passing through the various stages of her struggles and triumphs."[235] Fabiola and Callista served as models for other dedicated authors, "and though the list is short, it is select."[236] The idea of the Catholic novel immigrated to the United States where Mrs. Mary Anne Sadlier and Mrs. Anna Hanson Dorsey were revered as "the pioneers of the Catholic novel in America."[237] The Catholic novel, however, was just one of the mediums. More writers professing the Catholic faith, though not writing on exclusively Catholic subjects, produced fine, worthwhile reading. Among Brother Azarias' list of favorites, there were many names already familiar to us: Lady Georgiana Fullerton, Kathleen O'Meara, Rosa Mulholland, John Boyle O'Reilly, Christian Reid, Richard Malcolm Johnston, Marion Crawford, "with some exceptions"[238] the Rev. John Talbot Smith, James Jeffrey Roche, Charles Warren Stoddard, Maurice Francis Egan, Louise Imogen Guiney, Agnes Repplier, Eleanor C. Donnelly, Katherine Conway, Mrs. Mary E. Blake, and Mrs. Margaret F. Sullivan.

So far, the particular non-fictional efforts of three ladies and five men have demonstrated the love and concern these talented people held for their co-religionists. With criticism and praise, they attempted to shape Catholic opinion, to encourage a healthy interest in art and literature, and defend the Church against the insinuation that she was detrimental to the advance of education,

---

[235]Ibid.
[236]Ibid.
[237]Brother Azarias, Books and Reading, p.55.
[238]Ibid.

science, and medicine. Miss Agnes Repplier, the moremost essayist
of her time, with her graceful pot-shots at American life, was able
to instill more than a hint of Catholicism into the secular
journals. Meanwhile, Miss Katherine E. Conway, writing more
exclusively for Catholic periodicals, gave many a reminder of
gentle, proper conduct. Miss Eliza Allen Starr virtually carried
on a one-woman war to make Catholics aware of their heritage in fine
art. Conde Pallen and Maurice Francis Egan as writers and critics,
expanded the effort to make Catholics more aware of the pleasantries
and significance of art and literature. In addition, Catholicism
was well served when Egan became minister to Denmark and Pallen
absorbed with the Catholic Encyclopedia. Then, there were the
defenders: Father Smith, the stage; Brother Azarias, the Christian
Schools; and Doctor Walsh, the Catholic contributions to science and
medicine.

The dedicated eight were not alone. For example, John A. Mooney
(1839-1903) deserved to rank with them. The independently wealthy
Mooney, whose life abruptly ended in a mountain climbing accident
(1903), was free to write, so, he became Catholicism's trouble-
shooter filling such journals as American Catholic Quarterly Review,
New World (Chicago), Seminary, The Catholic World, Catholic News
(New York City), and the Rosary with timely articles. The compiler
of a Mooney bibliography said of him:

During the last years of his life Dr. Mooney spent his time and abilities without thought of recompense wherever he hoped to advance the cause of truth and to defend the faith of which he was so sturdy a champion.[239]

His historical defenses of Catholicism varied in subject matter: Columbus, he felt, received cavalier treatment from the historians Hustin Winsor and Charles Kendall Adams;[240] Pope Pius IX had been sorely tried with "liberalism;"[241] the priest-historian Johannes Janssen's Geschickte des Deutscher Volkes seit dem Ansgang de Mittelalters presented the world with a model history.[242] Leaving the realm of history for the popular arena, variety once more was present in his discussions of the school question in Belgium, of the drinking problem in the United States, or of the Baltimore Lay Congress of 1889.

Energetic Americans, engrossed in a variety of subjects, announced their discoveries in one essay after another. Naturally, Catholics and their contemporaries, oftentimes, commented on similar subjects. Father Smith's role as guardian of the stage approached those of the diligent drama critic, William Winter (1836-1917), and Brander Mathews (1852-1929), the serious student of the theatre. Where Charles Dudley Warner (1829-1900) optimistically urged his

---

[239]Elizabeth P. Herbermann, "John A. Mooney and His Literary Work," United States Catholic Historical Society, Historical Records and Studies, XIII (May, 1919) 120.

[240]John A. Mooney, "Columbus and the Scientific School," American Catholic Quarterly Review, XVII (October, 1892) 844-5.

[241]John A. Mooney, "Pius IX and the Revolution 1846-48," American Catholic Quarterly Review, XVII (January, 1892) 159.

[242]John A. Mooney, "Professor Janssens and Other Modern German Historians," American Catholic Quarterly Review, XII (July, 1887) 437.

fellow citizens to seek a higher, personal culture, Katherine Conway
and Eliza Allen Starr quietly indicated this course to their co-
religionists. Brother Azarias' interest in the philosophy of
education was equaled, if not surpassed by that of William T. Harris,
United States Commissioner of Education (1889-1906). Literary
criticism, the province of Edmund Clarence Stedman (1833-1908) and
Paul Elmer More (1864-1937), also profited from the comments of
Egan and Pallen. Of course, some essayists resisted this loose
comparison. Yet, the fact remained: the persistent essays of the
Catholics, religious and lay people alike,[243] contributed much to
the welfare of their co-religionists and to their fellow citizens.

---

[243]John A. Mooney's untimely death was a quiet reminder that
some of these talented Catholics died before the period (1880-1915)
terminated. Continuing their zealous program were other men and
women whose literary careers barely commenced during this period,
and who lived on to achieve greater fame in another generation. The
convert Katherine Bregy was (and still is) typical of this group.
Her sensitive, critical articles appeared as early as 1905 in The
Catholic World; (1) while The Sign printed a Bregy book-review in
its issue for July, 1955. (2) To this specific period, therefore,
those departed and those alive contributed much toward Catholic
welfare, leadership, and improvement. Religious and lay people
alike were persistent in their exertions.

[1]Katherine Bregy, "The Poetry of Francis Thompson," The Catholic
World, LXXXI (August, 1905) 614.

[2]The Sign, National Catholic Magazine, XXXIV (July, 1955) 65,
66.

CHAPTER V

SOME ADVICE AND LEADERSHIP FROM THE HIERARCHY

Many admirable Catholics, laymen and religious, at this time (1880-1915), were pre-occupied with writing material suitable for their fellow Americans, Catholic or otherwise. Fiction, poetry, and essays came from them in abundance as they sought to advance the cultural status of Catholicism. With this noble scheme, the American hierarchy was very much in accord.

Yet, the writings of the American bishops and archbishops to whom the English language was native, oftentimes, achieved a direct simplicity in an attempt to reach more people with their observations and good advice. The sum total of their creations might not have constituted a lasting literary, effort, but, it did represent the sound counsel and solicitation of a hierarchy, whose capabilities as a group have never been excelled in the United States. Moreover, in addition to their published books, these men succeeded in placing their articles in the secular magazines as well as in the Catholic periodicals. Among the secular magazines, the _Arena_ and the _North American Review_, probably, printed the highest number of the prelates' articles; while their Catholic voice was not entirely alien to the pages of the _Century_, _Putnam's_, _Independent_, and

Outlook.[1]

Within the hierarchy's writings, three themes constantly
developed: the affirmation of Catholic loyalty and patriotism to
the United States; the explanation and defense of Catholicism and
Christianity in general against agnostic and pseudo-scientific
critics; and, an indication of the various prelates' particular
educational objectives. These men were individuals and not always
in agreement as to the solutions to the vexing problems of the day;
but, to their credit, they did recognize the hazards confronting
American society and sounded the alarm.

The ranking member of the hierarchy during the greater part of
this period 1880-1915 was Cardinal James Gibbons, a gifted leader
and an ambitious writer. Cardinal Gibbons' views on patriotism were
stated in a sermon inspired by Chicago's Haymarket Riot. Those few
preaching the gospel of anarchy, socialism, and nihilism, he branded
as pirates, seeking to destroy rather than to build.

> The government of the United States is a government
> for the benefit of the people. Strangers from every part
> of Europe are welcomed to our shores. Like the sun that
> shines over all, the Government of our country sheds its

---

[1]Cardinal James Gibbons, "Divorce," Century, LXXVIII (May, 1909)
145-149.
_____. "Moral Aspects of Suicide," ibid., LXXIII (January,
1907) 401-407.
_____. "Organized Labor," Putnam's, III (October, 1907) 62-
67.
_____. "Benefits of Arbitration," Independent, LII (October
11, 1900) 2423-2424.
Rt.Rev. John Lancaster Spalding, "Spalding on Americanism,"
Independent, LII (September 29, 1900) 2285-2287.
Archbishop John Ireland, "The Religious Condition in Our New
Island Territory," Outlook, LXII (August 26, 1899) 933-934.

genial rays upon all classes without regard to race,
nationality or religion. The glorious banner of our
country protects alike the humble and the poor, the
mighty and the rich. Every man in the United States has
the opportunity for carving for himself an honest livehi-
hood and many have opportunities of acquiring private
fortunes.[2]

Six years later (1892), the North American Review carried some of

the cardinal's other reflections regarding patriotism. At this time,

he succinctly stated the relation of a clergyman to politics.

I have no apology to make for offering some reflections
on the political outlook of the nation; for my rights as a
citizen were not abdicated or abridged on becoming a Christian
prelate, and the sacred character which I profess, far from
lessening, rather increases my obligations to my country.[3]

After defining patriotism as a rational instinct "placed by the

Creator in the breast of man,"[4] his article offered to the patriotic

citizen a six-point program for the elimination of stuffed ballot

boxes and other voting malpractices. Stricter laws, enforced and

interpreted by an independent judiciary; a better informed public

created by a responsible press; the school's indoctrination of the

public with knowledge of our country's heroes and patriots; a more

hearty celebration of national holidays; and, the continuation of

the party system,[5] one to check the other, constituted several means

for improving the American commonweal.

---

[2] Allen Sinclair Will, Life of Cardinal Gibbons, Archbishop of
Baltimore, I, 211.

[3] Cardinal James Gibbons, "Patriotism and Politics," North
American Review, CLIV (April, 1892) 384.

[4] Ibid., p. 387.

[5] Ibid., pp. 398-399.

A grave application of the cardinal's patriotism appeared at the death of President William McKinley. At the conclusion of a short eulogy of the late president, The Independent printed the cardinal's plea for his fellow citizens to rally round Theodore Roosevelt and "sustain him in bearing the formidable burden suddenly thrust upon him."[6] Nor was Cardinal Gibbons reluctant to disclose his American heritage in his short character study of Leo XIII written for The Century Magazine. After telling of the Pope's interest in the United States and the pleasure he received from The Messages and Papers of the Presidents, a gift from President Roosevelt, Cardinal Gibbons commented upon the ability of the citizens of the United States to deal with the current social problems.

> ...I have no doubt that with God's blessing these problems will be solved by the calm judgment and sound sense of the American people, without violence or revolution or any injury to individual rights.[7]

In this fashion, Cardinal Gibbons helped destroy the notion that Catholics were unpatriotic.

At least three of the cardinal's articles appearing in the North American Review attempted to make Catholicism better understood in the United States. The Bible, he asserted, was one of the most important studies for ministers and priests.[8] Protestants, too

---

[6]Cardinal James Gibbons, "President McKinley," The Independent, LIII (September 26, 1901) 2272.
[7]Cardinal James Gibbons, "The Character of Leo XIII," The Century Magazine, LXVI (September, 1903) 795.
[8]Cardinal James Gibbons, "The Preacher and His Province," North American Review, CLX (May, 1895) 513.

often, did not appreciate the Catholic regard for the Bible. To
avoid making similar mistakes, he urged a closer intermingling of
Christians.

> Some of our separated clerical brethern are not infre-
> quently betrayed into similar errors by ascribing to their
> Catholic fellow citizens religious doctrines and practices
> which the latter repudiate. A caricature instead of a
> true picture, is held up to the public gaze, because the
> information is drawn from books, hearsay, or tradition, and
> not from contact with living men.[9]

Continuing this vein of reconciliation years later, his aim was to
help the non-Catholic who did not easily "grasp our regard for the
Pope." To the popes of the French Revolution, Pius VI and Pius VII,
through their personal courage and independence: "...is owing the
recrudescence of Catholic affection for a See which, in these
bishops, showed itself truly apostolic."[10] Although great obstacles
disturbed the unity of Christendom, he believed it possible, if
prayers were fervent enough, "...this incalculable boon would be
again granted, that we might all own one God, one faith, one
baptism."[11] On another occasion, his description of the Vatican
Council (1869) contained the prediction of the greater roles to be
played by American and English bishops in future councils. Thus,
the spectre of a Church controlled by mysterious foreigners found
itself pushed further into the background by the words of Cardinal
Gibbons.

---

[9] Ibid., p.514.
[10] Cardinal James Gibbons, "Catholic Christianity," ibid.,
CLXXIII (July, 1901) 86.
[11] Ibid., p.90.

... I venture to hazard the prediction that at the next
Ecumenical Council, if held within fifty years, the representatives of the English language will equal, if they do
not surpass those of any other tongue.[12]

As important as Cardinal Gibbons' magazine literature was, it
did not bring the fame awarded his books. His first book, The Faith
of Our Fathers (1876) was an immediate success;[13] and, by 1914, the
busy cardinal could remark that its sales had exceeded those of
Uncle Tom's Cabin.[14] The Faith of Our Fathers constituted a clear
and comprehensive explanation of the teachings of the Church and
aimed to help the sincere non-Catholic understand. Moreover, it
defended the Church from the slanders of Maria Monk and Peter
Parley. His missionary work in North Carolina inspired this work
for, in his own words,

> He has often felt that the salutary influence of such
> instruments, especially on the occasion of a mission in
> the rural districts, would be much augmented if they were
> supplemented by books or tracts which would be circulated
> among the people, and could be read and pondered at
> leisure.[15]

Several interesting sidelights attended the publication of this,
Gibbons' most successful book, which sold over two million copies[16]
before he died. The poet Father Tabb[17] read the copy and suggested

---

[12]Cardinal James Gibbons, "Personal Reminisces of the Vatican
Council," North American Review, CLVIII (April, 1894) 388.

[13]John Tracy Ellis, The Life of James Cardinal Gibbons, Archbishop of Baltimore, I, 146.

[14]Albert E. Smith, Vincent de P. Fitzpatrick, Cardinal Gibbons,
Churchman and Citizen, p.885.

[15]Cardinal James Gibbons, The Faith of Our Fathers (1892)
edition), p.vii.

[16]Allen Sinclair Will, op.cit., II, 879.

[17]John Tracy Ellis, op.cit., I, 146.

certain stylistic changes; while it was an enthusiastic Father
Hudson[18] who prompted the book's German translation. Moreover, many
Catholics announced that The Faith of Our Fathers was the source of
their conversion.[19]

Whereas this first book adhered more strictly to Catholic tenets
of belief; Our Christian Heritage (1889) offered to all Christians
"... the right hand of fellowship, so long as they unite with us in
striking the common foe." He gladly acknowledged: "... That most
of the topics discussed in this little volume have often found, and
still find able and zealous advocates in Protestant writers.[20]
This particular volume did not aspire "to influence free-thinkers,
agnostics, and other avowed enemies of Christianity;" instead it
hoped to reach those estranged from the specific teachings of the
Gospel, those having only a vague and undefined conception of
Christianity.[21] Actually, Our Christian Heritage was a handbook for
all Christians, as it interpreted current affairs in the light of an
intelligent Christian's thinking.

A critic of that day (1890) wrote that Our Christian Heritage
was destined to attract wide-spread attention from persons of all
sects and of no sect. "It is a part of contemporary religious
thought and deserves careful attention by those who wish to keep

[18]Ibid., p.149.
[19]Ibid., pp.150-151.
[20]Cardinal James Gibbons, Our Christian Heritage, p.1.
[21]Ibid., p.4.

abreast of the times."[22] In the critic's mind, the cardinal hardly appreciated the depth or the social problems[23] and his position on evolution was "far beneath the advanced tone of the rest of the work."[24] Yet, the critic experienced no difficulty in reconciling Our Christian Heritage with his own liberal inclinations.

> There is nothing in the spirit of the work which need prevent the most advanced liberal from welcoming his efforts to lead his fellow Catholics in the path of progress. And the book itself is but the outward evidence of an inward leaven which is waking in the minds of all deeply religious people and which promises the best results for the moral, social, and political future of the United States and of the world at large.[25]

The general nature of Our Christian Heritage did not succeed to The Ambassador of Christ (1896), which was aimed directly at the Catholic clergy, "I do not think that any age or country ever presented a more inviting field for missionary labor than that which the United States exhibits today."[26] The United States, in his mind, presented a most thriving environment for Catholicism. While the diplomatic cardinal acknowledged that the Church had accommodated itself to every form of government, "it has a special adaptability to our political system and to the genius of the American people."[27] Americans living under a government of constitutional freedom,

---

[22]Thomas B. Preston, "Cardinal Gibbons' Late Works," The Arena, I (February, 1890) 336.

[23]Ibid., p.337.

[24]Ibid., p.341.

[25]Ibid., p.342.

[26]Cardinal James Gibbons, The Ambassador of Christ, p.v.

[27]Ibid., p.ix.

experienced the greatest measure of liberty compatible with law and order; and, it was the cardinal's desire to see "... the kingdom of Christ extending its spiritual empire throughout our beloved country."[28] In keeping with this goal, the clergy was to be not only zealous and pious, but also learned. Once more, the worth of fine reading was extolled.

> The reader will find in his books delightful companions to enrich his mind with the treasures of knowledge, to entertain and cheer him in his solitude, to console him in adversity, to support and strengthen him in temptation, to caution him against impending dangers, to rebuke him in his transgressions.[29]

Although the study of history revealed much; still, biography was the "most entertaining and instructive of all companions."[30] One book, he argued, might be the means of signal conversions and other blessings. "Many a Christian luminary has found in a single page or sentence the germ of his moral reformation."[31] With his beloved clergy still in mind, he published Discourses and Sermons for Every Sunday and the Principal Festivals of the Year 1908. These were the fruit of nearly fifty years of serious meditation and he believed that their brevity "will also commend them to the reader; for long discourses are usually tedious and fatiguing."[32] (The insistence on

[28]Ibid., p.xl.
[29]Ibid., p.178.
[30]Ibid., p.181.
[31]Ibid., p.185.
[32]Cardinal James Gibbons, Discourses and Sermons for Every Sunday and Principal Festivals of the Year, p.v.

brevity also bespoke of the cardinal's love for his flock.)

In the twilight of his brilliant career in 1916, Cardinal
Gibbons published the more significant of his past essays in a
volume entitled <u>A Retrospect of Fifty Years</u>. One of the essays in
this collection summarized the cardinal's ideology. The evils
confronting American civilization, Cardinal Gibbons had warned, were
five: Mormonism and divorce; an imperfect and vicious system of
education; desecration of the Christian Sabbath; unreasonable delay
in executing the sentences of our criminal courts; and the gross and
systematic election frauds.[33] Common sense filled his analysis.
Secular education was not evil; it simply was not sufficient to
produce "not only learned but pious men."[34] As for Sunday, the
Church desired that day "to be cheerful without sadness and
melancholy."[35] Innocent recreation, of course, was permitted.
Votes, bartered and sold, were done so in violation of a sacred
trust.[36] Christianity, he avowed, held the secret of our social
stability and order. The future of America was to be involved in
the observance of those "wise laws based on Christian principles,
and which are the echo of God's eternal law."[37] The preface of
<u>A Retrospect of Fifty Years</u> revealed the cardinal's confidence in

---

[33]Cardinal James Gibbons, "The Dangers That Threaten Our
American Civilization," <u>A Retrospect of Fifty Years</u>, pp.484-485.
    [34]<u>Ibid</u>., p.491.
    [35]<u>Ibid</u>., p.505.
    [36]<u>Ibid</u>., p.507.
    [37]<u>Ibid</u>., p.482.

the Americans' ability to cope with the succeeding years.

> Younger men may trouble for the future of this country, but I have nothing but hope when I think what we have already passed through, for I can see no troubles in the future which could equal, much less surpass, those which afflicated us in bygone days. If only the American people will hold fast to that instrument which has been bequeathed to them as the palladium of their liberties, the Constitution of the United States, and fear and distrust the man who would touch that ark with profane hands, the permanence of our institutions is assured.[38]

Cardinal Gibbons' great concern for the United States and for

the Catholics within her borders was shared by his friend the

Archbishop of St. Paul, John Ireland. For Archbishop Ireland,

patriotism assumed the characteristics of a virtue. "I would have

Vatholics be the first patriots in the land."[39] When the unfor-

tunate Spanish-American War broke out, the archbishop in a sermon

typical of the response of the American hierarchy spoke:

> The supreme authority of this republic has declared war against another nation. What is the duty of Christians in our country's present crisis? It is to accept manfully, lotally the mandate of the supreme power of the nation; it is to co-operate in all manner of means within our reach as far as we may be demanded to do so with the government in the prosecution of the war. Beyond all doubt this is our solemn religious duty.[40]

Flag-waving, obviously, was not reserved to any one sect.

It was equally important for the archbishop to illustrate that

there was no conflict between the United States and the Catholic

---

[38]Cardinal James Gibbons, A Retrospect of Fifty Years, p. xi.
[39]John Ireland, The Church and Modern Society, I, 91.
[40]George Barton, "A Dvory of Self Sacrifice," Records of the American Catholic Historical Society of Philadelphia, XXVII (1926) 112.

Church, that the principles of the Church were in thorough harmony
with the interests of the Republic. Furthermore, it was desirable
that our fellow citizens of other religious preferences understand
that our "love of country and love of Church blend in sweetest
harmony."[41] When the one-hundredth anniversary of the establishment
of the American hierarchy was celebrated November 10, 1889, his outlined program was more ambitious: it was our mission "to make
America Catholic, and to solve for the Church universal the all
absorbing problems"[42] which confronted religion at that time.
Americans possessed the know-how, he believed, the earnestness, the
aggressiveness to lead the world.

> They are utterly incapable of the indifference to living
> interests and of the apathy which, under the specious name
> of conservatism, characterize European populations.[43]

An inherited misfortune was the alienation of non-Catholics in
America from the Church. However, since the traditional prejudices
against the Church were declining,[44] the time had arrived for
Catholics "to think, work, organize, speak, act, as circumstances
demand, ever anxious to serve the Church, and to do good to their
fellow men."[45] On the twenty-fifth anniversary of the episcopal
consecration of the Cardinal Archbishop of Baltimore, October 18,
1893, Ireland once more urged Catholics to be in harmony with the

---

[41]Ibid., I, 26.
[42]Ibid., I, 73.
[43]Ibid., I, 76.
[44]Ibid., I, 81.
[45]Ibid., I, 99.

generation.

> The age loves knowledge, let us be patrons of knowledge,
> let us be the most erudite historians, the most experienced
> scientists, the most acute philosophers; and history,
> science, and philosophy will not be divorced from religion.[46]

Since liberty and good government, social justice and the amelio-
rization of the masses, inventions and discoveries, of American life;
Catholics should embrace every reasonable opportunity to support and
enhance these properties, so that "no man will dare to speak to the
Church a word of reproach in the name of progress."[47]

At the Columbian Exposition in Chicago, one in which he took a
lively interest and "in which he was the initiator of the activity
of the hierarchy," the Archbishop spoke before the Parliament of
Religious where "invited representatives of all the great historic
faiths"[48] presented the tenets of their beliefs in a congenial
atmosphere designed to eliminate controversy and compromise. In
anticipation of the Parliament of Religions, he had announced to the
World Congress Auxillary of the Columbian Exposition, October 21,
1892,

> No discussion, no controversy will be allowed during the
> sessions of the Congress; the one purpose of the Congress
> will be to set forth calmly and dispassionately the con-
> fessions of faith and the labors of religion at the present
> time.[49]

Such a liberal attitude did not attain universal acceptance in the
Church either in America or abroad; and on September 18, 1895, in a

---

[46]Ibid., I, 120.
[47]Ibid., I, 121.
[48]Moynihan, op.cit., p42.
[49]John Ireland, op.cit., I, 149.

letter to the Apostolic Delegate at Washington, Leo XIII politely but firmly announced that it was "more advisable that Catholics hold their own meetings apart;"[50] thereby ending the period of toleration for Catholics attending the general assemblies of religion.

Although more controversy surrounded Archbishop Ireland's advocacy of the Faribault plan and the Catholic University of America, his attitude regarding State Education was interesting in the light of recent (1956) developments.

> I have assuredly no quarrel with the educational work of the State. In this matter, as in so many others, I am proud of my country. America understands the importance of education; she is most generous in founding and endowing schools, colleges, and universities. I praise America for her love of education...[51]

In the ideal institution, secular knowledge and religious truth were blended together in an inseparable union; but, according to the Archbishop, the State could not fashion such a union.

> And yet I do not condemn the State. In view of all the circumstances of the country, in view of public opinion to-day, what can the State do but leave out the teaching of religion from its course of instruction, and, in justice to all the people, strive to render its schools as unsectarian as schools can be? The State is doing all that the conditions of the country allow. Let us be fair to the State, praising it for the good it does, and excusing it for the defects which it cannot avoid.[52]

As for Catholic schools, they had no right "to stamp with the seal of religion on inferior instruction and expect it to pass current

---

[50]Ibid., I, 149-150 (footnote).
[51]Ibid., I, 247.
[52]Ibid., I, 247.

among Catholics."[53] The practical and useful subjects were not to
be denied the Catholic curriculum. As for the goal of this educational program, it was to produce lay leaders: erudite, staunch in
faith and morals, resolute and reliable, model citizens, who would
lead the mass of their fellow Catholics "before the country in all
movements making for truth and moral goodness."[54]

Religion, then, held an obvious position in the Archbishop's
aspirations for America. At this time, when organized labor sought
to advance its case before the nation's industrial giants, he wrote
that the spirit of Religion held the ultimate solution of this and
all other social difficulties.[55] For the immediate present, however, he had several ideas of his own. Labor had the right to
organize and to seek favorable legislation; and strikes, as the last
resort, were permissable. On the other hand, the striking unions
had no right to forcefully coerce or inflict violence upon the non-
union workingmen "who choose to work."[56] Peaceful, persuasive
arguments were to be the preferred means to convince the non-
members. Not only did he reject the closed shop, but he also
disallowed the union's claim that it could limit the individual
output of the various workers.[57] Labor and capital, it was hoped,
would learn to understand and appreciate each other. "I have not

---

[53]Ibid., I, 253.
[54]Ibid., I, 252.
[55]John Ireland, "The Marriage of Capital and Labor," The
Catholic World, LXXIV (January, 1902) 531.
[56]John Ireland, The Church and Modern Society, II, 335.
[57]Ibid., II, 360.

met the capitalist that (sic) has ever thought that man, whoever he
is, however weak, is a mere piece of machinery." At the same time,
the laborer was reminded that although an equality among men regarding political and legal rights existed, there was among men
"more or less inequality in the possession of the things of the
earth."[58] Yet, while this inequality prevailed, the realization that
all were children of the same great Lord and that all were willing to
help one another should dominate their lives. The occasion was not
at hand to place restrictions of a stringent nature upon capitalists.

> It is individual enterprise that has made America. The
> country's rewards have ever been open to the best, the
> bravest and the hardiest. America has been, above all other
> lands, the country of manhood. Reduce the talent and energies
> of her citizens to a dead level, America is no longer the
> country we have admired and loved, the country of opportunity
> and progress.[59]

Most of Archbishop Ireland's ideas under discussion appeared in
a notable two-volume work, The Church and Modern Society. Reviewing
these volumes, The Dial's critic hailed Archbishop Ireland as

> ... one of those who have helped us associate an earnest
> public spirit with high ecclesiastical position. It is a
> rare combination. "The Church and Modern Society," (sic)
> is, as the title implies, an expression of this interest.[60]

Furthermore, the style was so clear and direct. "Such simplicity
and dignity are sure to carry his words to the hearts of men."[61]

---

[58]John Ireland, "The Marriage of Capital and Labor," The Catholic
World, LXXIV (January, 1902) 533-534.
[59]John Ireland, The Church and Modern Society, II, 369.
[60]John Bascom, "The Orbit of Faith," The Dial, XXIII (March 16,
[61]Ibid.

The Catholic World, however, added a leveling note.

> ... His ideas have not always been acceptable all round;
> his pace to many has been too swift; his principles have
> been challenged as impracticable and utopian. But no one
> can deny the boldness and grandeur of his citizen ideals.[62]

Right or wrong, Archbishop Ireland placed his articles both in

the secular and religious periodicals. His attack on the saloon

first appeared in the North American Review, October, 1894. "The

American saloon is responsible for the awful intemperance which

desolates the land and which is the physical and moral plague of our

time."[63] There was a moderate and legitimate use of intoxicating

drinks and of their manufacture and sale; but the saloon keeper was

awarded hardly a modicum of toleration:

> Henceforth Catholic public opinion frowns upon the saloon
> and the saloon keeper; saloon keeping is accounted a dis-
> reputable business, and the saloon keeper, however correctly
> he conducts his particular saloon must not and will not,
> because of the general malodorousness of his business, be
> permitted to appear in any capacity as a representative of
> the Church or as a prominent Catholic; he must and will be
> kept aloof from all places of honor and distinction in the
> Church.[64]

The acceptable saloon keeper, one observing all the liquor regula-

tions, however, was not to be denied the sacraments of the Church.[65]

Archbishop Ireland was on much drier ground when the editors of The

Outlook sought his opinion in reference to the religious conditions

---

[62]"Talk About New Books," The Catholic World, LXIV (February,
1897), 704.
[63]John Ireland, The Church and Modern Society, I, 318.
[64]Ibid., p.313.
[65]Ibid., p.317.

in the territories gained from the Spanish-American War. "As a
Catholic, I cannot approve of any efforts of Protestants to affect
the religious duties of the inhabitants of the islands."[66] Still
referring to the islands' Catholic population, he continued:

> We must assure the Filipinos without delay that no
> churches will be looted, no vestments stolen, that Catholic
> churches and monasteries will be respected everywhere; that
> what we are introducing is a civilization under which Catholics
> and Protestants have equal rights under equal State protec-
> tion.[67]

As for the islands' pagan population, he would be tolerant of the
Protestants missionary efforts to convert them since he preferred
"partial or fragmentary Christianity to no Christianity."[68] For
The Catholic World, his clear, concise style showed itself to
advantage in the biographies Theobald Matthew[69] the temperance
leader and Matthias Loras,[70] first bishop of Dubuque.

Although Archbishop Ireland and Cardinal Gibbons wrote well and
often, their literary efforts did not surpass those of their friend
and contemporary, John Lancaster Spalding (1840-1916), Bishop of
Peoria. The gifted Bishop Spalding, as an essayist, "had no peer
in the priesthood,"[71] wrote the reputable historian, Richard J.

[66]Archbishop John Ireland (interviewed by Elbert F. Baldwin),
"The Religious Condition in Our New Island Territory," The Outlook,
LXII (August 26, 1899) 933.
[67]Ibid., p.934.
[68]Ibid.
[69]Archbishop John Ireland, "Theobald Matthew," The Catholic
World, LII (October, 1890) 1-8.
[70]_____, "Right Rev. Matthias Loras, First Bishop of Dubuque,"
ibid., LXVII (September, 1898) 721-731.
[71]Richard J. Purcell, "John Lancaster Spalding," Dictionary
American Biography, XVII (1935) 423.

Purcell. A recent (1953) critic, after surveying his generous

career, claimed:

> His greatest reputation seems to rest upon his published
> writings. He delved into the philosophy of education and
> modern social problems particularly socialism and labor.
> His essays on science, religion, art, and patriotism were
> written to lead his fellow men toward a more cultured way
> of life.[72]

In keeping with his good intention of raising the Catholic

cultural standard, Bishop Spalding wrote six months prior to the

opening of this period (1880-1915):

> If Americans in general are justly chargeable with lack of
> culture, may not this charge be brought home with even
> greater force to American Catholics? ... This self complacent
> temper does not dispose men to take a wide and enlightened
> view of the wants of the Church. So long as we are content
> with a progress for which we deserve little credit, and which
> is often more apparent than real, there is small hope that
> any serious effort will be made to create a higher spiritual
> and intellectual life among our Catholic people.[73]

After scanning the American scene and realizing that this

country was the "land of initiative, of individual self-confidence,

of individual power, of democracy, of liberty, of progress,"

Spalding was convinced that the influence of the Church in America

would be enhanced by the assimilation of those traits, "whereas

their absence or hostile rejection would cripple or arrest its

growth."[74] So, it was necessary for Catholics to make an adjust-

ment.

---

[72]Sr. M. Annella Garland, O.P., A.B., The Work of Bishop John
Lancaster Spalding in the Diocese of Peoria, 1877-1908, (thesis)
p.121.

[73]John Lancaster Spalding, "Religion and Culture," American
Catholic Quarterly Review, IV (July, 1879) 414.

[74]Rev. Franz de Hovre, Catholicism in Education, p.168.

... If we are to act along an inner line upon the life of America, we must bring to the task a divine confidence that our Catholic faith is akin to whatever is true or good or fair, that as it allied itself with the philosophy, the literature, the art, and the forms of government of Greece and Rome, so it is prepared to welcome whatever progress mankind may make, whether it be material or moral or intellectual; nay, it is prepared to co-operate without misgivings or afterthought, in whatever promises to make for higher and holier life.[75]

The key to this higher life, to Spalding, was education for "a public education is a people's deliberate effort to form a nobler race of men."[76] As for the teacher, he was placed at the side of the physician, the lawyer, the minister in the rank of social importance. "It is indeed difficult to exaggerate the worth of a true teacher."[77] Although acknowledging the worth of correct methods, good text-books, and a proper choice of subjects to be taught, he concluded that the greatest educational force was the teacher's personality, a combination of mind, character, and will.[78] The fact that a teacher passed an examination and was issued a certificate was not sufficient alone to qualify one with the teacher's office.[79] The ideal teacher should have not only knowledge, eloquence, tact and skill, but, also the ability to inspire the student to think and act. For the public schools, there was a particular plea:

[75]John Lancaster Spalding, Opportunity and Other Essays and Addresses, pp.76-77.
[76]_____. Thoughts and Theories of Life and Education, p.214.
[77]Ibid., p.222.
[78]Ibid., p.213.
[79]Ibid., p.228.

The fact that religious instruction is excluded makes it all
the more necessary that humanizing and ethical aims should
be kept constantly in view. Whoever teacher in a public
school should be profoundly convinced that man is more than
an animal which may be taught cunning and quickness.[80]

His other plea, that money and public opinion should be used to

"make the best men and women willing and ready to enter the teacher's

profession,"[81] had a familiar ring.

Transferring his attention to Catholic education, he proposed to

erect a central normal school where the various teaching sisterhoods

could send their younger members for instruction. "But a good

religious is not therefore a good teacher,"[82] was his reasoning.

Furthermore, the need of a similar institution for young men exis-

ted.

We must have an institution in which our Catholic young men,
while they live in an atmosphere of faith and reverence, may
acquire all the knowledge and skill as well as the mental
culture, necessary to success in teaching, that they may not
be excluded from a profession whose power in the world will
grow as civilization advances.[83]

Still more advanced and in keeping with the progressive tendencies

of the day was his demand that women had the right to the highest

education and that opportunities should be provided for such an

education.[84] Catholics should not lag behind in this matter for

[80]John Lancaster Spalding, "Scope of Public School Education,"
The Catholic World, LX (March, 1895) 763.
    [81]Ibid., p.767.
    [82]John Lancaster Spalding, "Normal Schools for Catholics,"
The Catholic World, LI (April, 1890) 95.
    [83]Ibid., p.97.
    [84]John Lancaster Spalding, Opportunity and Other Essays and
Addresses, p.66.

"it were blindness in Catholics to rest content with what they have
done or are doing."[85]

Paramount in Bishop Spalding's scheme for the American educational advance was his advocating an industrious program of reading.
At the base of this was self-instruction, a discipline in which the
reader could learn from the great teachers of the age. "The best
knowledge," wrote Spalding, "on all subjects is now within the reach
of many readers."[86] The importance of reading books resided not in
the information they contained, but the exercises of the mind they
impelled.[87] Magazine and newspapers were soulless, therefore, to
be shunned in favor of the great literature and history. Of this, a
modern educator (1951) wrote:

> Bishop Spalding sees in great books an influence almost
> equal to that of human beings; he portrays them as con-
> tainers of great men's thoughts, lying there awaiting the
> magical touch of the reader. Even while realizing what
> harm books may do to the unprepared reader, the bishop
> insists that one ought to know how to seek out what is true
> or high, even though these thoughts may be mixed in with
> matter that is somewhat base, as is sometimes the case in
> literature and history.[88]

Parents, teachers, priests, Bishop Spalding charged, were to select
the books "best suited to rouse the young to mental and moral
activity;" and, so directing and encouraging them in their reading,

---

[85] Ibid., p.64.
[86] Ibid., p.63.
[87] John Lancaster Spalding, Thoughts and Theories of Life and
Education, p.202.
[88] Brother Laurian La Forest, C.S.C., "Bishop Spalding's Views
on Character Education," The Catholic Educational Review, XLIX
(October, 1951) 531.

they would doubtless render them higher and more lasting
service than any which may result from their admonitions,
lessons and exhortations.[89]

The Bishop of Peoria, one of the foremost Catholic exponents of
education, justly deserved the title of "the intellectual leader of
American Catholicism during the late nineteenth century."[90] He was
equally inspiring as a promotor of social welfare. His essay The
Religious Mission of the Irish People (1880) forthrightly announced
his plan to relocate the Catholic population from the slums into the
rural areas.[91] Rural America offered the beleaguered city-dweller
(particularly, the Irish immigrant) an escape from poverty and
political machines, the oppressors of his urban existence.
Generally speaking, the condition of the laboring man seemed to be
"the great anomaly in our otherwise progressive and brilliant
civilization"[92] since it reflected his inability to share our
material and intellectual growth.

> ... even dispassionate observers think that the tendency of
> the present system is to intensify rather than diminish the
> evils which do exist; and that we are moving towards a state
> of things in which the few will own everything, and the many
> be hardly more than their hired servants.[93]

To this latter group, Socialism issued its siren call with a
promise to erect a State "which will own both land and capital, and

---

[89]John Lancaster Spalding, Thoughts and Theories of Life and
Education, p.179.
[90]Father Thomas T. McAvoy, C.S.C., "Bishop John Lancaster
Spalding and the Catholic Minority (1877-1908)," The Review of
Politics, XII (January, 1950) 3.
[91]Ibid., p.3.
[92]John Lancaster Spalding, Socialism and Labor and Other
Arguments, p.1.
[93]Ibid., p.2.

will control both production and distribution."[94] Then, all men
would be free and equal. At this point, Bishop Spalding wisely
praised Socialism for its desire to relieve the miserable; yet, he
insisted that the social reformation could be better fashioned
within the existing American economic system. Indeed, any radical
change such as the introduction of Socialism would jeopardize our
liberty and independence.[95] The reader was advised that America was
passing through a transitional period, one bringing hardships,
nonetheless, it would be better to endure these transitory circumstances rather than rush headlong into visionary and untried schemes
of reform.[96] His words of counsel suggested action tempered with
moderation.

> Indeed, the present inequalities in the distribution of
> wealth affect the moral sense so painfully that we cannot
> look upon them as irremovable. We may not however trample
> on rights to secure greater distributive justice, or
> approve schemes which if they promise a greater abundance
> of material things to the poor, would lead to a general
> enfeeblement and lowering of human life.[97]

Besides leading his fellow Americans beyond the errors of
Socialism, Bishop Spalding found occasion to do verbal combat with
Colonel Robert Ingersoll in particular and the A.P.A. in general.
The agnostic Colonel Ingersoll was branded a "polemic guerrila" who
had falsely represented the founders of the American Constitution as

---

[94]Ibid., p.7.
[95]Ibid., p.19.
[96]Ibid., p.18.
[97]Ibid., p.23.

sceptical and irreligious. Prudence, not scepticism, contended

Spalding, prompted the founding fathers to leave the question of

religion to the several States. Furthermore, Colonel Ingersoll's

thesis that the recognition of God in the Constitution "must have,

as its natural result, a theocracy"[98] was untenable. Spalding's

defense sought to align a considerable Christian front against the

popular, taunting, platform lecturer and writer.

> The seventy or eighty thousand Christian ministers in
> the United States to-day, Protestant and Catholic, are free
> from all theocratic pretensions; they could repel, if it
> could be made, any offer of union of Church and State; they
> are lovers of liberty, civil and religious; they accept
> science as the natural revelation of God and the friend of
> man; they with their brethern are busy with every kind of
> work, which can comfort, console, strengthen, unlift, en-
> lighten, and purify the children of men.[99]

Equally regrettable was the vigorous anti-Catholic activity

promoted by the American Protective Association. Reviving the

traditional and inherited prejudices against the Church, the A.P.A.

attempted to place before the American public the notion that

Catholics were disloyal to the United States. Calling upon all

fairminded citizens, Bishop Spalding declared that American Catholic

patriotism was a proven thing. Protests were needless, futile.

> To protest is half to confess, as to exhort is to reproach;
> and to urge American Catholics to love their country, which
> is as dear to them as their heart's blood, is to imply that
> they fail in this duty.[100]

---

[98]John Lancaster Spalding, "God in the Constitution: A Reply
to Col. Ingersoll," Arena, I (April, 1890) 523.

[99]Ibid., p.526.

[100]John Lancaster Spalding, "Catholics and Apaism," The North
American Review, CLIX (September, 1894) 285.

Spalding, then, still refuting the A.P.A., assured his fellow
citizens, that although Catholics found the public schools wanting
in providing religious instruction, Catholics did not condemn the
public school.[101] Moreover, members of the A.P.A., installed in
favored positions on the railroads and in manufacturing concerns,[102]
were using a religious pretext to divide friends from friends. However, he did not conceal his optimism that this anti-Catholic hatred
would soon pass away; and, the sooner the better, for then, all
Americans could be about solving the really important problems of
the day.[103]

The style of Bishop Spalding's essays evoked various responses.
For comparison, the reviews of The Catholic World and The Dial
proved interesting. The Catholic World recommended his Education
and the Higher Life not only for its beautiful English[104] with the
charm of poetry but also for its bold philosophical approach to the
problems in American civilization. For this same work, The Dial
wrote in close support that this exquisite collection of essays
should be in the hands of every graduate. The Dial's reviewer
realized that Bishop Spalding was urging Americans to become
educated "to influence the world about you."[105]

[101]Ibid.
[102]Ibid., p.284.
[103]Ibid., p.287.
[104]"Talk About New Books," The Catholic World, III (December,
1890) 451.
[105]The Dial, XII (May, 1891) 22.

... Here, too, are thoughtful presentations of the value in
education of the classics, of historical study, of the
sciences, and a well reasoned demand for an American
literature.[106]

Thoughts and Theories of Life, with its aphoristic style, made

reading a positive pleasure to the intellect and heart, according to

The Catholic World.[107] Concerning this volume, The Dial offered:

... These discourses are not meant so much for information
as for inspiration; but, while the truth is mostly truism,
it is always earnestly and often eloquently rehearsed with
an Emersonian sententiousness.[108]

On another occasion, The Dial again complimented the bishop for his

clear and winning style and rejoiced in the fact that he was free

from the offensive habits often associated with the Churchman, since

his work was characterized by clear thinking, deep sympathy, and a

reverent faith in God and human nature.[109] Things of the Mind, The

Catholic World visualized as the exorcist for the spirit of

pessimism as it lead the search of mind and soul for the higher

things. It was conceded that this volume was for adults although

students might read it for style. The reviewer of this work, how-

ever, did not agree with Spalding's views concerning women in

politics and with his opinions of certain writers.[110] Although

Bishop Spalding, Archbishop Ireland, and Cardinal Gibbons all were

[106]Ibid.
[107]"Talk About New Books," The Catholic World, LXVI (March,
1898) 839,841.
[108]Hiram Stanley, "Some Recent Books on Education," The Dial,
XXIV (February 16, 1898) 118.
[109]The Dial, XX (February 16, 1896) 103.
[110]"Talk About New Books," The Catholic World, LX (December,
1894) 421.

complimented for clarity of style, to the readers of the present
generation still further removed in time and practice from
Emersonian sententiousness, Bishop Spalding, perhaps, proved to be
the most laborious reading.

Nonetheless, Spalding, Ireland, and Gibbons formed the literary
Big Three among the American hierarchy. Yet, they were not alone.
At this time 1880-1915, there were other bishops who had opinions
of their own and the ability to express them. These other bishops
had their own variations to the design for Catholic living in the
United States and the evidence of their plans was found in the
periodicals. Forum, The North American Review, and the American
Ecclesiastical Review printed the articles of the Bishop of
Rochester, Bernard J. McQuaid. That there was a difference of view-
points among the American hierarchy was expressed openly by Bishop
McQuaid, who insisted that "Cardinal Gibbons and Archbishop Ireland
were not the only Americans in the hierarchy of the Catholic Church
in America."[111] Particularly irritating to Bishop McQuaid were
Archbishop Ireland's political activities in behalf of the Republican
party.

> I contend that this coming to New York of the Archbishop
> of St. Paul, to take part in a political contest, was un-
> dignified, disgraceful to his episcopal office, and a
> scandal in the eyes of all right-minded Catholics of both
> parties. It was, furthermore, a piece of meddlesome inter-
> ference on his part, to come from his State to another to

---

[111]Rochester Union and Advertiser, (June 28, 1892)

break down all discipline among our priests and to justify
the charge of those inimical to us that priests are parti-
sans and use their office and opportunities for political
work. If Archbishop Ireland had made himself as conspicuous
in favor of the Democratic party, he would be just as blame-
worthy in my estimation.[112]

He was equally positive in praising the Catholic school. As for

the state school system, Catholics were not to antagonize it;

instead, "they are leaving it alone."[113] The State could, according

to Bishop McQuaid, "pay for all secular learning in any school,

parochial, private, corporate."[114] In this fashion, non-public

schools would attain their equity in the school-tax. Such an ideal

seemed far away. More easily accessible was his revised curriculum

for seminarians.

Careful and painstaking instruction in the English language
and literature should begin with the student's first day in
the Seminary, and end with his last. It should be the
language of the classes in history, scripture, and sciences,
leaving to Latin all other studies. It seems absurd in
striving to give a young man an all-round education, to keep
him from familiarity with the very language in which we have
to present his ideas and knowledge to the people for whose
souls he is to become responsible.[115]

Patriotism, like education, was another concern of the Bishop

of Rochester. When our Nation celebrated the centennial of the

signing of the Declaration of Independence, he decreed that a Fourth

of July Mass should be said in every church in the diocese having a

---

[112]Frederick J. Zwierlein, *Life and Letters of Bishop McQuaid,*
III, 208.
[113]Bernard J. McQuaid, "Religious Teaching in Schools," *Forum,*
VIII (December, 1889) 381.
[114]Ibid., p.387.
[115]Bernard J. McQuaid, "Seminaries," *American Ecclesiastical
Review,* XVI (May, 1897) 471.

resident pastor.

> It will be advisable for pastors on that day, or on some
> convenient Sunday, to instruct their parishioners in the
> duties and responsibilities of good citizenship, the
> claims of every regularly constituted state in the reverence
> and obedience of its members and the principles underlying
> the right of command and the law to obey, well satisfied
> that no patriotism will avail to maintain justice and up-
> hold the weak that is not based on God's law.[116]

At the memorial services for General Grant and President

Garfield, Bishop McQuaid gave public addresses. One look at the

battlefield record of Catholics during the years 1776-1865 supplied

sufficient evidence for their patriotism. The taunt that when the

Catholics became the majority, "they will not tolerate others," he

branded "claptrap."[117] Neither was the argument acceptable that the

Catholics' refusal to support the re-introduction of Bible reading

in the public schools implied a lack of patriotism. He offered in-

stead:

> Earnest and devout Christians see that much of the growing
> contempt for the Sacred Scriptures is due to unwise and in-
> discriminate reading by young school-children, whose attention
> is called to passages suggestive of evil by perverted com-
> panions, or to its cold, hesitating, half-hearted, mechanical
> reading by sceptical masters.[118]

Where Bishop McQuaid was successful in presenting his views in

the secular press, Francis Silas Chatard, Bishop of Vincennes,

Indiana, preferred to contribute to the religious periodicals. The

---

[116]Frederick J. Zwierlein, op.cit., III, 364.
[117]Bernard J. McQuaid, "Religion in Schools," The North American
Review, CXXXII (April, 1881) 342.
[118]Ibid., p.341.

remarkable Paulist editor, Father Isaac Hecker, gave impetus to
Chatard's literary career,[119] when he first solicited the bishop's
articles for The Catholic World. Bishop Chatard, in 1894, re-
published selections of his work in a volume entitled Occasional
Essays. Here was the evidence that Chatard, too, subscribed to the
theme of The Era of Good Intentions, that his writings prompted his
co-religionists to seek culture and to adjust to the social environment about them.

Bishop Chatard, after admitting that Americans were not the most
cultivated, civilized, and well-informed people in the world, blamed
"especially Catholic parents" for putting "the greatest obstacles in
the way of those engaged in teaching."[120] Parents too often hurried
their progeny through school and acquiesced in their desire to dis-
card the study of Latin and Greek. It was desirable that foreign
languages should be learned at an early age along with the acquisi-
tion of reading skills. The study of literature was extremely
desirable. "The polish of the literary education is of great
necessity, as it is the one thing those educated in the non-Catholic
colleges may be said to excel us in."[121]

In the July issue of the American Catholic Quarterly Review for
1890, he insisted that the Catholics had a right to maintain
denominational schools and were entitled to a corresponding portion

---

[119]Francis Silas Chatard, Occasional Essays.
[120]Ibid., p.159.
[121]Ibid., p.164.

of the public school fund. If the latter idea was not acceptable to
all Americans, Catholics, at least, should be exempt from the taxa-
tion for schools. Moreover, an anti-Catholic influence had overtaken the normal school and the institute; and, if that was not
enough, freemasonry was busy with a scheme "to possess itself of
elementary education."[122] Perhaps, the environment of Indiana, one
that produced the hotbed of the K.K.K. in a later generation, gave
Bishop Chatard cause for alarm. Yet, he was not suspicious of all
non-Catholics, for he had reluctantly declined to receive their
children in his schools because there was no room.[123] When not
occupied with the problems attending Catholic education, Bishop
Chatard gave considerable attention to the temperance rally in its
extreme form, total abstinence.[124]

A contemporary of Chatard's residing originally in St. Louis
gave further evidence of the gifted leadership exhibited by certain
American prelates. For nearly thirty years Patrick John Ryan made
his way in the Mound City winning the esteem of its citizens, non-
Catholic and Catholic alike. When he left to become Archbishop of
Philadelphia, the Post-Dispatch honestly reported, "His departure is
a loss, not alone to the Catholic Church, but to the city and State
wherein he has lived so long."[125] Philadelphians, too, soon
learned to admire this citizen and churchman.

---

[122]Ibid., p.305.
[123]Ibid., p.306.
[124]Ibid., pp.323-338.
[125]St. Louis Post-Dispatch, (August 18, 1884)

"In the public concerns of the Church, in the policy of adapting

it to its American environment," one fair-minded non-Catholic

journalist analyzed Ryan's position by saying that it was not "so

radical as John Ireland's, or so conservative as Michael

Corrigan's."[126] There was little doubt that Ryan played his

position well.

> During the agitation in the American Church, over certain
> important issues, a reporter one day asked the Archbishop
> where he stood, in a supposed difference between Cardinal
> Gibbons and Archbishop Corrigan. He laughingly replied;
> 'As Archbishop of Philadelphia, naturally I stand between
> New York and Baltimore.'[127]

The d. .ic Ryan approached the school question with charac-

teristic aplomb. 'We are one with the public schools in all that

pertains to intellect and memory,' announced the Archbishop; but,

when they declined to ascend to the higher region of religious in-

struction, 'we separate from them, with regret.'[128] Education

should combine the secular with the religious and the absence of the

latter could not be fully compensated for with the hour of in-

struction in the Sunday School. 'The daily education in religious

truth is necessary.'[129] Like his contemporaries, Archbishop Ryan

thought that this great Republic contributed to the growth of the

Church and looked to the future with optimism.

---

[126]Richard F. Crowley, The Episcopal Silver Jubilee of the Most
Reverend Patrick John Ryan, D.D., L.L.D., Archbishop of Philadelphia,
p.238.
[127]Ibid., p.229.
[128]Ibid., p.231.
[129]Ibid., p.232.

> In the American Republic we are left entirely free to act
> out her sacred and beneficial mission to the human race.
> She is free theoretically as well as practically, not merely
> by toleration, nor overshadowed by civil law, but by consti-
> tutional guarantee. Obstacles in her progress arising from
> ignorance of her true doctrines, and from hereditary pre-
> judices, are gradually disappearing, as Catholics and non-
> Catholics come to know each other.[130]

No doubt the Archbishop of Philadelphia believed that the faithful

sons of the Church made mighty fine American citizens.[131]

At least six of the American Catholic prelates exhibited a

willingness to use the printed word to criticize, comfort, and in-

spire those under their spiritual domain. With this effort, the Big

Three, Spalding, Gibbons, and Ireland produced numerous works and

received some literary recognition. McQuaid, Chatard, and Ryan,

perhaps, felt that the ultimate had not been stated by the other

three; since they did not hesitate to offer their own recommenda-

tions to the American Catholics. All six, however, shared the

impulse to do good and to help their fellow men. Oftentimes, the

periodical journals, religious and secular, served as excellent

mediums for their views.

In reference to citizenship and patriotism, it was an honest

aspiration for Catholics to attempt to be the first patriots in the

land. They had an obligation to vote honestly and to avoid corrupt

politics. Actually, there was no conflict between the interests of

the State and those of the Church, although Bishop McQuaid thought

---

[130]Ibid., p.234.
[131]Ibid., p.238.

Archbishop Ireland to be overly active in behalf of the Republican party. The hierarchy endeavored to explain Catholic doctrine to the reading public and to defend Christianity from Ingersoll and his affiliates.

Literary wise, not only the clergy but also the laymen were urged to cultivate a taste for good reading, especially the classics. There was, unfortunately, a general failure to appreciate the teachers' role in American life. In careful statements, the hierarchy announced a non-opposition to the public schools, but, stated, under prevailing conditions, religious education achieved its fulfillment only in parochial schools. A note of optimism pervaded the hierarchy's good advice, as though time and this constant effort to do better would place cultured comfort within the grasp of all.

CHAPTER VI

TWO PRIEST-EDITORS: FATHERS HECKER AND HUDSON

Certain members of the hierarchy realized the importance of
publishing to disseminate their concepts for encouraging and
guiding their co-religionists. Consequently, some of them like
Buffalo's Bishop Stephen Vincent Ryan, welcomed as allies the good
periodicals edited by capable, Catholic journalists. Regarding
these editors, the able Jesuit historian, Father William L. Lucey of
Holy Cross, wrote (1952): "Many were outstanding; some were
great."[1] Father Lucey, in four serialized articles, emphasized the
significance of these editors and their publications. Upon them,
he wrote, "the intellectual history of Catholicism" during the years
(1865-1900) "will lean heavily."[2] Of particular consequence were
the last two decades of the nineteenth century for they provided the
"spring-tide of Catholic journalism."[3]

Prior to this "spring-tide," however, several noteworthy
periodicals already were in existence. For example, 1865 witnessed
the founding of the monthly, The Catholic World, and the weekly,

---

[1]William L. Lucey, S.J., Ph.D., "Catholic Magazines 1890-1893,"
Records of the American Catholic Historical Society of Philadelphia,
LXII (September, 1952) 136.
[2]_____, "Catholic Magazines: 1865-1880," RACHSP, LXIII
(March, 1952) 21.
[3]_____, "Catholic Magazines: 1894-1900," RACHSP, LXIII
(December, 1952) 222.

214

Ave Maria; two magazines which have survived to the present day.
Only a month selarated their appearances, The Catholic World was
published first, April, 1865.[4] The inspiring force directing the
establishment of The Catholic World was supplied by Orestes
Brownson's friend and fellow convert, Father Isaac Hecker, C.S.P.
The first of the Paulists, Father Hecker, combined religious zeal
and patriotic fervor in amazing proportions.

> When the nature of the American republic is better under-
> stood, and the exposition of Christianity is shaped in the
> light of its universal principles so as to suit the peculiari-
> ties of the American mind, the Catholic Church will not only
> keep her baptized American children in her fold, but will at
> the same time remove the prejudice existing in the minds of
> a large class of non-Catholics, and the dangers apprehended
> from the influence of republicanism will be turned into
> fresh evidence of the Church's divine character.[5]

The coming of the "Golden Day" was to hastened by bombarding the
country with an accurate Catholic press, one disseminating truth and
culture. As for The Catholic World, "Its purpose was to speak for
religion in high-grade periodical literature."[6] In 1870, in an
unsigned article, The Catholic World estimated its progress in providing Americans with the best Catholic magazine available. With
perfect candor, The Catholic World announced that it was "more
successful than any former Catholic magazine... the leading organ of
Catholic thought and... Catholic sentiment."[7] Catholics, however,

---

[4]Ibid., p.223.
[5]Isaac T. Hecker, "The Catholic Church in the United States,"
The Catholic World, XXIX (July, 1879) 455.
[6]Rev. Walter Elliott, The Life of Father Hecker, p.349.
[7]"Catholic Literature and the Catholic Public," The Catholic
World, XII (December, 1870) 404.

were slow in supporting their periodicals.

Nor was it only in neglect of periodical literature that
Catholics showed "a meagre appreciation of the religious uses of the
press."[8] Too many Catholic laymen failed to look at the literature
of their own denomination, while the sizable libraries of rich
Catholics often were devoid of Catholic books. To offset this
apparent apathy, the Paulists helped create The Catholic Publication
Society with the two-fold purpose of providing the "religious works
which people of culture and taste would like to have in their
libraries,"[9] and of making less expensive books available to the
poorer Catholics. In general, the Catholic publisher, in order to
make money, had to rely on the sale of prayer books and school books.

> Their best customers are devout people of the poorer class,
> who have generally too little education to take an interest
> in literature, and for whom books of piety must be manu-
> factured in the cheapest possible way.[10]

Adding to the woe, was the failure of the Catholic college
graduate, "this great army of young educated Catholics"[11] to do anything to foster Catholic literature. The colleges, perhaps, failed
to create a literary taste.

> We know that in some colleges young men are never taught to
> think of reading as one of the employments of their future
> life, never iniated into the delights of literature, or
> trained to make any other use of books than to get sound

---

[8] Ibid.
[9] Ibid.
[10] Ibid., p.405.
[11] Ibid.

Catholic ideas of the outlines of general history, and
principles of metaphysics, with a knowledge of Greek, Latin,
mathematics, physics and Christian doctrine.[12]

Parents, too often, were to blame for rendering their houses into

literary wildernesses. The Catholic World urged them to buy books

as presents for the children and to replace the reading of trashy

magazines and newspapers with the treasures of Catholic literature.

Ten years later, The Catholic World saw signs of general improve-

ment as periodical literature "assumed a new form to meet the

longing for multifarious knowledge and the discussion on all sides

of questions."[13] The best of the Catholic periodical writing of

Europe and America, The Catholic World prophesied, gradually would

form "a large and important part of the solid and permanent

literature."[14] Actually, the distinguished writers of these

periodical pieces were promoting the welfare of their fellow men.

> The light and active operations of the periodical press
> are most especially suited to the present and immediate
> exigencies of the cause we have in hand, the diffusion of
> Catholic knowledge, the dissipation of popular errors, the
> general promotion of religion, virtue, intellectual, moral,
> social, and political well-being, by the inculcation of
> Catholic principles... And those who aid in any other way
> to increase the circulation and enhance the influence of
> Catholic periodical literature are rendering one of the
> best kinds of service to the cause of truth, of good morals,
> and of the improvement of the social order.[15]

Since this article also was unsigned, Father Hecker was not

credited positively with its authorship although it was published

[12]Ibid., p.406.
[13]"Introductory," The Catholic World, XXXI (April, 1880) 2.
[14]Ibid., p.3.
[15]Ibid., p.4.

during his period of editorship, 1865-1889. Such hesitancy on the
author's part was prompted by the knowledge that Father Hecker,
never a robust man, was taken seriously ill in 1871 and did not
fully recover. In connection with his absence from office, Thomas
F. Meehan, the Catholic Encyclopedia authority on the periodicals of
the United States, supplied the information that when Father Hecker
"was absent abroad for several long periods he made Father A. F.
Hewit, his associate editor in charge of the Catholic World."16

An intimate glance into the life of the ambitious Father Hecker
was revealed in his letters to Orestes Brownson, the distinguished
convert. Doctor Brownson, in his declining years, felt that his
writing no longer held an appeal for American Catholics, so that the
Paulist editor repeatedly declared his "most sincere appreciation of
the value and high importance of the contributions of your pen."17
Hecker and Brownson did not always agree in interpreting certain
subjects, so that in refusing Brownson, Father Hecker had to write,
"In my judgment it would seriously impair the influence of the C.W.
to bring out in its pages conflicting views on such important
subjects."18 Still, another expression of Brownson's true worth

---

16Thomas F. Meehan, "The First Catholic Monthly Magazine,"
Historical Records and Studies, United States Catholic Historical
Society, XXXI (1940) 144.
17Rev. Isaac T. Hecker to Orestes Brownson, (August 26, 1869)
Brownson Papers. UNDA.
18Rev. Isaac T. Hecker to Orestes Brownson, (January 8, 1872)
Brownson Papers. UNDA.

came from the pen of the ever-grateful priest.

It seems to me that if you would continue to write such
articles as you have done the last two years or more in
refutation of the calumnies of the enemies of the Church,
in supplying Catholic principles to the social and political
questions of the day, in directing the young Catholic mind
how to judge and act in the midst of existing difficulties,
which never were greater or more threatening. And in boldly
confronting and silencing the leading advocates of heresy
and error, you would promote to the greatest degree Catholic
interests, give the highest satisfaction to the hierarchy
and interest most the readers of the magazine.
Believe me Dear Dr. you can have no idea of the great
good which you have done by your pen employed in this direction. I who am in more direct contact with the readers of
the Catholic World hear the satisfaction expressed on all
sides and by all classes for articles of this nature, all
rejoicing that in you they have found a champion of their
faith and a master who teaches them how to harmonize their
duties as Catholics with the best interests of society and
state.[19]

Here, in this letter to Doctor Brownson, Father Hecker indicated

many of the aspirations which guided him and his successors in

editing The Catholic World. After Father Hecker's death, Father

Augustine F. Hewit, C.S.P., became the magazine's editor (1889-

1897); and, in turn, Father Hewit was followed by Father Alexander

P. Doyle, C.S.P., (1897-1904) and Father John J. Burke, C.S.P.,

(1904-1920). These editors, like the magazine they fashioned,

promoted the wellbeing of Catholics in America. An issue of The

Catholic World was apt to contain fiction, poetry, and several

illuminating articles regarding pertinent events. In this fashion,

---

[19]Rev. Isaac T. Hecker to Orestes Brownson, (January 30, 1871)
Brownson Papers. UNDA.

the general trend toward social, political, educational, and
religious reform was treated within its pages. Here was recorded
the development and decline of the Reading Circle and of the
Catholic Summer School movements. In several ways, The Catholic
World offered to guide its readers to the best in current
literature.

For the members of the various reading circles, The Catholic
World conducted a department, "The Columbian Reading Union," which
served as a clearing house in reporting the activities of the
different circles. Humphrey J. Desmond, this department suggested,
had composed A Reading Circle Manual, a little volume of cardinal
importance to "beginners seeking guidance in the choice of books."[20]
The more advanced reader, particularly the financially solvent, was
alerted to the forthcoming publication of Reuben Fold Thwaite's The
Jesuit Relations, for wealthy Catholics "should need no urging to
subscribe to such a worthy object."[21] When Edith Wharton's poem
"Margaret of Cortona" aroused the religious sensibilities of
Catholic readers who wrote letters to protest to Harper's Magazine,
the publisher of the poem; The Catholic World printed Harper's
apology and the opinion of another Catholic editor;

---

[20]"The Columbian Reading Union," The Catholic World, LXXVII
(June, 1903) 424.
[21]"The Columbian Reading Union," The Catholic World, LXXII
(December, 1900) 423.

"If intelligent Catholics always acted with the promptness and vigor which have distinguished many of them in this case, the interests of truth and morality would be grandly served."[22]

Maintaining this spirit of indignation, the Columbian Reading Union charged that Marie Corelli's The Master Christian was an attempt to burlesque the modern theological novel which specifically portraying Roman Catholic clergymen as "monsters of vice and iniquity."[23] At the same time, Miss Gertrude Atherton's Senator North merited strong condemnation.[24] Hence, the Columbian Reading Union, in praising some books while denying others, compiled with its avowed purpose of counteracting the "indifference shown to Catholic literature" and of suggesting a course for "acquiring a better knowledge of standard authors."[25]

"Talk About New Books," however, provided the regular column for reviewing current literature. Extremely favorable criticism was given to Lindsay Swift's Brook Farm[26] and to the American Winston Churchill's The Crisis; the latter volume gave "greater justifica-tion to the writer's claim for literary rank."[27] Praise, given to Churchill's latest fictional effort, was not withheld from An American Anthology. "The work is admirable,"[28] wrote The Catholic

[22] Ibid., LXXIV (February, 1902) 696.
[23] Ibid., LXXII (November, 1900) 287.
[24] Ibid.
[25] Ibid., LXXII (October, 1900) 140.
[26] "Talk About New Books," The Catholic World, LXXI (June, 1900) 406.
[27] Ibid., LXXIII (July, 1901) 531.
[28] Ibid., LXXIII (February, 1901) 676.

World, as it described the last of Edmund Clarence Stedman's four
volumes "devoted to a critical review of British and American
poetry." Whereas the social historian, John Bach McMaster merited
the words "vigorous narrative," "well proportioned," "touching on
all matters of real importance"[29] attached to his Primary History of
the United States; the revised edition of John O'Kane Murray's,
Catholic Pioneers of America, was admonished:

> The author's object was to offset the partial and incomplete
> records of non-Catholic historians. The present revised
> edition, however, reveals no change in spirit or in method
> from the original edition; and in these days of critical
> and scholarly works, like The Jesuit Relations, must be
> ranked as passe.[30]

When the representative stories of Father Finn, Maurice Francis
Egan, Mary T. Waggaman, Ella Lorraine Dorsey were collected and
published as a Juvenile Round-Table, the reviewer exulted that "the
stories possess those qualities which are well calculated to awaken
noble sentiments in young minds."[31] Also recommended was Miss
Katherine E. Conway's visits to the Catholic shrines of Europe, an
experience she recorded in New Footsteps in Well-trodden Ways.[32]
Another member of O'Reilly's Pilot staff, James Jeffrey Roche, wrote
By-ways of War, an account of the rise and fall of American fili-
bustering which was considered "a real contribution to American

---

[29]Ibid., LXXIII (August, 1901) 680.
[30]Ibid., LXXIII (May, 1901) 256.
[31]"Talk About New Books," The Catholic World, LXXIV (March,
1902) 821.
[32]Ibid., LXX (March, 1900) 843.

history."[33] "A fascinating account of conversion,"[34] was the
garland awarded <u>A Troubled Heart and How It Was Comforted at Last</u> by
Charles Warren Stoddard. Molly Elliot Seawell, another convert,
bestowed a "rare, sweet individuality" upon her character, a Jesuit
martyr, who died on the scaffold for James II. The author, wrote the
reviewer, presented a new view of James II as a victim of the
fiercest bigotry in his generation. Never a villain, James was
honest, brave, and yet, narrow and inadequate as a ruler.[35] The
combination of the Polish author, Henryk Sienkiewicz, and his
American translator, Harvardman Jeremiah Curtin, who presented the
inspiring Quo Vadis to this country, received only lukewarm approval
for <u>The Judgment of Peter and Paul on Olympus</u>, as the notation was
made that the volume "does not possess any striking merit as far as
thought is concerned... but it does appeal to the artistic sense."[36]

The same varied reception was given to non-Catholic authors.
For example, Frank Banfield's <u>John Wesley</u> was admired as a model
biography, clear, pleasant, concise, not a whitewash "but a true
picture of the man who did so much to elevate and spiritualize the
English Middle Classes."[37] Equally admirable was Sanford H. Cobb's
<u>The Rise of Religious Liberty in America</u>, only the reviewer wished

[33] Ibid., LXXIII (August, 1901) 677.
[34] Ibid., LXXII (February, 1901) 687.
[35] Ibid., LXXI (December, 1900) 405.
[36] Ibid., p.412.
[37] Ibid., LXXII (March, 1901) 816.

that Cobb had substituted "Catholic" or "Roman Catholic" for "Romanists" and "Romanism."[38] However, the author of Every Inch A King, Josephine Caroline Sawyer, was objectionable for "as is usual with a large class of non-Catholic writers, her treatment of things Catholic is a trifle offensive."[39] Marie Corelli, again, was a favorite target of the reviewers, who were so accustomed to alerting their readers to a forthcoming Corellian blasphemy, that the words regarding Boy seemed tame:

> The construction of the story is simple, and in its worst aspects not bad;... almost wholly free from the weird improbability which has characterized some previous novels by the same writer.[40]

In addition to departments such as "The Columbian Reading Union" and "Talk About New Books," The Catholic World also printed longer, featured articles of literary interest. Georgina Pell Curtis, a zealous convert, reminded her co-religionists to be proud of the fact that Ludwig van Beethoven was a Catholic. The great Prussian composer throughout

> ... his whole life expressed the glory of his faith, and that in his mortal illness he asked the Ursuline Sisters to pray for him, and received humbly and prayerfully the last sacraments of the Church.[41]

The novels of Henry Harland, particularly The Cardinal's Snuff Box and The Lady Paramount were considered at length by the Paulist

---

[38]Ibid., LXXV (July, 1902) 675.
[39]Ibid., LXXIII (May, 1901) 246.
[40]Ibid., LXXI (September, 1900) 854.
[41]Georgina Pell Curtis, "Ludwig van Beethoven," The Catholic World, LXXVII (July, 1903) 521.

Father John J. Burke. In the former, the teachings and practices of

the Church were treated frequently, intelligently, and sympathe-

tically. Father Burke lamented:

> Oftentimes non-Catholics are under the impressions that
> Catholics can not live and act as human beings if they are
> true to the teachings of their faith.[42]

Rose F. Egan, writing in 1902, maintained that the Catholic novel of

the nineteenth century was, for the most part, literary pabulum with

monotonous religious discussions filling page upon page and abetted

not a bit by noble, faithful but highly impossible heroes and

heroines. That this sort of novel no longer served to satisfy our

Catholic people was not surprising for many obvious reasons.[43]

However, the twentieth century promised reform if the American pub-

lished novels of the Irish curate, Patrick A. Sheehan, were any

indication. His _My New Curate_ and _Luke Delmege_ were books

> that are the results of influences that have been long at
> work, but that likewise mark a turn in a new direction.
> They show us the power and far-reaching influence of novels
> based on Catholic truth, and illuminated by Catholic ideals.[44]

Also vastly encouraging were the deep-reaching essays of Bishop

Spalding, which, according to Rose Egan, gave a glimpse of the

immense possibilities of an educated Catholic people. "He is doing

more to enliven the Catholic truth, and to show its application to

---

[42]Rev. John J. Burke, "Mr. Henry Harland's Novels," _The Catholic World_, LXXV (June, 1902) 400.

[43]Rose F. Egan, "The Basis of a Catholic Novel," _The Catholic World_, LXXVI (December, 1902) 316.

[44]Ibid., p.327.

modern life, than any other writer since this era has begun.[45]

Nearly seven years later, the progress of Catholic writing in America, again, was evaluated in The Catholic World by two more famous critics, Agnes Repplier and Louise Imogen Guiney. Father John Talbot Smith was the instigator of their articles since he had published in the St. John's Quarterly (July issue), Syracuse, New York, an article entitled, "The Young Catholic Writer: What Shall He Do?" Father Smith's indictment was a melancholy one. The Catholic crowd was indifferent to the young writers and the Catholic press was helpless to aid them.[46] Consequently, Father Smith advised the young writer to enter the secular arena and to give no evidence of his faith in his writing. Concerning this advice, Miss Repplier did not object to the first part; but, the second brought a sharp retort:

> The average editor is not looking out for Episcopalian, or Unitarian, or free-thinking contributors. What he wants is timely and readable matter, and very little of it can he get.[47]

Drawing from her own experience, she proclaimed that no editor or publisher had ever asked her to omit or to alter any sentence "that proclaimed my religious beliefs."[48]

Louise Imogen Guiney, in some respects, used the same rebuttal and, also, introduced some ideas of her own. To Father Smith's

---

[45]Ibid.

[46]Louise Imogen Guiney, "On Catholic Writers and their Handicaps," The Catholic World, XC (November, 1909) 204.

[47]Agnes Repplier, "Catholicism and Authorship," The Catholic World, XC (November, 1909) 169.

[48]Ibid., p.173.

regret that John Gilmary Shea was virtually unknown to most
Catholics, Miss Guiney advised that surely he knew "that fiction
only is what the illiberal general public now wants and pays for?"[49]
Miss Guiney was hopeful. Not only had the tone of the lesser
American Catholic publications improved visibly; but also the
secular magazines, notably those in England, were more "hospitable
than ever before to our scholars and apologists."[50] In her mind, the
situation called for a greater effort.

> What we want from our writers is a harvest of great books;
> productions so lofty and masterful that there can be no
> doubt about their reception. As no one of us has yet pro-
> duced a really great book, it is, perhaps, too soon to
> compain of the cold world's chilling blight.[51]

Thus, The Catholic World, through its articles and departments,
reminded its readers of the aspiring task that awaited Catholic
writers. While The Catholic World, during this period (1880-1915),
had four different editors, the Ave Maria had only one, Father Daniel
E. Hudson, C.S.C. The "Big Man" in everything but stature, Father
Hudson became editor in 1875 and did not relinquish the position
until he retired in the year of the Great Depression, 1929. The Ave
Maria, under this remarkable priest, gained in "importance and
prestige throughout the English speaking world."[52] Equally edifying

---

[49]Louise Imogen Guiney, op.cit., p.206.
[50]Ibid., p.212.
[51]Ibid., p.215.
[52]William L. Lucey, S.J., Ph.D., "Catholic Magazines: 1865-1880,"
RACHSP, LXIII (March, 1952) 25.

was the increased circulation to 22,000 (1897).[53] Giving less space
to the strictly, literary article than did The Catholic World, the
Ave Maria included more devotional literature and a juvenile department. (Both magazines could be counted upon for lucid comment
aroused by current conditions.) Moreover, the Ave Maria was far from
ignoring the literary scene as its pages attested. Fiction (often in
serial form), poetry, the departments: "Notes and Remarks," "The
Latest Books," "With Authors and Publishers," and "Notable New Books"
gave some indication of the editor's taste and judgment.

The Latest Books department was headed by a short paragraph of
explanation.

> The object of this list is to afford information concerning
> new publications of special interest to Catholic readers. The
> latest books will appear at the head, older ones being dropped
> out from time to time to make room for new titles. As a rule
> devotional books, pamphlets and new editions will not be
> indexed.[54]

In addition to listing books by Catholic and non-Catholic authors,
the department also announced that the books could be ordered either
from the Ave Maria or the publisher. "With Authors and Publishers"
gave gossipy, short-notices regarding the trade. When the Benziger
Brothers published ten volumes of Short Stories by the Best Catholic
Authors, "With Authors and Publishers" declared them to be well
written, instructive without being didactic, and of a pocket-size

suitable for traveling.[55] Current comment on all pertinent questions was dispensed in "Notes and Remarks," but, even this department had an occasional literary bearing. For "Notes and Remarks"
supported America in censoring certain Catholic book-catalogue
publishers. Both magazines insisted that catalogues intended for
general circulation should include no works "likely to prove mental
and moral poison rather than intellectual and spiritual sustenance."[56]
Occasionally, a short feature article would appear such as "Some
Books for Catholic Teachers." Thoughts on Education and Counsels for
the Young by the Anglican Bishop Creighton and E. L. Kemp's History
of Education were recommended with the caution:

> To ignore such books, as these because they happen to be
> non-Catholic pens and to contain a few slurs on the Church
> and some historical errors is the height of folly.[57]

The burden of significant literary reviews was carried by
Notable New Books, a feature whose appearance in the Ave Maria,
varied, usually, from three to six or eight times during a six-
month's period. "Notable New Books" greeted the initial volume of
The Catholic Encyclopedia with great admiration.

> The Catholic Encyclopedia at once takes rank among the most
> important reference works to be found in English and its
> publication may well be considered an epoch-making event in
> the history of the Church in English speaking countries.[58]

---

[55]"With Authors and Publishers," Ave Maria, LXXIII (July 15,
1911) 95.
[56]"Notes and Remarks," Ave Maria, LXXIII (July 29, 1911) 151.
[57]"Some Books for Catholic Teachers," Ave Maria, LXVII (October
10, 1908) 469.
[58]"Notable New Books," Ave Maria, LXV (August 17, 1907) 214.

William Allen White's novel on "mammonism," <u>A Certain Rich Man</u>, it regarded "a realistic presentation of a dominant phase of American life in the twentieth century."[59] Prognostication was not beyond Notable New Books since it declared that Allen S. Will's <u>Life of Cardinal Gibbons</u> "...will prove of a very material assistance to the future chronicler who tells the story of Catholicity in the United States."[60] Reaching across the ocean to England with its literary scope, Notable New Books was delighted with <u>The Life of John Henry Newman</u> by the noted Wilfrid Ward. "Let us hope that a cheaper edition of this biography of Cardinal Newman may soon be put within the reach of a wider circle of readers. It is a work to do the world good.[61]

Since Father Hudson signed none of the above articles, his correspondence is valuable in confirming the notion that here was a fair-minded man dedicated to bring inspiration, gratitude, common sense, and historical and literary insight into the lives of his fellow men. The letterheads of his incoming correspondence varied: England, Ireland, Italy, Father Damien's Molokai, New Zealand, China, and Austria harbored some of his far-flung friends. Among his American correspondents were authors, editors, publishers, political figures, high-ranking clergymen, no-ranking clergymen, interested

---

59"Notable New Books," <u>Ave Maria</u>, LXIX (November 13, 1909) 631.
60"Notable New Books," <u>Ave Maria</u>, LXXIV (March 25, 1912) 376.
61"Notable New Books," <u>Ave Maria</u>, LXXIV (June 22, 1912) 825.

Americans, and little boys and girls thanking Father for a book or two or some stamps which he had sent. Father Hudson, in turn, sent to his corresponding multitude letters full of encouragement, advice, and friendly feeling.

One indication of the extent of Father Hudson's letter writing was contained in the-day-after Christmas lines he sent to his old friend, Charles Warren Stoddard. "This is my thirty-first letter this week already; and it is only Monday night! Three times as many more must be written at intervals during the week.[62] Indeed, this was an amazing output for a man actively engaged in publishing a quality, weekly magazine. Stoddard, by this time advanced in age and lonely, needed Hudson's gentle prodding. "Your place can not be filled and the vacancy is a trial to your admirers."[63] Thus, did the editor preface his remarks to the essayist. Something, anything by Stoddard would be acceptable for the Ave Maria's New Year number. Nor was Father Hudson thinking of himself when he urged Stoddard to submit a manuscript to the Atlantic.

> The present editor of the latter seems to be a nice man.
> Do you know him, Bliss Perry? I am thinking he would
> be glad to welcome you to the Atlantic, which impresses me
> as being now more life its old self.[64]

---

[62]Rev. Daniel E. Hudson, C.S.C., to Charles Warren Stoddard, (December 26, 1905) Hudson Papers. UNDA.
[63]Rev. Daniel E. Hudson, C.S.C., to Charles Warren Stoddard, (December 4, 1906) Hudson Papers. UNDA.
[64]Rev. Daniel E. Hudson, C.S.C., to Charles Warren Stoddard, (April 29, 1907) Hudson Papers. UNDA.

As for Stoddard, most of his letters were filled with the complaints of a man in poor health. Nonetheless, he did appreciate the friendly, little editor. "After all you seem to be the only consistent Catholic editor in the country; all Catholic publications barring the "Ave Maria" should be suppressed by law, I think!"[65]

Fortunately, this conviction of suppression was not shared by Father Hudson. Although Father Hudson believed some Catholic papers to be worthless as he admitted to Henry F. Brownson,[66] he was not parsimonious in his praise of the good ones. Thomas Daly, the McAroni Ballad poet, wrote thanking Hudson for the generous words in the Ave Maria commending some of his verses. Daly, at this time, disclosed what a flutter was "occasioned in our editorial rooms" as Father Hudson's letter to Mr. O'Shea spoke so handsomely of The Catholic Standard and Times (Philadelphia) as 'the leading Catholic newspaper.'[67] Two years later, John J. O'Shea thanked Father Hudson for the encouraging words given to the Catholic Standard and Times for its attempts "to do in defense of our holy faith and our sorely tried Pontiff."[68] Previously, William J. O'Shea had written a letter indicative of Hudson's effect upon his fellow editors.

---

[65]Charles Warren Stoddard to Rev. Daniel E. Hudson, C.S.C., (January 26, 1901) Hudson Papers. UNDA.
[66]Henry F. Brownson to Rev. Daniel E. Hudson, C.S.C., (March 14, 1903) Hudson Papers. UNDA.
[67]Thomas Daly to Rev. Daniel E. Hudson, C.S.C., (April 3, 1908) Hudson Papers. UNDA.
[68]John J. O'Shea to Rev. Daniel E. Hudson, C.S.C., (April 23, 1910) Hudson Papers. UNDA.

I owe it to the generous appreciation of Catholics like
yourself in spirit that I have been encouraged to put forth
what little power I possess to uphold and defend our great
cause...
     The first duty of a Catholic editor is, in my humble
belief, to forget his own personality completely, in so
far as his public teaching is concerned, and bear in mind
the great principle upon which our glorious Church is
founded, respect.[69]

Obviously, Father Hudson had earned the respect and confidence

of his co-religionists. He was in a position to do them favors and

this he enjoyed. Early in 1901, Bishop Spalding wrote: "I see the

Digest (sic) has noticed by Roman Discourse. This is due to your

influence."[70] Later that year, Spalding penned his gratitude "for

your notice of Alphonsius (sic.) McClurg tells me the book is

having a very good sale."[71] Monsignor John A. Ryan, the avid

interpreter of the Catholic advance in social thinking, wrote:

     Permit me to thank you heartily for your kind reference
to me in the Ave Maria of the 14th inst. Your appreciation
of the quality of specificness encourages me more than
perhaps you are aware. For years I have been neglecting
every other property of literary expression in order to
secure if possible this quality and the kindred one of
clearness, as these seem to me to be the supreme requisites
in the kind of writing time I have to do with. I assure you
that I am glad to be told by one whose opinion is of value
that I am succeeding in my efforts.[72]

---

[69]William J. O'Shea to Rev. Daniel E. Hudson, C.S.C., (September
4, 1909) Hudson Papers. UNDA.
     [70]Bishop John Lancaster Spalding to Rev. Daniel E. Hudson,
C.S.C., (January 21, 1901) Hudson Papers. UNDA.
     [71]Ibid., (August 18, 1901)
     [72]Mgr. John A. Ryan to Rev. Daniel E. Hudson, C.S.C., (March 21,
1908) Hudson Papers. UNDA.

To these, Louise Imogen Guiney could add her appreciation for the review of *Campion*, a work she enjoyed writing for "I love the man and the background."[73] Father Thomas J. Shahan thanked Father Hudson for the *Ave Maria's* kind references to the *Encyclopedia* and to his translation of Bardenhewer's *Patrology*.[74] Within forty-one days in 1910, the encouraging editor had letters from three different people acknowledging their indebtedness to him. Whereas Frank H. Spearman had been inspired by a little talk,[75] Benjamin B. Lindsey[76] and Father James Field Spalding were grateful for the "kind" references to their respective works.

This assistance was given as unsparingly that others did not hesitate to seek his help. Benziger's, a respected Catholic publishing firm, for example, asked the courtesy of a notice for a book they deemed important.

> We have this day mailed you a copy of Fr. Oechtering's little book *Capital and Labor*, and kindly ask you to give it a notice in your paper. This is the only book that has been published on this subject from a Catholic standpoint, and we send it to you at the suggestion of the Reverend author who feels that if it is only noticed by the Catholic Press it will help create a demand for it and spread it amongst the masses of working people where   will do the most good.

[73]Louise Imogen Guiney to Rev. Daniel E. Hudson, C.S.C., (September 17, 1909) Hudson Papers. UNDA.

[74]Rev. Thomas J. Shahan to Rev. Daniel E. Hudson, C.S.C., (October 20, 1909) Hudson Papers. UNDA.

[75]Frank H. Spearman to Rev. Daniel E. Hudson, C.S.C., (July 14, 1910) Hudson Papers. UNDA.

[76]Benjamin B. Lindsey to Rev. Daniel E. Hudson, C.S.C., (July 8, 1910) Hudson Papers. UNDA.

The object of the work you will notice is to create peace
and unity amongst the employers and employee's and to avoid
strikes...[77]

It was doubtful whether the Bishop of Covington, Kentucky, Camillus

P. Maes, wanted a public notice of Dr. Philip Zenner's Education in

Sexual Physiology and Hygiene; but, he did seek his friend's

opinion.

Today I send you Dr. Zenner's book about which I spoke to
you... Have you people ever felt the need of such a text
book from which a Catholic medical man might talk to your
boys? For, I think, if anything is done, it must be done
by word of mouth and to small classes of homogenous
characters.[78]

Of a different nature and one more familiar to an American's

ears was the plea of the renowned scholar Dom F. Aidan Gasquet who

was engaged in organizing a new edition of the Vulgate. It was for

money. Since Pius X had turned him into a "beggar," Dom Gasquet

wondered whether Father Hudson would say a word to his wealthy

friends and readers. Every contribution including the smallest was

to be thankfully received and promptly acknowledged. For this

effort, "I shall be more indebted to you than I am already."[79] In

reference to this worthy project, Bishop McQuaid borrowed some

---

[77]Benziger Brothers, (Cincinnati), to Rev. Daniel E. Hudson,
C.S.C., (March 9, 1889) Hudson Papers. UNDA.

[78]Camillus P. Maes, Bishop of Covington, to Rev. Daniel E.
Hudson, C.S.C., (undated, archivist assigned the year 1910).
Hudson Papers. UNDA.

[79]Dom F. Aidan Gasquet to Rev. Daniel E. Hudson, C.S.C.,
(January 8, 1908) Hudson Papers. UNDA.

breezy words from the business world and made a further request.

> Do something to set the ball rolling to raise some money
> for the commission in charge of the revision of the Vulgate
> under the direction of Dom Gasquet. It is a much needed
> work, is in good hands, and ought to be helped by educational
> institutions and clerics in America.[80]

All of the requests that came to the editor-priest were not from
fellow clerics. For example, the Cleveland industrialist, M. A.

Fanning, asked the Ave Maria to say something about his articles on

social subjects that the Catholic Universe was publishing. The

civic-minded Fanning noted that most Catholics were so engaged in

the struggle for existence as to be deprived of the leisure or

opportunity to properly study the current movements in civic life.

Thus, there was need of a "body of wise and well-informed counselors

in every city" to focus the attention of the Catholic population upon

the impending municipal reforms. Would the Ave Maria support this

lay action? When the Ave Maria promptly gave favorable notice to the

articles, the enthusiastic Fanning wrote again to Father Hudson.

> If we had a dozen men in each community who would give up the
> idea that our vast Catholic influence should be traded for
> political jobs and adopt the idea that Catholic influence
> should be wielded for the public benefit along the line of
> Catholic ideals, we could do a great deal to shape municipal
> life in this country.[82]

---

[80]Bishop Bernard J. McQuaid to Rev. Daniel Hudson, C.S.C.,
(February 18, 1908) Hudson Papers. UNDA.
    [81]M. A. Fanning to Rev. Daniel E. Hudson, C.S.C., (April 27,
1908) Hudson Papers. UNDA.
    [82]Ibid., (May 8, 1908)

Cleveland, the city of the reforming Thomas "Golden-Rule" Jones had produced another remarkable man, this time a Catholic layman.

Not only did the reformers seek out Father Hudson, but, likewise, those being reformed. An inmate of the Jeffersonville, Missouri, prison stated that the institution's Methodist chaplain was permitting the Catholic inmates to submit a booklist along with his to the next legislature in the hope of having $1000 appropriated for Catholic purposes.

> This place should be flooded with Catholic literature... Inmates are somewhat receptive, if judiciously handled... There is a good Catholic Librarian here, and he and I can do a lot, if we only meet a little assistance and moral support.[83]

A similar idea occurred to T. A. D. Lucasz, head clerk of the Judge Advocate General's office in Madras, when he requested the _Ave Maria_ "with an object of disseminating virtuous actions amongst the Catholic congregations of this country which is flooded with anti-Catholic journals."[84] A more unusual request came from Francis McCullagh who desired Butler's _Lives of the Saints_ in payment for an article he had submitted. His letter explained:

> I am sure you will sympathize with a Catholic in a place like Tokyo where the second hand book shops are filled with Huxleys and Spencers but where not even the Imperial Library contains a single Catholic (religious writer), not even one volume of Newman.[85]

---

[83]Francis Furey to Rev. Daniel E. Hudson, C.S.C., (November 28, 1910) Hudson Papers. UNDA.

[84]T.A.D. Lucasz to Rev. Daniel E. Hudson, C.S.C., (October 8, 1881) Hudson Papers. UNDA.

[85]Francis McCullagh to Rev. Daniel E. Hudson, C.S.C., (January 15, 1901) Hudson Papers. UNDA.

Justice, like charity, was courted by Father Hudson. When
G. P. Putnam's Sons printed a volume particularly offensive to him,
he accused them of being anti-Catholic publishers.[86] To their
protestations, he answered:

> You do not realize that you have given any offence or done
> any injustice, therefore you can not be expected either to
> express regret or to refrain from publishing books like
> that of Dr. McKim, though Catholics I assure you, regard
> them as insulting, unjust, and injurious.[87]

Putnam's, then, suavely suggested that some scholarly authority,
"for instance youself,"[88] should compose a volume making a specific
reply to Dr. McKim. The MacMillan Company, in a similar situation,
had the perfect answer, "The book referring to Father Ralph is
neither published nor imported by us."[89] Naturally, it was not
always necessary for him to use the "mailed fist." Often, the
opposite was true. The editor of the Independent, William Hayes
Ward, recognized this kindness.

> ... I should not neglect to thank you for your generous
> recognition of the spirit which I mean should characterize
> the Independent in its relation to the Catholic Church.
> I recognize that the better class are more generous in their
> criticism.[90]

---

[86]G.P.Putnam's Sons to Rev. Daniel E. Hudson, C.S.C., (October
28, 1914) Hudson Papers. UNDA.

[87]Rev. Daniel E. Hudson, to G.P. Putnam's Sons, (October 31,
1914) Hudson Papers. UNDA.

[88]G.P.Putnam's Sons to Rev. Daniel E. Hudson, C.S.C., (November
4, 1914) Hudson Papers. UNDA.

[89]The MacMillan Company to Rev. Daniel E. Hudson, C.S.C.,
(June 6, 1913) Hudson Papers. UNDA.

[90]William Hayes Ward to Rev. Daniel E. Hudson, C.S.C., (August
25, 1912) Hudson Papers. UNDA.

The author of If I Were a Pastor Again, L. P. Winter was grateful for the brotherly words. "I appreciate them deeply, and all the more because of your Church relation and my own."[91] Equally indebted was Gamaliel Bradford, Jr. "Thank you very much for your courtesy in printing by little note. I hope that other Catholic papers will copy. I do not like to be judged by careless expressions."[92] Whereas the Bradford courtesy had been accomplished in print, Father Hudson could evoke a strong, favorable response with a letter. After reading his sermon in the Detroit Free Press, Hudson tended his congratulations by mail to Eugene R. Shippen of the Congregational Unitarian Church. Shippen was moved.

> I feel very strongly in regard to the anti-Catholic prejudices which poisons so many Protestants. By personal acquaintance with high minded lay members of your Church, and my casual acquaintance with the writings of some of your thinkers to say nothing of my convictions in regard to Christian unity, have happily saved me from such prejudice.[93]

No doubt, the Hudson pen was an instrument of good. Both the printed word and the intimate letter as products of this pen presented him to many Americans as an intelligent priest, who was anxious to serve them his country, and his Church. Yet, this was not the limit of his services. As editor of the Ave Maria, he paid

---

[91] L. P. Winter to Rev. Daniel E. Hudson, C.S.C., (March 25, 1913) Hudson Papers. UNDA.
[92] Gamaliel Bradford, Jr. to Rev. Daniel E. Hudson, C.S.C., (February 6, 1913) Hudson Papers. UNDA.
[93] Eugene R. Shippen to Rev. Daniel E. Hudson, C.S.C., (April 20, 1910) Hudson Papers. UNDA.

for its articles, poems, and stories. As a paymaster, he was
prompt, sometimes even in advance. The rate was not always the
highest and there were complaints, but, the general impression was
given that the Ave Maria would extend itself in an effort to make
its contributors comfortable. For example, early one March,
Mrs. Anna Hanson Dorsey asked, "Will you send me a check for as much
as you can spare on acct?"[94] By the fifteenth, she acknowledged
receiving $100,[95] not an untidy sum in 1886. Nor was Christian
Reid, in 1909, too reluctant to ask for an advance of "another
$300."[96] One of those complaining was Thomas Walsh, who thought
his "A Feast Day in Cordoba" merited $15[97] instead of the $8.50 it
brought. Lucile Nuncia Kling had a most fair grasp of the situation.
After stating that the Associated Sunday Magazines had paid her
seventy-five dollars for a three thousand word story, she announced:

> ... Now don't think I expect the Ave Maria to pay for this
> story at such a rate. I realize that secular magazines
> can afford to pay more than those that appeal only to
> Catholics.[98]

Beyond being as generous as circumstance would allow with pay-
ments, Father Hudson treated his contributors with much tact and

[94]Mrs. Anne Hanson Dorsey tp Rev. Daniel E. Hudson, C.S.C.,
(March 1, 1886) Hudson Papers. UNDA.
[95]Ibid., (March 13, 1886)
[96]Christian Reid to Rev. Daniel E. Hudson, C.S.C., (February 27,
1909) Hudson Papers. UNDA.
[97]Thomas Walsh to Rev. Daniel E. Hudson, C.S.C., (January 9,
1908) Hudson Papers. UNDA.
[98]Lucile Nuncia Kling to Rev. Daniel E. Hudson, C.S.C.,
(November 13, 1910) Hudson Papers. UNDA.

understanding. He must have communicated to them his intense

desire to help as one thankful author wrote:

> I think the story was much improved, for your young
> readers, by the paragraphs and touches you added. There
> is always such a pleasure in writing for your magazine,
> because of the hearty appreciation my efforts meet.[99]

Anna T. Sadlier elaborated on this same theme:

> ... your encouragement extended so kindly and so dis-
> criminately has been I am sure the prime factor in much
> literary incentive. I know it has been a great help to
> me. And, in fact, no less, except perhaps Catholic
> editors, need stimulus more than Catholic authors, who
> have to write in the face of an indifferent, if not
> hostile public, and with comparatively little apprecia-
> tion from their co-religionists.
> The "Ave Maria" is as I have said, a great power for
> good, one which has always maintained its high standards,
> safe in its opinions, and each number contains flavor and
> variety...[100]

Evidently, Father Hudson was appreciated by his contemporaries

and it was gratifying that they did not hesitate to praise him for

the great effort. His Holiness, Pius X, sent a "special blessing to

you and to all others engaged in this useful and interesting

publication."[101] Equally stimulating to Father Hudson, in my

opinion, was a four page letter of appreciation written by one

Joseph F. Fieg. Just what Joseph Fieg's position was in this life

has not been determined by the writer. However, the Ave Maria, to

him, was a "treasure worthy of preservation" so he had his

---

[99]Flora Haives Longhead to Rev. Daniel E. Hudson, C.S.C.,
(April 4, 1908) Hudson Papers. UNDA.
[100]Anna Sadlier to Rev. Daniel E. Hudson, C.S.C., (February 8,
1909) Hudson Papers. UNDA.
[101]Thomas F. Kennedy to Rev. Daniel E. Hudson, C.S.C., (June 4,
1910) Hudson Papers. UNDA.

accumulated copies bound.

> Altogether, Our Lady's magazine has been, and is a power
> for good amongst us. Besides being a power to educate and
> cultivate the mind it is helpful in bringing the heart
> nearer to God and to His Blessed Mother.102

From the high and the humble, the gratitude was great.

Father Hudson and Father Hecker were priests and editors.
Impressed by the opportunities offered Catholics in the United
States, they worked diligently to direct their co-religionists in
the manner of the cultivated citizen. They made it easier to obtain
good books. Two fine magazines, The Catholic World and the Ave
Maria, each bearing the individual stamp of its editor, introduced
quality reading material into the Catholic home. Fiction, poetry,
and non-fiction were provided for entertainment and inspiration.
Not only did the editors inspire their readers but also their
contributors, giving the latter praise and money as well. These two
Americans, Fathers Hecker and Hudson, served their fellow men with
love and intelligence.

102Joseph F. Fieg to Rev. Daniel E. Hudson, C.S.C., (February 13,
1908) Hudson Papers. UNDA.

CHAPTER VII

SOME EDITORS AND SOME JOURNALS

A distinguished pace for Catholic periodicals was established by
Father Isaac T. Hecker, C.S.P., and Father Daniel E. Hudson, C.S.C.
The two priests correctly interpreted the role of editor as guide to
their co-religionists and as a voice of Catholic opinion. Happily,
at this time (1880-1915), there were other Catholic editors, who had
the ability to edit equally impressive journals. The Catholic World
and the Ave Maria, from 1876 until 1924, had an extremely worthy
companion in The American Catholic Quarterly Review. The success of
this latter magazine, as in the cases of the former two, rested in
the capability of its chief-editor, Monsignor James Andrew Corcoran.
In reference to this ability, Archbishop John J. Keane, the founder
of the Catholic University of America, wrote in 1889:

> The reputation of his name at once placed the Quarterly
> in the front rank of learned periodical literature; and
> during the fourteen years of its existence, his matchless
> ability, joined with his quiet but untiring energy, has
> kept it in its high place of honor.[1]

Archbishop Keane deemed Monsignor Corcoran one of the three great
American Catholics of his generation. Whereas, Orestes Brownson was
"our great philosopher," and Father Hecker, "our great missionary,"

---

[1]Archbishop John J. Keane, "In Memoriam: Monsignor Corcoran,"
American Catholic Quarterly Review, XIV (October, 1889) 740.

Keane hailed Corcoran as "our living encyclopaedia of sacred
learning."[2] Corcoran the theologian, having participated to an
advantage in the Twelfth Ecumenical Council at the Vatican and in the
Third Plenary Council at Baltimore, enjoyed an international reputation; Corcoran, the writer and editor, deserved to be better known.

Periodical literature served as the major outlet for his
writings since that medium gave him the best opportunity to answer
"the honest questions and the dishonest sophisms of the erring and
hungry souls around him."[3] Whether defending the church or en-
lightening the faithful, the scholarly editor made interesting
reading. There was a barb to his review of an apostate's work.

> Dr. Schulte's book has been hailed in some quarters as a
> work of great power and originality, and a "deathblow to
> popery." But the latter clause can only be a publisher's
> stereotyped flourish, as we remember having heard it re-
> peated in the case of a thousand and one books of the sort,
> from Maria Monk's Awful Disclosures to the late, stupid,
> mendacious book of R. W. Thompson, who sits by the side of
> John Sherman in the new cabinet, and is the representative,
> we suppose, of its Christian statesmanship.[4]

He could be equally sharp with his co-religionists as he chided the
Catholic King of Bavaria for permitting the busts of Franz von
Sickingen and Friedrich von Schelling to remain in the Ruhmeshalle
of his capital, "thereby teaching his people that highbrow cutthroats

[2]Ibid., p.738.
[3]Ibid., p.741.
[4]Very Rev. James A. Corcoran, D.D., "Schulte's Roman Catholicism:
The Plea of an Apostate," The American Catholic Quarterly Review,
II (April, 1877) 331.

and windy pantheists are worshipful heroes when born on Bavarian soil."[5] A note of caution was injected into his review of the case of Sister Anne Catherine Emmerich. The visions of the poor, uneducated, German girl had evoked widespread interest, so that Monsignor Corcoran commented:

> ... She may be canonized for her heroic virtues deserve the honor, but her visions and revelations will find no approbation, unless they rest on safer authority than that of Brentano or Schmoeger.[6]

On the other hand, optimism was not foreign to his outlook; and he rejoiced in Pope Leo XIII's endorsement of Thomistic philosophy.

> Of the many documents that have come forth from the Holy See within the memory of living men, few can be counted that surpass in importance the Encyclical which we have considered it a duty to place on record in the pages of our Review. In this noble effusion of apostolic zeal and learning our Holy Father Leo XIII, following in the footsteps of his illustrious predecessors has thought fit warmly to recommend, both to those who are already learned and to those who are striving after true knowledge, the study of the volumes of St. Thomas Aquinas, known in the schools as the Angelic Doctor. He further discloses a praiseworthy anxiety to restore the scholastic philosophy of the Middle Ages and of our fathers to the old place of honor which it once held, and whence it has been cast down, or allowed to fall, through the contempt or negligence of our supercilious and superficial day and generation.[7]

To guide the people of his generation, Monsignor Corcoran wrote numerous articles and edited a quality magazine, The American Catholic Quarterly Review. It was his good fortune to be aided from

---

[5]Very Rev. James A. Corcoran, D.D., "Martin Luther and His American Worshippers," ibid., IX (July, 1884) 538.

[6]_____. "Anne Catherine Emmerich," ibid., X (July, 1885) 570.

[7]_____. "The Recent Encyclical Letter of Pope Leo XIII," ibid., IV (October, 1879) 719.

the outset by Father James O'Connor (later Bishop of Omaha) and
George Dering Wolf,[8] another remarkable convert and a former editor
of The Catholic Standard of Philadelphia. Their initial volume
announced "... we shall not forget the duty we owe our non-Catholic
countrymen."[9] At the same time, the trip expected to explain and
defend Catholic truth and to show the operation of the Catholic
principle in the history of the world, "in the lives of great and
good men, and in the destinies of nations."[10] This need of sound
guidance for all Americans was reiterated by a later writer and
editor of the magazine, Father James F. Loughlin. The priest of the
future, wrote Father Loughlin, "will be a literary veteran from his
youth, with a discursive mind, a ready tongue, and a well sharpened
quill."[11] Nor, was it unreasonable to expect from him an occasional
contribution to a magazine. That same year, Archbishop John Patrick
Ryan, upon assuming his episcopal duties in Philadelphia, announced:

> The mission of the Review is to the higher intellects Catholic
> and non-Catholic of the country. That mission becomes more
> momentous every day. Catholics suffer most from the ignorance
> of learned men, learned in almost everything but Catholic
> doctrine, history, and tradition.[12]

---

[8]"Some Philadelphia Catholics," American Catholic Historical
Society Records, XXXIII (June, 1922) 266.
[9] American Catholic Quarterly Review, I (January, 1876) 4.
[10]Ibid., p.1.
[11]Rev. James F. Loughlin, "The Higher and Lower Education of
the American Priesthood," The American Catholic Quarterly Review,
XV (January, 1890) 121.
[12]Archbishop Patrick John Ryan, "Salutatory," The American
Catholic Quarterly Review, XV (July, 1890) 385.

The Archbishop also indicated that the Review would continue "to be
thoroughly American. The fact is, that in this century the American
and Catholic spirits seem identical."[13]

Under the supervision of the original trio, Monsignor Corcoran,
Bishop O'Connor, and George Dering Wolf and their successors,
Archbishop Ryan, Father Loughlin, and Monsignor James P. Turner.
The American Catholic Quarterly Review furnished its readers with
numerous scholarly articles meditating upon philosophy, theology,
sociology, history, and biography. To show that Catholics had no
need to fear science, a regular feature of the earlier issues was
the "Scientific Chronicle" recording the latest discoveries in that
field and the discussion of them by a competent authority. Another
regular feature, of course, was the section devoted to book notices.
Monsignor Corcoran's book notices,[14] according to Father Loughlin,
won much of the original prestige for the Review. Coupled with this,
was the fact that many of the current, top-flight, Catholic writers
wrote for the magazine.

Almost any issue was a testimonial to its general excellence.
Consequently, the index for the 1883 issue[15] revealed that Cardinal
James Gibbons was the author of the article, "The Law of Prayer."
For the same volume, the prominent Chicagoan, William J. Onahan,

[13]Ibid., p.388.
[14]James F. Loughlin, "Corcoran, James Andrew," The Catholic
Encyclopedia, IV (1908) 356.
[15]"Index," The American Catholic Quarterly Review, VIII (1883)
iv,v,vii,viii.

wrote "The Catholic Church and Popular Education;" while, the noted

historian, John Gilmary Shea, analyzed Bancroft's History of the

United States, in addition to estimating the influence of converts

in the United States. Bishop O'Connor considered "Socialism" and

Monsignor Corcoran wrote "How Church History is Written." An over-

all view of the many excellent Catholics writing for the Review was

established in an author and subject index compiled by Mr. Paul R.

Byrne, a former librarian of the University of Notre Dame. This

unpublished index[16] indicated that the following published at least

three times in The American Catholic Quarterly Review. (Some, of

course, exceeded this limit many times.) Included as writers were:

Brother Azarias, Bishop Francis Silas Chatard, Richard H. Clarke,

Father Charles Warren Currier, Cardinal James Gibbons, Charles

George Herbermann, Father Augustine Francis Hewit, Father William J.

Kerby, Father James F. Loughlin, John A. Mooney, William J. Onahan,

John Boyle O'Reilly, John J. O'Shea, Conde Pallen, Father Reuben

Parsons, Father Augustus Thebaud, Marc F. Vallette, James J. Walsh,

George Dering Wolf, and Father John A. Zahm. Added to this imposing

array of talent, were a few of the better European writers. One of

these foreign Catholics, Hilaire Belloc, in 1910, advised his co-

religionists to create more historical writings since

---

[16]Paul R. Byrne, "Author and Subject Index, Volumes 1-49,
(1876-1924)" The American Catholic Quarterly Review, 7,32,37,47,69,
76,77,94,102,117,126,127,128-129,131,134,168,172,175-176,178,180.

> ... that minority of Catholics who speak the English
> language have not as yet in the English tongue a litera-
> ture which can make them familiar with these general
> truths.[17]

Obviously, the editors of The American Catholic Quarterly Review

shared Belloc's convictions for seldom did an issue come from the

press that did not contain some well-written piece involving the

history of the church either in the United States or abroad. The

same conservative tone, which was apparent in these historical

presentations, also pervaded the articles treating the current

educational, political, social, and cultural developments.

Conservatism was also a characteristic of the American Ecclesi-

astical Review. It was the good intention of its editor, Father

Herman B. Hauser, to maintain the cultural interests of the American

priests after they had left the seminaries. The lead article in the

first issue affirmed that a sound knowledge of current literature was

calculated "to make the priest efficient, whether in church, or

chool, or the homes of his people, or the assemblies of strangers.[18]

> Moreover, with the spread of that general culture which
> comes principally from reading, the priest is supposed to
> keep pace. If in his teaching he shows himself familiar
> with what men consider the special prerogative of the edu-
> cated, his influence upon them must needs be greater than
> without such knowledge.[19]

---

[17]Hilaire Belloc, "The Need for Catholic History," The American
Catholic Quarterly Review, XXXV (October, 1910) 594.

[18]"Literature and the Clergy," American Ecclesiastical Review,
I (January, 1889) 15.

[19]Ibid., p.6.

In keeping with this counsel, the American Ecclesiastical
Review, as regular features, printed book reviews in a section
entitled "Criticism and Notes" and announced the shorter observations
and criticisms in the "Literary Chats" section. By design, many of
the articles and reviews appearing in the magazine held an especial
appeal for the American clergy. The guidance program conducted so
successfully won for Father Heuser the following praise: "No man
in the country has exercised so large or helpful an influence or
placed the priests of America under so deep a debt of gratitude."[20]

During Father Heuser's period of editorship (1889-1926), for
three too-short years, 1902-1905, the American Ecclesiastical Review
sponsored The Dolphin, a magazine designed for the "educated gentleman and lady who are especially interested in the Catholic Church."[21]
There was a need for such a magazine.

> Much indeed, of what is beautiful in the Church, our music,
> painting, architecture, decoration, symbolism, rites and
> customs of the Church, is being discussed in our well
> edited Catholic periodicals. Yet it is not done systemati-
> cally or with special reference to principles so as to serve
> a permanent or consistent purpose.[22]

In presenting an intellectual and liturgical magazine to American
Catholics, The Dolphin obviously borrowed the format of the American
Ecclesiastical Review.

20"Chronicles," The American Catholic Historical Review, XII
(April, 1926) 128.
21The Dolphin, I (January-June, 1902) 1.
22Ibid., p.4.

In addition to feature articles and the department, "Student's Library Table" with its scholarly treatment (with footnotes) of Scripture, Philosophy, Science, The Dolphin presented criticisms and notices from the world of books. Because The Cardinal's Snuff-Box had given an exquisite and truthful description of Catholic life, the latest of Henry Harland, The Lady Paramount, was eagerly awaited.[23] The Dolphin,[24] also, proudly announced to its readers that they might expect an article by the deft Miss Repplier to appear in a forthcoming issue. Father Finn and Smith and Ella Dorsey, Eleanor Donnelly, Anna Sadlier, Clara Mulholland, and Mary Waggaman were other Catholic writers winning approval.[25] Non-Catholic writers meriting an inclusion in its notices numbered Henry James, Arthur Train, H. G. Wells, Edith Wharton, Bret Harte, and H. Rider Haggard.[26] In spite of the leveling influence of book notices, a Georgetown Journal[27] and the Providence Visitor[28] objected that The Dolphin was exceedingly lofty and that there were not enough educated Catholics to support the venture. Whatever the case, the American Ecclesiastical Review announced January, 1906, that the

---

[23]"Book Notes," The Dolphin, I (April, 1902) 501.
[24]Ibid., p.500.
[25]Ibid., I (January, 1902) 119.
[26]"Recent Popular Books," The Dolphin, VIII (November, 1905) 624-629.
[27]"Catholic Higher Education and The Dolphin," The Dolphin, I (May, 1902) 590.
[28]"Book Notes," The Dolphin, I (April, 1902) 502.

object for which The Dolphin had been founded, was superseded by
another organ, Church Music,[29] and The Dolphin ceased publication.

1889, the year of Father Heuser's founding of the conservative
American Ecclesiastical Review, also witnessed the establishment of
the most vituperative of the Catholic magazines, The Globe
(Philadelphia). Reflecting the personality of its editor, William
Henry Thorne, The Globe was reasonable in stating:

> The work of some of my best friends has been rebuked in
> The Globe: and when I fail, as they have failed, I hope
> they will rebuke me in language ten thousand times stronger
> than my own.[30]

Yet, just what could have been stronger than his reference to one of
his competitors as "that toilet paper affair called Donahoe's."[31]
Moreover, The Catholic World, because of its imbecility and per-
petual blunders, should have failed; "but the Paulists' money bags
and a lot of priestly palaver have kept it nominally alive to this
day."[32] These words from the Philadelphia editor were far from
brotherly and his exhortation to another editor regarding the
embattled Father Henry A. Brann was no better.

> For God's sake, Mr. O'Malley, if you take any notice of The
> Globe at all, read it and be an honest man. Brann is no-
> body... (and two pages later, the description continued)...
> this defunct clerical politician, this place-seeker; this
> untaught blundering booby...[33]

---

[29]"Literary Chat," American Ecclesiastical Review, XXXIV
(January, 1906) 108.
[30]William Henry Thorne, "Carnegie, Bellamy and Company," The
Globe, I (September-November, 1890) 299.
[31]_____. "Globe Notes," The Globe, IX (March, 1899) 109.
[32]Ibid., p.106.
[33]William Henry Thorne, "Rev. Dr. Brann and Co.," The Globe,
IX (March, 1899) 70,72.

Showing the same disregard for the hierarchy, he intimated that the Archdiocese of St. Paul and the United States in general would have profited if "Archbishop Ireland would stay at home and mind his own business."[34]

On the positive side, he appreciated Charles Warren Stoddard. The ease of Stoddard's prose style, more beautiful than most men's poetry, presented an unrivaled literary work in his South Sea Idyls. Of almost equal merit was Cruise Under the Crescent, a work "that Protestants will read as gladly as Catholics."[35] Stoddard and Maurice Francis Egan stood apart from their co-religionists.

> I consider Egan and Stoddard the only literary men in the Catholic Church in this country. The other gentlemen are well enough in their way, but their way is the way of amateurism. Were I to make any exception to this I should except Walter Lecky... Conde Pallen, Mr. Randell, but no others.[36]

Egan, however, would not be remembered as a novelist, although his Jack Chumleigh at Boarding School "will do good and lots of it, the more it is read."[37] Much more worthwhile in Thorne's mind was Egan's Studies in Literature with the general effect of:

> ... the beautiful insistence throughout the essays that literature is not merely or primarily for amusement, but an expression of human life with bonds laid upon it to

---

[34]William Henry Thorne. "Catholic Journal and Criticism," ibid., IX (September, 1899) 285.

[35]_____. "A Lot of New Books," ibid., IX (June, 1899) 214.

[36]_____. "Globe Notes," The Globe, IX (March, 1899) 123.

[37]Ibid., IX (December, 1899) 498.

express the highest life, the whole of life, but supremely
the life of faith in the supernatural, and that the greatest
writers have done this, which simple truth so utterly ignored
by the literary hacks of the last fifty years, we have been
trying to make plain in the pages of this magazine during the
last ten years.[38]

Eleanor C. Donnelly, a fellow Philadelphian, was commended for
Stormbound, a Romance of Shell Beach and her poems, The Rhymes of
Father Stephen and Christian Carols of Love and Life;[39] and, the
much maligned Ella Wheeler "had poetic genius albeit she was a little
slovenly in the use of it."[40]

With negative criticism, Thorne, at times, was relatively
gentle. A poethumous collection of Mrs. Madeline Vinton Dahlgren's
works, he acknowledged, contained many passages of characteristic
strength and fine touches of local coloring; yet, honestly compelled
him to say, "Books that catch the eye of the world are somewhat
different than this."[41] He even admitted that Marie Corelli's
Master Christian was superior to her other offerings as a literary
work; but, still filled with the clap-trap of reform, the prattled
glories of science, and the general misinterpretation of Christian
living.[42] As for the realists, Howells and James, they caught only

[38] Ibid., p.499.
[39] Ibid., VIII (June, 1898) 230.
[40] William Henry Thorne, "Novels and Criticism," The Globe, I
(October-December, 1899) 84.
[41] William Henry Thorne, "A Lot of New Books," The Globe, IX
(June, 1889) 217.
[42] _____. "Books and Authors," ibid., XI (March, 1901)
75,80.

the shoestrings of life while missing the soul of things.[43] The
critics, George Ripley, New York Tribune, and George William Curtis,
Harper's, were mere book-tasters for the publishers and first class
hacks.[44] Now (1889) warmed to his task, Thorne thought that the
weekly literary edition of the New York Times was only a "rehash of
old anecdotes about books and authors."[45] Worse yet, The Critic
(New York) was a "sort of a stupid female aid to publishers to sell
their useless publications."[46] Occasionally, careful literary
reviews appeared in the Literary World (Boston) and in the Chicago
Dial.[47]

Transferring his attention to Catholic journalism, editor Thorne
divided the Catholic papers into two groups; those for the professional and more cultured class and those for family reading and
religious instruction. Of the early family journals, he preferred
the Freeman's Journal to the Pilot, since he admired the "genius of
McMaster."[48] In 1899, he adjudged The New World (Chicago) as the
best family paper presenting the prevailing Catholic opinion; the
Sacred Heart Review was almost as good save for its idiotic treatment of current events. Infrequent bursts of brilliance characterized Philadelphia's Times-Standard.[49] However, the strong editorship

---

[43]William Henry Thorne. "The Heroic and Commonplace in Art,"
Ibid., I (October-December, 1889) 35,36.
   [44]_____. "Catholic Criticism and Journalism," ibid., IX
(September, 1899) 292.
   [45]Ibid., p.294.
   [46]Ibid.
   [47]Ibid.
   [48]Ibid., pp.284-285.
   [49]Ibid., pp.286,289.

of Father Louis A. Lambert elevated the Freeman's Journal to a
position "equal to the best Protestant weeklies in the country."[50]
Thorne considered that Father Lambert was the only priest in the
United States capable as a thinker and writer of editing a Catholic
journal.[51] More of a non-family journal than Lambert's paper was
Arthur Preuss' The Review (St. Louis). It was a genuine paper with
many excellencies.[52] (Two years later after Preuss had criticized
Thorne, the wounded Philadelphian declared (1901) that any mention
of Preuss was beneath his notice or contempt.)[53] As for Catholic
criticism, much of it was of a minus quality; yet, good criticism
had been achieved in the Sacred Heart Review, The Catholic World, the
Times-Standard, The New World, and The Review.[54]

Any mention of Thorne, usually, brought to mind a recollection
of his sometimes friend, Arthur Preuss. Both men had a rough manner
with words and tactfulness seemed non-essential to their literary
compositions. The format of The Review, when it was founded in 1893,
resembled that of a newspaper; however, the content of its observations and short suggestions bore more resemblance to those found in

[50]Ibid., p.286.
[51]William Henry Thorne, "Globe Notes," The Globe, VIII (March,
1898) 110.
[52]_____. "Catholic Criticism and Journalism," The Globe,
IX (September, 1899) 290.
[53]_____. "Globe Notes," ibid., XI (June, 1901)
252.
[54]_____. "Catholic Criticism and Journalism," The Globe,
IX (September, 1899) 294.

the magazines. This latter fact, perhaps, became more noticeable, as the title and format were altered to accommodate a new frequency of publication, hence The Catholic Fortnightly Review. No matter what the format, Arthur Preuss was a stimulating, ire-arousing critic, who never quite attained Thorne's state of vituperation. Critic Preuss, a precise man, whose many translations from the German into English gave him an air of scholarship, apparently enjoyed his role. After noting "We are told that we have been neglecting our duties as 'censor of the Catholic press,'"[55] he promptly reduced Maurice Francis Egan to "a shallow dabbler in many branches,"[56] and, L. W. Riley, editor of the Catholic Columbian, was advised to eschew his offensive methods of puffery for the paper's sake. He branded the Catholic News (New York) as a clipping bureau newspaper[57] of no consequence and the editor of the Chippewa Falls Catholic Sentinel "obviously has little philosophy and less theology."[58] The Catholic Citizen (Milwaukee), a good paper, was guilty of yellow journalism.[59] So, it must have surprised no one when Preuss declared "three fourths of the Catholic papers should discontinue publication."[60]

---

[55] The Review, (September 3, 1903)
[56] Ibid.
[57] The Review, (July 6, 1899)
[58] Ibid., (May 4, 1899)
[59] Ibid., (June 22, 1899)
[60] Ibid., (May 11, 1899)

Since the articles in The Review were extremely short in length,
whether original or reprints from other journals, little time was
wasted in making a point. Allowing that Louise Imogen Guiney was an
"excellent contemporary," The Review objected to Aubrey Beardsley as
the subject for her article in The Catholic World. There were many
better examples of the penitent. Why Beardsley? His artistic work,
"apart from its moral aspect, was nasty and debasing."[61] The Two
Standards, the latest novel of the Irish priest Dr. William Barry
was so improbable and wearisome that "few will care to read it at
all."[62] To the proposal that The Review should help publish the
poetry of a Catholic citizen of Louisville, writing under the name
of A. Winter, there was a quick rejoinder:

> ... as newspaper rhymes they were good and readable... but
> they have not in them the note that marks the great poet.
> We have too much mediocre Catholic verse in book form al-
> ready; The Review is not willing to increase the bulk
> needlessly.[63]

After reading the advertising blurb for Bernard Francis Moore's new
play The Rough Riders, Preuss wrote, "We sincerely hope that this
new production will never disgrace the stage of any Catholic
hall."[64]

---

[61]Ibid., (May 18, 1899)
[62]Ibid., (April 27, 1899)
[63]The Review, (July 6, 1899)
[64]Ibid., (July 27, 1899)

The Review, in reprinting a Catholic Universe opinion, ques-
tioned the generosity of Andrew Carnegie's fund for the public
libraries. Too many people besieged the fiction department, in
marked contrast to the few who sought "more solid entertainment in
the departments of history, science, literature, or philosophy."[65]
These frothy and trashy novels, especially the historical ones, were
foisted upon the public by clever advertising. Favorable newspaper
reviews plus the enthusiasm created by the literary magazines owned
by the publishing houses enabled many a mediocre work to be demanded
by the public.[66] Furthermore, the Catholic booksellers were guilty
of other indiscretions. P. J. Kennedy, for example, offered a
shallow work, University of Literature; and, even at a price reduced
from $70 to $15, it was not to be "conscientiously recommended."[67]

> Benziger Brothers offer for sale a book which should not be
> on the list of Catholic publishers or booksellers at all.
> It is sufficient to mention that the author is C. M. Wieland,
> 'sus germanica.'[68]

Sadlier's were guilty of the same thing in offering The Arabian
Knights, Gulliver's Travels, and Byrce's Holy Roman Empire. Some of
Whittier's poems were anti-Catholic and not good poetry besides;
whereas, Olive Schriener's Story of an African Farm "is a veritable
crime to put in the hands of a Catholic child."[69]

---

[65] Ibid., (October 15, 1903)
[66] Ibid., (April 14, 1904)
[67] Ibid., (May 25, 1899)
[68] The Review, (May 25, 1899)
[69] Ibid., (July 1, 1907)

On the other hand, The Review supported the Catholic publishers exclusively in the sale of school books. "We are in favor of Catholic books, published by Catholic firms, for all of our Catholic schools."[70] This directive was aimed at the American Book Company's, "it is a trust" selling Catholic text-books. When one of the brightest names in American architecture, Ralph Adams Cram, brought forth The Magazine of Christian Art, Preuss was so impressed with the magazine's interpretation of the Middle Ages that he felt confident that the magazine "will strive to do justice to the Catholic point of view on the questions which it will find within their purview to treat."[71] For Preuss, this was a strong endorsement because the editors, "as far as we know are not Catholics."[72] Also worthy of support was the periodical, American Catholic Historical Researches (Philadelphia). So far, the clergy had been the chief supporter.

> Surely there must be at least a few hundred among our many intelligent readers who are sufficiently interested in Catholic American history to sacrifice a dollar per anum for this good cause, especially when this dollar entitles them to four numbers of a quarterly magazine brimful of valuable and absorbingly interesting researches.[73]

To counter the charge that the main body of English literature was under papal ban, the study of the Jesuit Father Ernest R. Hull

---

[70]Ibid., (August 11, 1904)
[71]The Catholic Fortnightly Review, (February 1, 1907)
[72]The Catholic Fortnightly Review, (February 1, 1907)
[73]The Review, (October 13, 1904)

was used to show that, probably, there were no more than one hundred
and twenty books written in English on the Index. In the prolific
nineteenth century, some thirty English and forty American books had
failed to pass the judgment of the Index Congregation.[74] As for
Preuss's own judgment, although Thackeray was a gifted author, his
Vanity Fair should not be recommended for it based upon the false
and pernicious principle that human nature was totally depraved,
"virtue therefore impossible and religious practice a sham."[75] Nor
should Catholics have glorified Francis Parkman.

> What is the use of having a Catholic press at all if it does
> not instruct the Catholic public in the truth, but simply
> re-echoes the errors and lies of secular newspapers and
> magazines.[76]

Where Preuss and Thorne confronted their readers with bellicose
opinions and The American Catholic Quarterly Review used a more
scholarly technique for the purpose of educating their co-religionists, The Catholic Reading Circle Review maintained the most systematic approach for the same cause. Established in 1891 by Warren E.
Mosher, The Catholic Reading Circle Review adhered to a primary
design of indoctrinating its readers with a generous dosage of
scientific, historical, literary, artistic, philosophic, and
religious material which held an acknowledged cultural content for
those days. Admittedly, some issues resembled text-books in their

---

[74]The Catholic Fortnightly Review, (August 15, 1907)
[75]The Review, (November 19, 1903)
[76]Ibid.

best and worst features, informative and dull. Perhaps, the educational level of its readers required this fundamental simplicity and
dryness.

At any rate, The Catholic Reading Circle Review was an integral
part of its editor's fine plan for organizing the available educational forces at a popular level. Warren E. Mosher, promoter and
editor, conceived the idea that his Review would be the guiding force
and connecting link for the various Catholic reading circles established throughout the country. Besides acting as a medium of inter-
communication for the different circles, the Review offered an
organized approach to "good reading" through its Catholic Educational
Union.

The C.E.U. presented a four year reading course with an appropriate syllabus, a required list of readings, and a short bibliography.[77] Week by week from October to July, the syllabi led the
ambitious readers through the prescribed courses. At the same time,
the Review served as an auxiliary, several departments "being
conducted with the view of assisting readers to a better understanding of the subjects contained in the books recommended."[78]

A conductor of one department, Thomas O'Hagan, the eminent
Canadian scholar, advised the readers taking his course, Study of

---

[77]"The Catholic Educational Union," The Catholic Reading Circle
Review, I (September, 1891) 396.
[78]Warren E. Mosher, "Introduction," The Catholic Reading Circle
Review, I (January, 1891) ii.

American Literature, that justice would be done to every American
writer of note, Catholic and non-Catholic alike. Obviously,
Brownson, Shea, O'Reilly and Ryan would be evaluated; however, he
refused to "galvanize mediocrity into greatness simply because an
author has professed the Catholic faith."[79] The writers of individual articles likewise comprised talented men and women.
Naturally, "The Christian Interpretation of Art,"[80] fell within the
province of Miss Eliza Allen Starr; while Teddy Roosevelt's friend,
Charles P. Neill, of the United States Bureau of Labor, certainly
was qualified to discuss the organization of labor and municipal
ownership in the light of Catholic teaching.[81] The erudite brother
of Brother Azarias, Father John F. Mullany, contributed "Short
Sketches of the Evangelists."[82]

With the passing years, the magazine confined itself "more
strictly to the field of educational work on the lines of home
reading."[83] In the meantime, Warren E. Mosher had helped to promote
the successful establishment of a "Catholic Chautauqua," the
Catholic Summer School of America at Cliff Haven, New York. Here,

---

[79]Thomas O'Hagan, "Study of American Literature," ibid., IX
(October, 1896) 66.
[80]Eliza Allen Starr, "The Christian Interpretation of Art,"
ibid., IX (February, 1897) 322.
[81]Charles P. Neill, "Economic Study," Mosher's Magazine, XVII
(March, 1901) 396.
[82]Rev. John F. Mullany, "Short Sketches of the Evangelists,"
ibid., p.397.
[83]The Champlain Educator, XXII (August, 1903) 184. (Mosher's
magazine in an effort to attract a wider circulation changed its
name from The Catholic Reading Circle Review to Mosher's Magazine
and, finally, to The Champlain Educator.)

many members of the reading circles and other well-intentioned
Catholics gathered to pursue culture along the resort-lined shores
of Lake Champlain. Mosher's magazine had done its work. The
Catholic Reading Circle Review was a magazine with a purpose of
devoting its energies to the spreading of popular education among
Catholics. Unfortunately, it did not survive the death of its
editor, March 22, 1906.

However, 1906 witnessed the establishment of a new and vastly
different periodical Extension, the monthly publication of a society
devoted to bringing the Church to the more remote parts of the United
States. Although much space was devoted to the expansion efforts of
the society, current literature and its writers received more than a
bit of consideration. Fiction in the guise of short-stories and
serials appeared in every issue. Mrs. Sallie Margaret O'Malley was
the author of the serial The Brown Princess[84] while Doctor James J.
Walsh[85] contracted to deal with the weighty problems of education on
the American scene. Julia R. Doyle's installments regarding "Who's
Who in Catholic Journalism" and Father John Talbot Smith's serialized
reminiscence, "Old Times in Catholic Journalism,"[86] paid tribute to
the Catholic editor.

---

[84]Sallie M. O'Malley, "The Brown Princess," Extension, II
(September, 1907) 21ff.
    [85]James J. Walsh, "Catholic School and Education," ibid., II
(December, 1907) 39.
    [86]Rev. John Talbot Smith, "Old Times in Catholic Journalism,"
ibid., IX (September, 1914) 8.

Julia R. Doyle noted that a doctor two-times over, Thomas P.
Hart, M.D., Ph.D., valiantly rescued the bankrupt Catholic Telegraph
(Cincinnati) and edited it, so important did he deem the necessity
of having a capable outlet for Catholic truth. Father John J. Burke
(The Catholic World), Martin I. J. Griffin[87] (American Catholic
Historical Researches), John Paul Chew (The Church Progress), John
J. O'Shea (The Catholic Standard and Times), and Charles J.
Phillips[88] (The Monitor) exemplied some other devoted men anxious to
guide their co-religionists to the proper concepts of American
Catholic life. In addition to these brief biographies, Katherine E.
Conway wrote two lengthier articles concerning John Boyle O'Reilly[89]
and James Jeffrey Roche.[90] Father Tabb[91] was given a similar
consideration.

At varied times, the stage was evaluated, whether it was praise
for Chauncey Olcott[92] or condemnation for immorality by Archbishops
John M. Farley and John Joseph Glennon.[93] As for the Catholic
writers, Extension noted that most of them did not write to grow
rich; instead, they were instilled with the importance "of their

[87]Julia R. Doyle, "Who's Who in Catholic Journalism," ibid.,
II (September, 1907) 7,27.
[88]Ibid., II (November, 1907) 9.
[89]Katherine E. Conway, "The Anecdotal Side of John Boyle
O'Reilly," Extension, III (December, 1908) 7.
[90]_____. "The Anecdotal Side of James Jeffrey Roche," ibid.,
III (January, 1909) 5.
[91]Patrick Dempsey, "The Anecdotal Side of Father Tabb," ibid.,
III (February, 1909) 5.
[92]James F. Byrnes, "Chauncey Olcott, The Actor and The Man,"
ibid., III (January, 1909) 6.
[93]Extension, III (April, 1909) 17.

message and therefore are satisfied with the spiritual returns."[94]
(In this same article for 1915, the more favored authors still in-
cluded Father Finn, Father Smith, Monsignor Benson, Maurice Francis
Egan, Mary T. Waggaman, and Kathleen Norris.)

The "spiritual returns" also greatly interested the devotional
magazines. Within the pages of this type of periodical, were recorded the inspiring messages and the activities of Christian people
united in prayer for special intentions. From Brainerd, Minnesota,
the Third Order of Saint Francis of Assisi issued its first monthly
bulletin, Annals of Our Lady of the Angels (1874).[95] Far to the
east in Watertown, New York, the Archconfraternity of the Sacred
Heart published The Annals of Our Lady of the Sacred Heart (1877).[96]
In an effort that was promotional as well as devotional, the Jesuit
fathers, in their desire to erect a pilgrim shrine to the memory of
Rene Goupil, Father Isaac Jogues, and Catherine Tegawita, brought
forth The Pilgrim of Our Lady of the Martyrs (1885).[97] That same
year, because of the growth of the Ave Maria "in another direction,"[98] the publication material for the Confraternity of the
Immaculate Conception was taken from its pages and placed in a new
magazine, The Annals of Our Lady of Lourdes. In southern Indiana,

---

[94]S. A. Baldus, "With Catholic Authors and Publishers," ibid.,
IX (January, 1915) 22.
[95]Annals of Our Lady of Angels, I (1874).
[96]The Annals of Our Lady of the Sacred Heart, I (June, 1877).
[97]The Pilgrim of Our Lady of Martyrs, I (1885).
[98]The Annals of Our Lady of Lourdes, I (April, 1885) 1.

The Poor Soul's Advocate proposed (1888) to explain and defend the
Catholic doctrine of purgatory; and, at the same time, to encourage
its readers to pray for the poor souls.[99] For the most part, these
devotional magazines just considered, seldom deviated from the themes
announced on their bannerheads. However, other devotional journals
printed articles calculated to attract a more general interest.

Representatives of this latter group included The Rosary (1891),
The Magnificant (1907), The Lamp (1909) and the much earlier one,
The Messenger of the Sacred Heart of Jesus (1866). The Dominicans
established The Rosary not only to foster a devotion to our Blessed
Mother and to strengthen piety and religion but also to encourage
the literary efforts of Catholics and to "spread good, sound, wholesome reading"[100] among their co-religionists. Charles J.
O'Malley,[101] the editor and poet, prepared for its pages a review of
the Catholic writers of Chicago, men and women, who were contemporaries of the great names of the "Chicago Renaissance:" Vachel
Lindsay, Edgar Lee Masters, and Carl Sandburg. The Bishop of Peoria,
John Lancaster Spalding, true to his profound interest in education,
discussed "The Physician's Calling and Education,"[102] in the March
issue (1905). Articles by the art critic, Mary F. Nixon-Roulet,[103]

---

[99] The Poor Soul's Advocate, I (September, 1888) 4.
[100] "With the Editor," The Rosary, XXVI (May, 1905) 549.
[101] Charles J. O'Malley, "Catholic Literators of Chicago," ibid.,
(January, 1905) 17-24.
[102] Rt. Rev. John Lancaster Spalding, "The Physician's Calling
and Education," ibid., (March, 1905) 306-315.
[103] Mary F. Nixon-Roulet, "The Annunciation in Art," ibid.,
232-237.

and the prolific John J. O'Shea[104] appeared in the same issue.

Another "American shrine" to the Blessed Mother, The Magnificat, gave evidence of a strong literary interest in the lead article of its initial volume, "The French Crisis and French Literature."[105] In succeeding volumes, American attention was focused once more on the literary accomplishments of their foreign contemporaries. Father Matthew Russel, S.J., the splendid editor of the Irish Monthly, introduced The Magnificat's readers to Hilaire Belloc, naturalized Englishman, Catholic, man of letters, and member of parliament.[106] Another author advanced the Englishman Francis Thompson as "The Poet of Catholicism."[107] "The Irish Dramatic Movement," came under the scrutiny of the Canadian Thomas O'Hagan.[108] Among the novelists, one critic favored the Europeans Canon Sheehan, Father Benson, Mrs. Wilfrid Ward, Rene Bazin and the American Father Finn.[109]

Among the devotional magazines, The Lamp, perhaps, held one distinction. Prior to 1909, it served the spiritual and literary interests of those of the Anglican persuasion. After that year,[110] when numerous members of the Society of the Atonement (Anglican) were converted to Catholicism, The Lamp was added to the list of

[104]John J. O'Shea, "Cervantes' Troubled Life," ibid., pp.226-231.
[105]Rev. E.L. Rivard, C.S.V., "The French Crisis and French Literature," The Magnificat, I (November, 1907) 4.
[106]Matthew Russel, S.J., "Hilaire Belloc, Man of Letters and Member of Parliament," The Magnificat, VII (February, 1911) 201.
[107]J. Corson Miller, "The Poet of Catholicism, Francis Thompson," ibid., XV (September, 1915) 250.
[108]Thomas O'Hagan, "The Irish Dramatic Movement," ibid., p.265.
[109]Katherine Hearne Kelley, "Confessions of a Literary Snob; The Catholic Novelist," ibid., VII (December, 1910) 75.
[110]"Then and Now," The Lamp, X (February, 1912) 30.

Catholic journals. In the change, some subscribers were lost; but,
The Lamp retained a spiritual and literary aspect in making a
particular appeal to converts. The Lamp was never as well known
among American Catholics as one of its predecessors, The Messenger
of the Sacred Heart of Jesus. The monthly bulletin of the Apostle-
ship of Prayer, this Jesuit inspired magazine organized the prayers
of the faithful in support of Catholic action. At the same time,
The Messenger directed its co-religionists to create a demand for
Catholic books in the public libraries. Firmly convinced that it
was opportune time to place the standard Catholic works where the
poorest could find them, The Messenger cautioned its readers that
the sum total of Catholic literature amounted to more than the "goody
goody story-books about angels and saints, and bright youths whose
piety betokened a vocation to the priesthood."[111]

This same mixture of sound, conservative advice and spiritual
inspiration, administered in monthly doses, enabled The Messenger to
be a welcome visitor in Catholic homes for more than fifty years.
However, as the tempo of American life increased, the editors of
The Messenger felt that the needs of their fellow Catholics were
"too numerous, too urgent, too frequent to be satisfied by a monthly
journal."[112] So, in their zeal to educate the American Catholic
into becoming an informed and active citizen, they brought forth a

---

[111]J.F. O'Donovan, S.J., "Catholic Books in Public Libraries,"
The Messenger of the Sacred Heart of Jesus, XXXII (April, 1897) 318.
[112]"Editorial Announcement," America, (April 17, 1909)

Catholic review of the week America.

> America will take the place of the monthly periodical
> The Messenger, and continue its mission. It is in reality
> an adaptation of its precursor to meet the needs of time.[113]

Father John J. Wynne, S.J., editor and encyclopedist, described the

evolution essential to the establishment of the new weekly.

> It was with the greatest interest we developed what was
> hitherto a pious magazine, The Messenger of the Sacred Heart,
> into a monthly of general events, a choice book-review. It
> had its exquisite pictures and its editorials, and it brought
> out many a writer who would otherwise have been unknown to
> fame. It accustomed thousands to take an interest in world
> affairs. It was this Messenger of the Sacred Heart, which
> still exists and now perhaps with the largest circulation of
> any religious magazine, that led up to the publication of
> America, which was founded with the purpose of getting
> Catholics to take an interest in public affairs. I spent
> only a year at the work of establishing America, since by
> that time, in 1909, The Catholic Encyclopedia was absorbing
> the attention of its editors and requiring every moment of
> our time.[114]

Father Wynne in that brief time, however, made at least one

appointment which contributed positively to the America's success.

His selection[115] of Thomas F. Meehan to the staff assured America

of the services of a versatile, extremely capable journalist. As a

working reporter, he was a New York correspondent for the Baltimore

Sun, Philadelphia Ledger, Richmond (Virginia) Times, De Maasbode

(Rotterdam, Holland) and a member of the editorial staffs of the New

---

[113]Ibid.
[114]The Xavier Alumni Sodality, Fifty Years in Conflict and
Triumph, Golden Jubilee of Rev. John J. Wynne, S.J., pp. 97,98.
[115]Francis Talbot, "A Noble Catholic Layman Passes From Our
Midst," (July 18, 1942)

York Herald, the Brooklyn Eagle, and the Brooklyn Citizen.[116]
Meehan, the copy editor and staff contributor, remained with America
for thirty-three years through a succession of editors, thus, in-
suring the magazine's continuity from an auspicious beginning
April 17, 1909. Imbued with a sense of history and the desire to
publicize the Catholic contributions to American civilization, the
earnest layman wrote myriad articles and devised other means to meet
this end. Thus, Meehan, the friend of John Gilmary Shea and Dr.
Charles G. Herbermann, served as chairman of the editorial board of
the United States Catholic Society and was responsible for in-
augurating the society's monograph series.[117] In a similar manner,
he was one of the prime movers and editors of the five volume
comprising The Catholic Builders of the Nation (1923).[118] Some
years previous, he had supervised the printing layout for the
earlier issues of The Catholic Encyclopedia, in addition to writing
numerous articles for that excellent publication. While contributing
to the Encyclopedia, Meehan caught the attention of Father Wynne,
who drafted him for the America.

This review and news-journal fashioned by Wynne and Meehan
discussed the life and literature of the day, defended sound
doctrine, recorded religious progress, and related the position of
the Church in the thought and activity of modern life. America

---

[116]Ibid.
[117]Ibid.
[118]Ibid.

studied current affairs at length and the literary scene in brief accuracy. It hailed Gilbert Keith Chesterton's Orthodoxy as a brilliant apology for Christianity and a "paradox which may well confound the modernists;"[119] and, another Englishman, Monsignor Benson wrote the best non-historical novel of his career in An Average Man.[120] As for Americans, Stoddard's[121] island essays and Dr. Walsh's scientific expositions[122] were most praiseworthy; while Richard Aumerle's juvenile novel, Between Friends, lacked delicacy and refinement in reducing studies to a secondary importance to baseball and football.[123] Much worse was the July issue of Cosmopolitan, a sadly fallen magazine, which Father Finn branded as "dirty, vulgar, pagan, immoral,... bad for all."[124]

Of the Catholic magazines, America favored the Ave Maria, The Messenger of the Sacred Heart, The Catholic World, the Rosary, and Extension.[125] Moreover, it expressed amazement at the rapid growth of Father John S. Noll's Our Sunday Visitor, Huntington, Indiana, whose circulation increased to 160,000 within a year. (Father Noll, America noted, had established his paper to counteract the widely circulated Menace and other papers of that ilk.) What was so amazing about Our Sunday Visitor was its ability to attract so many

---

[119]America, (April 24, 1909)
[120]Ibid., (October 4, 1913)
[121]Ibid., (May 1, 1909)
[122]Ibid., (May 22, 1909)
[123]Ibid., (June 12, 1909)
[124]Ibid., (July 12, 1913)
[125]America, (October 21, 1911)

readers, since it specialized only in apologetics and religious instruction.[126] America, in its drive to help the better publications, also appealed to all Catholics to subscribe to the Historical Records and Studies of the United States Historical Society.[127] (Meehan, perhaps, inspired this appeal.) Obviously, The Catholic Encyclopedia received (and deservedly so) generous notices as its volumes appeared.[128]

This concern for putting the proper reading material into Catholic hands, led to the publishing of Father Finn's statement that a number of English, Irish, and American Catholics including Canon Sheehan, Monsignor Benson, John Ayscough, Henry Harland, Olive Katherine Parr, Frank Spearman, Alice Dease, Maurice Francis Egan, and Mrs. Wilfrid Ward had written books "which in every respect would be superior to any of the recorded 'best sellers' of the last four or five years."[129] Again, Catholics were urged to read and acquire a first hand knowledge of books themselves and not be content with perusing books of criticism.[130] Still, there was another side to this effort.

> Those, moreover, who staunchly support Catholic editors and authors may feel assured that they are doing more to stay the spread of irreligion and immorality in our land than if they built a score of churches; for Catholic books and periodicals can be made to reach and influence those who never enter a church.[131]

[126]Ibid., (August 23, 1913)
[127]Ibid., (June 19, 1909)
[128]Ibid., (February 10, 1912)
[129]America, (October 21, 1911)
[130]Ibid., (June 28, 1913)
[131]Ibid., (October 21, 1911)

America's exhortation to support Catholic editors was not given
for the sole benefit of those publishing magazines. For among their
contemporaries, there were priests and laymen editing numerous
weekly Catholic newspapers. The characteristic urge to acquaint
their co-religionists with the proper cultural attributes, to
educate them, as well as to fortify their religious convictions also
appeared in this latter group of editors. With equally good intent,
their advice poured forth, sometimes in delightful language, sometimes barbed.

No other editor was more colorful, perhaps, than the self-
nominated[132] "dean of the Catholic press of the United States,"
Father David S. Phelan of the Western Watchman (St. Louis). The
modest Father Phelan's opinions were strong and not always fair so
that he made good copy for anti-Catholic newspapers.[133] His caustic
comments spread broadcast included many aspects of religious,
political, and social life in the United States.

The Western Watchman (1868) spared no cordiality for the various
Protestant denominations. The Western Watchman or Father Phelan
branded Martin Luther as a "coarse, profane, brutal bully;"[134] and,
rejoiced in the lament of the Baptists that "there is something in
the climate or people of the United States that will not allow their

---

[132]Western Watchman, (January 26, 1911)
[133]Richard J. Purcell, "Phelan, David Samuel," Dictionary
American Biography, XIV (1934) 521.
[134]Western Watchman, (November 10, 1882)

sect to thrive."[135] The Episcopal burial service given a deceased
Indian, aroused the barb: "Now, Spotted Tail was a heathen and up
to his death enjoyed the society of four wives. But then, the
author of Episcopalianism had eight."[136]

Politicians fared no better. During President Garfield's
struggle for life, he lashed out at the "Stalwart" senator from
New York.

> ... Conkling is a ghoul, and cannot refrain his grins while
> the president is in agony. We sincerely hope Mr. Garfield
> will recover, as we do not wish our presidents to be elec-
> ted by bullets.[137]

Roscoe Conkling and Chester A. Arthur, according to Phelan, did not
possess "the fine sense of honor" so desirable in public figures.
For "Teddy" Roosevelt, he held no affection;[138] and, although professing to respect President Taft, he described the portly golfer as
a "big polar bear being borne on an iceberg toward tropical
waters"[139] by his abominable party. Furthermore, navalist Alfred
Thayer Mahan's appeal to England "to get ready for the inevitable
conflict with Germany"[140] seemed exceedingly puerile.

Where Arthur Preuss was the guardian of German interests in
St. Louis, Father Phelan was the critic and he missed few
opportunities to remind them of their failings. Phelan was at his

---

[135] Ibid., (October 29, 1881)
[136] Ibid., (September 10, 1881)
[137] Ibid., (July 9, 1881)
[138] Western Watchman, (May 12, 1910; July 7, 1910; September 1, 1910)
[139] Ibid., (May 12, 1910)
[140] Ibid., (August 4, 1910)

best (and worst) on June 18, 1881:

> The "Anzeiger" of this city, prophesying on the future of
> the colored race, declares that Sunday Observance and
> Temperance will kill them politically. A German physician,
> last year, gave it as his deliberate judgment based on many
> years of professional practice, that many of the diseases
> prevailing among us were owing to excessive cleanliness.
> The negroes will probably escape the perils lurking in the
> bar of soap, so they must discover antidotes only for
> sobriety and piety.[141]

The hierarchy in St. Louis received his scrutiny. The "greatest
prelate in the American Church"[142] was Bishop Kenrick. "Archbishop
Glennon preaches ten sermons a year. They are good, and their few-
ness is all that ails them."[143] Father Phelan felt that the Sunday
sermon was one of the most effective means of instructing the faithful, hence the advice to Archbishop Glennon. In keeping with his
belief, the Western Watchman printed the weekly sermons delivered by
pastor Phelan at his church, Our Lady of Mount Carmel. At least two
volumes of his sermons appeared in print and the preface to the
first, The Gospel Applied to Our Times, A Sermon for Every Sunday in
the Year, stated his credo:

> I have long felt that only parish priests know the secret
> of preaching effectively. They have their finger on the
> pulse of the public and their ear close to their throbbing
> heart, and they alone can find the word that cheers and
> consoles them.[144]

Further advice was to be found in the Western Watchman.

Catholics were dishonest to subscribe to Catholic periodicals and,

---

[141]Ibid., (June 18, 1881)
[142]Ibid., (December 1, 1910)
[143]Western Watchman, (January 26, 1911)
[144]Rev. David S. Phelan, The Gospel Applied to Our Times, A
Sermon for Every Sunday in the Year, iii.

then, to refuse to pay for them. "The Catholic publishers should publish the names of these leeches ... for mutual protection."[145] The efforts of the leading Catholic publishers in the United States to reduce the selling price of books by a fair-trade agreement among themselves was a notable move; since Catholic books were never so high, due to mismanagement.[146] Moreover, Phelan objected to the Federation of Catholic Societies' practice of transferring

> ... its name and prestige to a committee of four or five, who constitute themselves a tribunal for the settlement of all the differences between the Church and the American public. This committee comes together at a moment's warning, and speaking in the name of the 25,000,000 Catholics under the American flag, they issue their pronouncements to the world.[147]

Not only was the committee too prone to beat the "big Catholic drum" at the slightest provocation; but also, it was usurping the office and function of the American hierarchy. Various other phases of Catholic activity did not escape the editor's attention. Applause greeted the appointment of Edward Douglass White,[148] the second Catholic to be appointed Chief Justice of the Supreme Court of the United States. Literarywise, the English poet Adelaide Procter[149] and the Americans Father Ryan[150] and James Ryder Randall.[151] caught his eye. Regarding a fellow newspaperman, France's Louis Veuillet

---

[145] Western Watchman, (August 13, 1881)
[146] Ibid., (August 26, 1882)
[147] Ibid., (November 3, 1910)
[148] Ibid., (December 22, 1910)
[149] Ibid., (May 7, 1881; April 22, 1882)
[150] Ibid., (February 18, 1882)
[151] Ibid., (May 5, 1910)

praise issued forth:

> He was the Church's great small talker in the nineteenth
> century. Ours is a flippant age... Veuillot answered them
> in their own chosen style and vanquished them with their
> own sharp swords ... But, Veuillot could brook no opposition
> and in his wrath he often mistook a mitre for the Red Cap of
> the Communist. But we believe his heart was right; at least
> he was respectful and obedient to Rome.[152]

(Evidently the American editor could sympathize with Veuillot's

feuding with the hierarchy for he himself indulged in the practice.)

Of this, Phelan's biographer noted that the editor of the Western

Watchman caustically criticized "priests and bishops with whom he

did not agree.")[153]

Father Phelan, pugnacious as he was, alerted, informed, and

educated his co-religionists. Throughout the United States, the

Western Watchman, during his long editorship, was known, respected,

feared. The Western Watchman reflected one man's opinion of the

civilization in the American Democracy and the Catholics' relation

to it. Naturally, other editors existed, who were anxious to shape

impressions and impose standards upon their fellow men. Fitting

into this mold was Patrick Valentine Hickey, editor of the Catholic

Review (New York, 1872).

Newspaperman Hickey, the year following the conclusion of the

Civil War in the United States, wrote to his sister in Dublin and

outlined his journalistic ideals.

---

[152]Western Watchman, (April 14, 1882)
[153]Richard J. Purcell, op.cit.

My darling project however, is to start an illustrated
periodical, to supplant the abominable, cheap literature
that now floods the market. From the pages will be
excluded everything containing the slightest tinge of
immorality. It will be printed on the best paper, with
the best type. The best artists, writers, etc., will be
employed... I will enter on this undertaking not merely as
a speculation that will make me a wealthy man... but also
with, I trust, a higher motive. I don't intend to make
it purely Catholic except in bias and insinuation as that
would deprive me of a large number of readers whom I intend to influence. Yet, I shall obtain for it the approbation and support of the highest ecclesiastical authority
... If I can succeed in accomplishing this idea, I shall
regard my life as well spent.[154]

In fulfilling this ideal, the ambitious Hickey established The

Catholic Review, Illustrated Catholic American, Holy Family Magazine,

American Catholic, and The Vatican Library. The last named was a

publishing venture which offered for a quarter-sale such Catholic

"literary classics" as Cardinal Wiseman's Fabiola.[155] The most

successful of these publications, perhaps, was The Catholic Review.

Mrs. Anna Hanson Dorsey, a contemporary, labeled it "the model

Catholic newspaper in the country."[156] In surveying the various

journals of that day, Thomas F. Meehan judged it "a very high-class

paper much before its time."[157] These laudatory opinions were

echoed by a later (1954) historian:

---

[154]John K. Sharp, History of the Diocese of Brooklyn 1853-1953,
The Catholic Church on Long Island, I, 214.
[155]Ibid., p.242. (Father Sharp, with a slip of the pen, in-
correctly gave Cardinal Newman as the author of Fabiola.)
[156]Mrs. Anna Hanson Dorsey to Rev. Daniel E. Hudson, C.S.C.,
(March 16, 1889) Hudson Papers. UNDA.
[157]Thomas F. Meehan, "The Catholic Press," The Catholic
Builders of the Nation, IV, 223.

Its urbanity was an innovation in the field of Catholic journalism which hitherto had appealed to Irish sentiment or to violent political or theological polemics. Yet, the Review was a fearless and tireless Crusader.[158]

No doubt Hickey's thorough training with secular journalism contributed to the Catholic Review's success; since, as an associate reported, he relinquished an "important and profitable position"[159] with the New York World in order to publish 'in the cause of the Church and for the benefit of their fellow citizens.'[160] For this effort, Hickey was honored here and abroad. Pope Pius IX made him a Knight of St. Sylvester, and Pope Leo XIII, a Knight of St. Gregory. On at least two occasions, Leo XIII praised The Catholic Review and its conductors for their services to the Catholic cause.[161] The University of Notre Dame bestowed upon him the Laetare Medal in 1888. These honors were significant of the general recognition that Patrick Hickey had raised the level[162] of Catholic journalism in the United States.

The early issues of this sixteen-page journal proudly carried the box announcement that The Catholic Review was "A Weekly News-paper Suitable for Sunday Reading in Catholic Families."[163] It regularly reported the news items concerning the archdiocese of New York and the diocese of Brooklyn and sporadically noticed the

---

[158]John K. Sharp, op.cit.
[159]John McCarthy, "Patrick Valentine Hickey," The Illustrated Catholic Family Annual of 1890, p.44.
[160]John K. Sharp, op.cit.
[161]John McCarthy, op.cit., p.46.
[162]Notre Dame Scholastic, XLII (February 23, 1909) 412.
[163]The Catholic Review, (July 14, 1883)

occurrences in other Catholic centers. Poems, book notices, and publication "blurbs" did not appear in every issue; and, the fictionalized serial did not become a weekly feature until after the paper had been published a number of years. Obviously, the attraction of The Catholic Review resided in the well-expressed observations of its editor.

Patrick Hickey had his own version of what was good for Catholics. They were to acquire a knowledge of the classics, for to go without would place them under a lasting disadvantage of which no brilliancy could relieve them.[164] Moreover, he favored the continued development of the denominational schools since "... you cannot teach religion in our public schools as at present constituted, without giving offence... to classes of religionists."[165] Thus, the Faribault plan did not appeal to him. As early as 1883, Hickey supported the proposed Catholic University, which he visualized as an intellectual practicing ground "where all the approved schools of Catholic thought may meet and grow strong by generous contention."[166] Yet, it was sad to report that so few Catholic college and convent graduates exhibited a strong religious spirit in the secular world. Too often, they engaged in the "pleasures and frivolities of society with as much apparent zest... as the most pronounced devotees of ambition and pleasure."[167]

---

[164]Ibid.
[165]Ibid., (July 28, 1883)
[166]The Catholic Review, (December 1, 1883)
[167]Ibid., (January 8, 1893)

Perhaps, their teachers were at fault.

On the general literary scene, he advised young girls and their mothers to avoid reading the pernicious trash[168] masquerading throughout the country as the romantic novel. This condemnation did not apply to Christian Roid, who did a most praiseworthy work in "... supplying our people with a sound, healthy Catholic literature..."[169] However, in his opinion, the American Catholic writers of 1893 failed to carry the standard set by Orestes Brownson, John Gilmary Shea, and John R. G. Hassard. "What has become of our Catholic American literature," he asked, "which twenty-five years ago gave promise of generous development?"[170]

Nor was Catholic art progressing.

> ... there is a crudeness of idea, a poverty of invention, a coarseness, or even complete absence, of taste in many of our attempts at professedly Catholic art going to show that as yet the cultivated element among us exercises little or no control in these matters.[171]

The remedy for this situation, he advised, might be a worthy project of discussion before the Catholic Columbian Congress (Chicago) or the Catholic Summer School (Cliff Haven, N. Y.). On the other hand, Hickey the defender of Catholicity, challenged the boasted culture of New England in indicating that the two most popular public characters representing the "Athens of America" were John L.

---

[168]Ibid., (November 17, 1888)
[169]Ibid., (October 6, 1888)
[170]Ibid., (August 19, 1893)
[171]The Catholic Review, (April 15, 1893)

Sullivan and Colonel Robert Ingersoll. The same cause engaged both:
the developing of the brute instinct in man; one by loosening the
restraints of religion; the other by exhibiting scenes of blood and
savagery. He continued:

> ... The fact is, New England culture, which to some extent
> influences the culture of the country, is fast learning to
> ignore the supernatural and despise the ideal of the angelic
> Christian virtues, and consequently, in spite of the ele-
> gancies of aesthetics, the fascinating realism of art and the
> external refinements of society, the brute instincts of
> human nature are fast coming to the surface and being stimu-
> lated to an unnatural degree...[172]

The Catholic Review was one of the periodicals proudly
announcing the return of another editor-publisher whose career was
interrupted by severe financial reverses. This was a happy event.
The words were warm.

> 'Patrick Donahoe, re-enters the field in which for more
> than forty years, he rendered such good service to his
> countrymen and co-religionists... He was the founder of...
> the oldest, certainly the most successful Irish paper pub-
> lished at this side of the Atlantic... As a publisher of
> Catholic books, Mr. Donahoe was liberal, enterprising, and
> judicious, giving us many valuable books at moderate prices
> and in excellent style. Of the misfortunes which swept away
> his princely estate and compelled him in his own age to begin
> the world again, we feel that they were sufficient to depress
> most men, but certainly he seems to us to have borne them with
> dignity and courage. It appeals to every one's sense of
> admiration for pluck and enterprise to see this old man
> attempting the work of youth, and we are glad to notice that
> the Catholic press of the United States and Canada have wished
> well to the new enterprise and its publisher.'[173]

---

[172]Ibid., (August 18, 1883)
[173]Donahoe's Magazine, I (December, 1878) 91. (Quoted the
Catholic Review.)

The new venture was called appropriately enough Donahoe's
Magazine; whereas, "the most successful Irish paper..." previously
mentioned was the Boston Pilot. The success of the Pilot was no
idle boast, for Donahoe, after assuming sole control in 1839, saw
the Pilot's circulation reach nearly 100,000 in 1872.[174] Four years
later, the collapse of his extensive business and charitable enter-
prises forced his sale of the paper. Making a partial comeback
within two years, Donahoe inaugurated the magazine bearing his name.
This magazine operated under the veteran's auspices from 1878 until
1892 and under later operators until 1908, when it combined with The
Catholic World. Another turn of events in the meantime saw Donahoe,
in 1890, re-purchasing the Pilot. Feeling inadequate as a publisher
of both a paper and magazine, he sold the latter.[175]

Donahoe's Magazine, published monthly, devoted itself with
"Tales, the Drama, Biography, Episodes in Irish and American History,
Poetry, Music, Miscellany, etc."[176] The magazine also featured a
juvenile department. Articles treating strictly of literature were
not always present in Donahoe's for the veteran editor was pre-
occupied with the Irish. He, having one ear in Boston and the other
in Dublin, printed stories calculated to stir the Irish pride. For
example, James Shields, the Union general and politician, was praised

---

[174]Sister Mary Alphonse Frawley, S.S.J., M.A., Patrick Donahoe,
p.79.
[175]Ibid., p.255.
[176]Donahoe's Magazine, II (July, 1879) Frontpiece.

for being Irish, Catholic, and loyal to the United States.[177]
Dr. Edmund Bailey O'Callaghan, who discovered, while residing in
Albany, so much primary material regarding the Dutch settlement, was
honored as an Irish-Canadian patriot.[178] One short notice even
claimed George Washington was of Irish descent.[179] Of more value,
perhaps, was the statement declaring that Lawrence Kehoe, manager of
the Catholic Publication Society, had done more to "raise the
standard of Catholic literature in the English language than any
other man in the country.[180]

Another elevating improvement desired was more support for the
Catholic paper. Catholics, as a rule, were not so well educated
that they could afford to overlook the admirable treatment of evolution which had appeared in the New York Freeman's Journal, December
6, 1884.[181] Furthermore, the general condemnation of novels was
not to be observed.

> It would be a sad day and lonely to lovers of letters if
> "Fabiola," "Callista," "Loss and Gain," the charming novels
> of Walter Scott, the delightful pen-pictures of human life
> of William M. Thackerary, and such similar productions,
> wore set aside by this swooping denunciation of all books
> denominated novels.[182]

---

[177] William J. Onahan, "General James Shields," Donahoe's
Magazine, XVII (May, 1887) 445.
[178] Hugh P. McElrone, "Edmund Bailey O'Callaghan," Donahoe's
Magazine, XXV (April, 1891) 429,430.
[179] "Was Washington an Irishman," ibid., (February, 1891) p.141.
[180] "Mr. Lawrence Kehoe," Donahoe's Magazine, XVIII (August, 1887)
284. Reprint from New York Freeman's Journal.
[181] Rev. John Conway, "Reading," Donahoe's Magazine, XVII
(January, 1887) 12.
[182] Ibid., pp.15,16.

"Read for the sake of instruction," the author concluded, "and with instruction is always added intellectual pleasure."[183] At another time, the reader was advised to cast a discerning eye over premium books, too many of them only amounted to "literary junk."[184] Since librarians were often grateful for suggestions, Catholics were at fault for not recommending the books of their own authors to be placed in the public libraries.[185] Generally speaking, the layman in the United States was too inactive.

> The great lesson must be taught the Catholic laity that there is work for them to do; that their lives and virtues; and best talents, must be enlisted in the work of the church.[186]

This country lacked figures like Windthorst, Daniel O'Connell, Count de Maistre, Frederic Ozanam, Frederich Lucas, and St. George Mivart. Only Brownson approached being the great Catholic layman in America.[187]

This same Orestes A. Brownson was the subject of a feature which rightfully proclaimed him as a renowned Catholic writer and the "practical applicant of Catholic principles to the leading questions of the day."[188] This contemporary critic thought that Brownson's

---

[183]Ibid., p.16.
[184]"Notes on Current Topics," Donahoe's Magazine, XVIII (July, 1887) 91.
[185]Ibid., XXIV (August, 1890) 190.
[186]"The Catholic Layman of the Future," Donahoe's Magazine, XXI (January, 1889) 24.
[187]Ibid.
[188]Michael J. Dwyer, "Dr. Orestes A. Brownson," Donahoe's Magazine, XIII (June, 1885) 499.

American Republic, with its interpretation of the Constitution and
its belief in the destiny of the American Nation, was his crowning
work. Donahoe's also valued the writings of Cardinal Newman.[189]
Another provocative figure of that day, Henry George, did not escape
Donahoe's scrutiny. Disagreeing with the Single-Tax economist, the
author advised his co-religionists; "Let him go in peace. His way
is not open to Catholics. For them to enter upon it would be to
dishonor their Church and deny their religion."[190]

Donahoe's Magazine, as successful as it was, never approached
the popularity and circulation of his first venture, The Pilot.
When disastrous fires gutted the foundation of his financial empire
and the walls tumbled, Donahoe sold the paper to Archbishop John J.
Williams and John Boyle O'Reilly.[191] Obviously, the change in
ownership did not influence the high standard of The Pilot and it
remained a guide and supporter of Catholic causes. Resuming control,
the septuagenarian owner had the good sense[192] to retain James
Jeffrey Roche and Katherine E. Conway. (Unfortunately, the untimely
death of O'Reilly provided the opportunity for the repurchase of the
paper.) Under O'Reilly, Roche, and Conway, the cause of Catholic
literature was well served.

---

[189] Ibid.
[190] L.W. Reily, "Henry George, the Socialist," Donahoe's
Magazine, XVIII (July, 1887) 7.
[191] "Patrick Donahoe, Founder of the Pilot," Donahoe's Magazine,
XXV (February, 1891) 101.
[192] S.S.J. Frawley, op.cit., p.289.

The Pilot furnished its readers with an ample supply of current
events, serialized fiction, poetry, a juvenile department, news from
the sporting world, and the most tantalizing advertisements for
patent medicines. Much space was given to the Irish Land League and
Total Abstinence causes while the Catholic Reading Circles and the
Catholic Summer School of America received solid and devoted support
from these well-meaning Catholic writers. Furthermore, their
interest in poetry and poets was reflected in the paper; and, the
names of O'Reilly, Roche, and Conway were affixed to poems appearing
there.[193] Longfellow was a great poet, one appreciated by Cardinal
Wiseman;[194] but, Lowell, although a good poet, was an "un-American
snob"[195] as our ambassador to England. From abroad, The Pilot indicated a preference for the poetry of Fanny Parnell,[196] sister of
the famed agitator; and that of Coventry Patmore, the Englishman
whose work approached the mystical and extolling the virtue of
married love.[197] Admiration was shown also for Paul Hamilton Hayne,
the Southern poet, whose efforts did not betray the straightened
circumstances of his life in the "reconstructed" South.[198] Among
the dialect poets worth considering were the Americans Lowell, James

[193]The Pilot, (March 25, 1882; June 24, 1882; May 6, 1893;
April 7, 1894)
[194]Ibid., (April 1, 1882)
[195]Ibid., (April 8, 1882)
[196]Ibid., (June 29, 1882)
[197]The Pilot, (June 10, 1893)
[198]Ibid., (August 5, 1882)

Whitcomb Riley, and Bret Harte, and Rudyard Kipling, a British
subject.[199] In this manner of publishing poetic criticism and
poetry, did The Pilot establish some poetical criteria for its
readers.

Another worthwhile service was the paper's brief summarizing o
the leading articles in the magazines each month. The reader was
touted to such periodicals as The Catholic World, the Month, The
Century, Ave Maria, Popular Science Monthly, Lippincott's, Rideout's
Potter's American Monthly, Harper's, Atlantic Monthly, and
Donahoe's.[200] Here, the best of the non-Catholic and Catholic
periodicals, were indicated as worthwhile reading. Similarly,
"Books and Bookmakers", a review section, scrutinized the newly
published books. The American Statesman Series, for example, was
devoted to a careful and impartial study, by specialists, "of the
lives and achievements of the more prominent American statesmen."[201]
Equally important was the new edition of Parkman's Oregon Trail.[202]
The Robber Count by Julius Wolf contained inaccuracies regarding the
faith which might have scandalized some Catholics, but the book was
fairly interesting "although one incurs no rash of repentance by not
reading it."[203] A reviewer was more severe with Dr. J.I. Mombert's

---

[199]Ibid., (November 4, 1893)
[200]Ibid., (April 8, 1882; April 15, 1882; May 27, 1882)
[201]Ibid., (April 29, 1882)
[202]The Pilot, (December 30, 1893)
[203]Ibid., (October 18, 1890)

A Short History of the Crusades, relegating its use to Catholics only as a record of events. "It would be folly for Catholics to expect a satisfactory history of the Crusades from the pen of a Protestant writer."[204] "Books and Bookmakers" was much happier in recommending The New Fifth Reader in the Catholic National Series, an eclectic reader selecting the best from non-Catholic and Catholic sources. As such, selections from Rip Van Winkle and Fabiola and from the historians Francis Parkman and John Lingard were among those able to give young students a love for literature. The book not only was free from objectionable matter but also did not leave the young reader ignorant of Catholic literature. "So far as a school book can make him a Catholic American gentleman, the 'New Fifth' will work that effect."[205]

This penchant for combing the best from non-Catholic and Catholic authors was carried over into the Pilot's lengthier articles. Among those so honored were William Cullen Bryant, Richard Henry Dean, Aubrey DeVere, Mary Elizabeth Blake, Charles Warren Stoddard, and Richard Malcolm Johnston.[206] It was a sad task to print the obituaries of Oliver Wendell Holmes, "last of the noble company of literary men,"[207] and that of Robert Louis Stevenson. The latter's place in literature was assured. "... and it is an enviable place,

---

[204] Ibid., (June 9, 1894)
[205] Ibid., (August 25, 1894)
[206] The Pilot, (August 24, 1894; September 8, 1894; March 4, 1893; June 17, 1882; September 8, 1894; November 18, 1893)
[207] Ibid., (October 13, 1894)

especially in these decadent days when the apostles of Realism
offer not pearls to swine but realism to everybody."[208] "Literary
Workers Who are Catholics", as the title suggested was reserved by
the paper to announce a new publication by a competent Catholic
author. This feature inaugurated by Miss Conway in 1893 included a
review of the present work, some references to past performances,
and the author's biography. Miss Conway hoped that such encouragement would enable the good writer to become an ideal one.

> The ideal literary worker would be for us Catholics, the
> writer with originality and a high degree of grace and
> strength of style, united to deep religious knowledge and
> intelligent zeal who could do for the Catholic life of
> this or any age or country what Hawthorne has done against
> the sombre background of Puritanism in early New England,
> in the "Scarlet Letter."[209]

The Catholic who could do this had not "revealed himself" but there
were capable Catholic writers with whom "the public should become
better acquainted." With this in mind, she began the series with
Maurice Francis Egan and his recently published poems. In addition
to Egan, some of the others spasmodically considered included Father
John Talbot Smith,[210] Louise Imogen Guiney,[211] and Mary Catherine
Crowley.[212]

The Pilot, like most of its contemporaries, reprinted what it
considered worthwhile articles from the other journals. When the

---

[208] Ibid., (December 22, 1894)
[209] Ibid., (February 11, 1893)
[210] The Pilot, (August 5, 1893)
[211] Ibid., (January 20, 1894)
[212] Ibid., (June 2, 1894)

Reverend Washington Gladden, a worthy advocate of social justice, alerted his fellow Protestants to the wrongs done Catholics by the A.P.A., the Boston paper printed Gladden's pleas which had originally appeared in The Century.

> Can we afford, as Protestants, to approve by our silence, such methods of warfare against Roman Catholics as this society is employing? For the honor of Protestantism, is it not high time to separate ourselves from this class of patriots?[213]

Returning to the strictly literary article, a reprint from the London Month declared that the Irishman in fiction was unreal because of the excessive dialogue put into his mouth. Even the good novels were overwhelmed by the jargon.[214] From the Poor Souls Advocate, The Pilot borrowed the literary criticism of the American editor, Charles F. O'Malley. Like Gladden and the London critic, O'Malley was in a reforming mood. The Catholic press left much to be desired since many failed to advance "the best, only the best" of history, philosophy, sociology, poetry, and fiction. As for the latter, "the bulk of American Catholic fiction is trite and vapid"[215] repulsive rather than attractive to readers of culture. Young writers, for instance, located their stories in lands they had never seen. Instead of commuting their visions to the paper, they revealed only their inexperience. More deplorable were the misrepresentations of Catholic life by non-Catholic writers.

---

[213] Ibid., (March 3, 1894)
[214] Ibid., (October 14, 1882)
[215] The Pilot, (October 28, 1893)

Mrs. Gertrude Atherton from spite and Mrs. Mary Hartwell Catherwood
from ignorance contributed some harm which the Catholics did little
to combat. O'Malley concluded:

> If we are Americans and Catholics let us present these
> aspects of our own, or a past civilization that are dis-
> tinctly American and Catholic. It is very evident that
> Catholics when producing work of a secular character can
> be very American; why can they not when treating subjects
> which are Catholic...[216]

With enthusiasm and criticism, both original and borrowed, The
Pilot of Boston showed Catholics the literature that might possible
be theirs. Down the coast in Gotham, the New York Freeman's Journal
maintained its own pattern for Catholic progress. Whereas criticism
from the Boston paper hit with the clean, sharp effect of well-
aimed, rifle fire, that from the New York one left the jagged wound
of shrapnel. The difference was in the personality of the editor of
the New York Freeman's Journal, James A. McMaster. An associate
politely gave the key to this personality, "If his zeal in the cause
of the faith seemed at times excessive, who shall honestly say that
it was a fault."[217] In other words, McMaster, the militant convert,
did not hesitate to criticize all Americans; and, his way with words
hurt unnecessarily. In his zeal to help, it was likely he made
enemies.

When the Bay City Catholic Chronicle (Michigan) gave favorable
mention to Dr. John Gilmary Shea and Mr. John O'Kane Murray in the

[216]Ibid.
[217]Maurice Francis Egan, "James A. McMaster," The Illustrated
Catholic Family Annual, XX (January, 1888) 44.

same paragraph, the New York Freeman's Journal was outraged. Shea
was a competent, thorough historian, while Murray left something to
be desired.

> If we are to have a sound American Catholic literature, we
> shall never get it by praising every man who puts "Catholic"
> on the title pages of his books. We are informed that
> Mr. John O'Kane Murray is an excellent young man; that rough
> criticism injures his health. If so, we hope that it may be
> injured just enough to prevent his writing more "Catholic
> histories."[218]

Another Catholic paper, the Iowa Messenger (Davenport) was condemned
for "publishing the lucubrations of putrefying minds."[219] The
occasion for the outburst was the printing of the translations of
Theophile Gautier's poetry. The translator, Miss Ella Wheeler,
belonged to "the Milwaukee School of fleshly poetesses."[220] Showing
no preferences, it branded the New York Times as an anti-Catholic
paper guilty of confounding "the principles of the Reformation with
the 'moral ideas' of the Republican Party."[221]

"We observe with pain," was the Freeman's Journal's reaction to
the favorable reviews given in other Catholic journals to Mrs.
Southworth's novels. They were literary nightmares, Mrs. Southworth
being the Madame Scudery of her time.

> We protest the introduction of this trash into Catholic
> homes. If a journalist has no time to read the books sent
> him for review, he had better not make book-notices which
> must be mischievous and misleading.[222]

---

[218] New York Freeman's Journal, (November 3, 1883)
[219] New York Freeman's Journal, (August 18, 1883)
[220] Ibid.
[221] Ibid., (September 29, 1883)
[222] Ibid., (June 9, 1883)

On the other hand, Eliza Allen Starr's Pilgrims and Shrines, it considered capable of creating and fostering a good taste for Catholic literature. "It is not cheap books we want, but good books,"[223] maintained the Journal. The indiscriminating praise given to every little thing printed under Catholic auspices, books well intentioned but entirely inadequate, should be discontinued. There were entirely too many namby-pamby stories and pamphlets.

> The lack of support given to Catholic literature must be laid at the doors of the colleges which neglect to encourage properly either the study of the Scriptures, which can be best done under proper guidance, or researches into the history of the Church.[224]

Not only were young Catholics not likely to know the Scriptures or Church History, but also they created no demand for books although the Catholic school graduates were multiplying each year. Part of the difficulty was that every boy was not a fit subject for higher learning. "The young man who would have been a successful grocer, like his father, wastes his time in becoming a mediocre lawyer or a physician without patients."[225]

Regarding the theatre, the Journal assumed the attitude that although some plays were immodest and the custom of the young play-goers' dining after the performance was deplorable,[226] the parents should direct their children's taste "and when a sound moral play is produced, prove to the manager that there is a public which knows

---

223 Ibid., (December 15, 1883)
224 New York Freeman's Journal, (June 23, 1883)
225 Ibid., (September 22, 1883)
226 Ibid., (November 10, 1883)

a good thing."[227] Far less reasonable was the paper's view of the young man's literary societies. Most of them were nothing but base-ball, billard, and picnic clubs not worthy of the saints' names the flourished.[228] Nor were they more ridiculous than when adopting their high sounding resolutions denouncing Bismarck,[229] shaming the French, and praising the Catholic Indian Bureau and the Catholic press. Generally, they were aimless, while some societies counted neither Catholics nor gentlemen among their ranks.

When McMaster died, December 29, 1886, other capable editors including Father Louis A. Lambert and Austin E. Ford manned the Journal. The Ford corresponderce revealed some of the frustrations and aspirations which befell these well-meaning men. Where Father Lambert could not be accused of being favorable to the Archbishop of New York, Michael J. Corrigan, Ford protested otherwise:

> ... I had at all times endeavored to fulfill my duty as an individual Catholic and a Catholic editor in inculcating respect for you as the guardian of souls in this great Arch-Diocese, and that there was nothing in my conduct to warrant the insinuation of personal antagonism to you; and this I reiterate to you direct so that you may judge of me not by what newspapers or sensational news-mongers may say, but by my own words.[230]

A much happier tone prevailed in Ford's appeal to Cardinal Gibbons. As a promoter of Catholic life in America, Ford solicited Gibbons' support of having a Roman debut of a mass composed by a

---

[227] Ibid., (June 16, 1883)
[228] New York Freeman's Journal, (June 16, 1883)
[229] Ibid., (June 2, 1883)
[230] Austin E. Ford to Archbishop Michael J. Corrigan, (August 6, 1892) Ford Papers. UNDA.

young American. This Solemn Mass honoring Leo XIII and the
Pontifical Jubilee was written by Frank G. Dossert, musical director
for St. Stephen's Church, New York City, and St. Bridgit's, Jersey
City. The editor pleaded his case:

> There is an opportunity for serving a worthy young American
> composer and at the same time securing a great distinction
> for our country in the way of precedence in a field where
> our genius has as yet had but little recognition.[231]

In summary, Ford concluded that this promotional scheme would prove
successful in emphasizing the position of the Church as the patron
of art; in encouraging higher musical efforts in America; in
calling forth "the grateful praise and recognition of His Holiness
from the people of this Republic."[232] Flattery and an honest
evaluation attended his words to the Cardinal, "I have felt that you
above all would appreciate and enter into the spirit of the
thing."[233]

The New York editor illustrated that the urge to good was not
confined to the pages of his paper. Working behind the scenes, in
two well-placed letters, he attempted to bring comfort and recognition to his fellow Americans. In Chicago, another editor, William
Dillon, had his variation to theme of educating and helping his
countrymen. Dillon's paper, The New World, was a sixteen page,
published on Saturday weekly that regularly reviewed books and

---

[231]Austin E. Ford to Cardinal James Gibbons, (October 5, 1892)
Ford Papers. UNDA.
[232]Ibid.
[233]Ibid.

magazines, exhibited poetry and fiction and had among other things:
an exchange column, a woman's and a juvenile department. Usually,
each issue contained one or two book reviews and several short
notices. Economics and politics obviously interested William Dillon,
since he wrote numerous signed articles such as those involving
bimetallism and the struggle between capital and labor.[234]

Aside from politics and economics, Dillon's other interest was
the strengthening of the cultural background of his co-religionists.
An acquaintance with the tremendous inheritance in art and architecture was presented in the various series of pictures appearing
periodicalls in The New World. Cathedrals such as the ones in
Guadalupe, Mexico, and Strasbourg, Alsace, and Notre Dame de Paris,
dominated one series; as the Italian painters Correggio and
Ghirlandago were a vital part of another.[235] To stimulate and
foster the literary interests of his co-religionists, the Chicago
editor was apt to publish a poem by "the great O'Reilly," a juvenile
serial by Anna T. Sadlier, the accurate prose of Eliza Allen Starr,
or a short biography of Father Tabb.[236]

The critical eye of The New World considered some of the
characters in Maurice Francis Egan's The Vocation of Edward Conway
to be unreal and that F. Marion Crawford's Tarquisara seemed crude

---

[234]The New World, (September 12,19, 1896; October 24, 1896;
February 20, 1897)
[235]Ibid., (December 12, 1896; January 9, 1897; February 20,
1897; March 20, 1897; June 26, 1897)
[236]Ibid., (September 19, 1896; December 19, 1896; January 30,
1897)

and unfinished when compared to his Saracinesca and his Saint
Ilario.[237] Father Finn was cherished for the "most delicately
beautiful" Ada Merton, while Ethelred Preston equalled past productions.[238] The collections of Brother Azarias' essays published
posthumously elicited the "raves" that this genius of the Christian
Brothers, through his research and comment, had done a service for
literature, history, and philosophy.[239] Also a real worth were
the translations of the first two volumes of Johannes Janssen's,
History of the German People at the Close of the Middle Ages. At
the conclusion of two lengthy columns of praise were the words, "We
want the rest of Janssen's History in English."[240]

The New World protested the inclusion of certain women writers
in the anthology Immortelles of Catholic Columbian Literature. "We
see no reason whatever why a Catholic who has written one or two
mediocre articles for an obscure magazine should be held up for
admiration."[241] Catholics, so often, to their detriment, honored
their writers with good hearts and no talents.[242] Agnes Repplier
had a comment for the American Sunday School literature, which was
repeated in the Chicago paper.

> There is no reason why the literature of the Sunday-
> School, since it represents an important element in modern
> bookmaking, should be uniformly and consistently bad.

[237] Ibid., (October 3, 1896; January 9, 1897)
[238] Ibid., (October 17, 1896; November 14, 1896)
[239] The New World, (November 7, 1896)
[240] Ibid., (January 16, 1897)
[241] Ibid., (March 20, 1897)
[242] Ibid.

There is no reason why all the children who figure in its
pages should be such impossible little prigs...[243]

Furthermore, Miss Repplier wrote that these books were so filled
with characters of dejection such as crippled lads, consumptive
mothers, innocent convicts, and famished families that one was led
to believe there was no joy in this world. Such a position was
untenable. Another object of protest was the ascending popularity
of the mystery story, glorifying crime and criminals. Elizabeth A.
Adams wrote for the paper: "Such literature is unworthy of our age
and nation. But it will take many summer and winter schools to
counteract the mischief done by this class of stories..."[244] The
New World inspired by Benziger's A Round Table of the Representative
Catholic Novelists, editorialized the state of affairs regarding
these same novelists. Benziger's was to be applauded for its effort
to make the Catholics of the United States "better acquainted with
the best work of our Catholic novelists."[245] When the publishers
sent copies of this work for review to the New York papers, The Sun
gave it a brief notice and the Post replied with an editorial
treating Catholic novelists as objects of disdain. On the contrary,
the Chicago view held many of these writers to be good, some
excellent. Obviously, since non-Catholics would not support these
novelists; Catholics, in the future, were to give their co-
religionists "at least sufficient encouragement to continue the good

[243]Ibid., (March 6, 1897)
[244]The New World, (November 14, 1896)
[245]Ibid., (December 19, 1896)

work they are engaged in."[246]

In addition to William Dillon, The New World boasted of another competent editor When Charles J. O'Malley assumed the position. This was the same Mr. O'Malley whom Thorne was so wont to advise. O'Malley, according to Charles Phillips of the San Francisco Monitor was not only a fine editor but also a poet of "great status." Egan went further and proclaimed him "our greatest poet."[247] O'Malley the editor acquired a vast experience working for the Angelus Magazine, the Pittsburgh Observer, Catholic Telegraph of Cincinnati, Syracuse Sun, The Midland Review, and The New World.[248] Therefore, it was honestly said that he devoted his life to Catholic literature and journalism.

While working in his native Kentucky editing The Midland Review (Louisville), he advanced several ideas involving his co-religion-ists. Noting that an English critic had declaimed that the bulk of pious literature still was translated from the French and the Italian; The Midland Review assented that it was time for Americans, as well as the English, to fashion their own books of piety. Now, there were too many translations in America.[249] In the beginning, translations served well; but, in interpreting the national character in the hope of influencing the same, it remained for the

[246]The New World, (December 19, 1896)
[247]The Monitor, (January 29, 1910)
[248]Ibid., (April 2, 1910)
[249]"In the Library," The Midland Review, IV (June 1, 1899) 7.

American Catholic to portray his religious experience in words
attractive to all. Transferring its attention from the devotional
to the political sphere, the Louisville paper applauded the action
of the Standard-Times' persuading McClure's to stop advertising
James M. King's latest book of infamous and disgusting lies calculated to stir up religious strife in the next presidential election.[250] The Century and Scribner's subscribed to McClure's good
example. However, since Munsey's, Harper's, Review of Reviews,
Forum, North American Review, The Chautauquan, and Frank Leslie's
continued to move "the thing," The Midland Review proposed a boycott
of these publications which "have no right to insult us."[251]

Within a year of the two aforementioned articles, editor
O'Malley, in 1900, made several observations regarding the advances
of Catholic literature in America. Nationalism was in ascendancy
while the racial and controversial characteristics in writing declined. (Twenty years ago, the Irish dominated the scene).[252]
Secondly, a substantial beginning "toward evolving a Catholic youth's
literature" had been established. Anent youth's fiction, it paid
not greatly but satisfactorily. Moreover, the children would read
almost anything they could get. Thirdly, many excellent essays came
from the pens of Bishop Spalding, Conde Pallen, Walter Lecky,

---

[250]"Again Facing the Twentieth Century," The Midland Review,
IV (October 5, 1899) 8.
[251]Ibid.
[252]Charles J. O'Malley, "The Catholic Literary Advance," The
Midland Review, IV (February 1, 1900) 6.

Maurice F. Egan, Humphrey Desmond and others; "... but probably since the essay appeals to older people, these have not been found in any strong demand."[253] Finally, slight was the demand for history and poetry.

When Charles O'Malley died, March 26, 1910, The Monitor of San Francisco asked, "Who can take his place?"[254] At that time, Charles Phillips, critic, college professor, and Polandophile edited The Monitor. Under the Phillips banner, the California paper professed a strong interest in the theatre as well as a general enthusiasm for the efforts of Catholic writers. He, like Father John Talbot Smith, found the stage fascinating, and in need of reform. The star of "L'Aiglon" thrilled him.

> ... not once does Miss Adams lose her grasp of character,
> or fail to reach its heights and so I say, Maude Adams is
> a great actress.[255]

The magnificent Madame Modjeska, the Polish actress, and the American Mary Anderson, he proudly noted, were Catholics;[256] and, so was Ada Rehan, the star of so many of the late Augustin Daly's successes. Miss Rehan, upon her retirement, declared that the theatre, solely interested in the box-office, was declining.[257] Poor Chauncey Olcott, it was not true that his wife was divorcing the Irish Catholic actor.[258] Again, the box-office was involved.

---

[253] Ibid.
[254] The Monitor, (April 2, 1910)
[255] Ibid., (August 3, 1907)
[256] The Monitor, (November 9, 1907)
[257] Ibid., (June 14, 1913)
[258] Ibid., (March 22, 1913)

In spite of the Catholic actor, writer, and producer the stage was in need of reform. It was left to the playgoer and the fathers of playgoers to bring the desired change. "Fathers of families... can do more to purify the stage than all the mayors and police in the country."[259] They were not to condemn all productions, just those of low moral tone. "There are clean actors and they should be supported,"[260] said Scranton's Bishop Hoban. The power of the stage that these good people felt was summarized by Bishop Peter J. Muldoon of Chicago. "After the pulpit, there is no such influence for good in the world as the theatre, when it seeks to do good."[261]

With this in mind, editor Phillips recorded (1913) that the Socialists "have secured a local theatre where they are presenting propaganda plays."[262] Appalled, he wondered whether simon-pure Marxist plays would soon find a place on the boards? Still perplexed, he inquired: "And where is the Christian drama strong with Catholic philosophy and pure with clean love and romance to offset the socialists' plays?[263]

---

[259] Ibid., (July 20, 1907)
[260] Ibid., (November 16, 1907)
[261] Ibid., (November 9, 1907)
[262] Ibid., (April 26, 1913)
[263] The Monitor, (April 26, 1913) (a partial answer to Phillips inquiry was supplied by Francis Deming Hoyt, author of The Coming Storm. The reviewer of The Live Issue, II (November 8, 1913) 3., hailed this socialist romance for presenting the Catholic viewpoint on such a vital problem. It was a timely novel entering an arena where Catholics had been exploited by the advocates of a new social order. Briefly, the story involved two intimate young men, one a Socialist and the other a Catholic. The romance matched the Socialist and the Catholic's sister. The characterizations were vivid and the novelist's understanding of the inner workings of Socialism was well grounded. Most important of all, the arguments against socialism was convincing. "It is a timely production," said the reviewer, "and should be an incentive to further effort.")

No such doubt plagued him when he came to the defense of Thomas
Daly's poetry. Daly's "To A Thrush," winner of The Lyric Year
Prize, was criticized by the new Poetry magazine as one guiltless of
expression and exhibiting a poor choice of words. "No, Daly's poem
stands," held Phillips, "a great lyric achievement and such criticism
as that of 'Poetry' cannot detract from its high fame."[264] He was
equally positive in praising Louise Imogen Guiney as one of the
"world's best Catholic authoresses;"[265] and, the retired editor of
the New Orleans Morning Star, James Ryder Randall, had contributed
greatly in raising the level of Catholic journalism.[266] Books to be
shunned by Catholics included Sapho, The Decameron, Balzac's Honore
and others. These books had been found in the library of a departed
citizen whose fall from virtue to degradation had been pitiful to
behold. Catholics finding these books in their own libraries were
to burn them.[267] Furthermore, the tasteful Catholic would hang the
pictures of the Madonnas on the front walls where they could be
seen; and, support was needed for the program of restoring the more
appropriate sacred music for all religious services.[268]

As for Catholic writers, Phillips' paper plainly revealed its
approval of their efforts. E. Francis Mohler, for example, wrote,
for The Monitor, a series of articles entitled "Living Catholic

---

[264] The Monitor, (February 1, 1913)
[265] Ibid., (November 2, 1907)
[266] Ibid., (August 17, 1907)
[267] The Monitor, (November 30, 1907)
[268] Ibid., (June 7, 1913)

Writers." In this giving of roses to the living, the writers considered varied from the juvenile specialis Father Finn,[269] to Monsignor Robert Hugh Benson,[270] the convert son of the Archbishop of Canterbury. A regular feature of The Monitor, "Under the Library Lamp," gave Mrs. Sallie Margaret O'Malley the opportunity to discuss the current literary trends. The widow of Charles J. O'Malley was impressed with the early success of Kathleen Norris. "Mrs. Norris is a Catholic writer who has won her place in the secular field without ever relinquishing one jot of her good pure Catholic philosophy."[271] This comment was inspired by Mrs. Norris' collection of short stories, Poor Margaret Kirby. Likewise, Miss Zona Gale, "the well known Catholic writer," enjoyed the enviable position of having her "Friendship" stories designated as "the most popular of all the year's output."[272] Mrs. O'Malley would not agree that Caroline D. Swan was the "foremost Catholic poet of the English speaking world."[273] Her criticism admitted that the poetry (sonnets) was flawless but cold. Without attempting an international ranking, Mrs. O'Malley installed the Englishman, Francis Thompson, as the "master of the winged prose of our day."[274] Madison Cawein, likewise, was attractive in holding his own "in the

[269] Ibid., (February 8, 1913)
[270] Ibid., (March 22, 1913)
[271] The Monitor, (May 10, 1913)
[272] Ibid., (May 31, 1913)
[273] Ibid., (June 7, 1913)
[274] Ibid., (July 19, 1913)

field of poetry for over twenty years." Cawein was not a Catholic as many supposed, "but is so genuine a man that I regret he is not of the Faith."[275]

On the other hand, Poetry magazine was not enhanced an iota by publishing the "rot" of Ezra Pound.[276] The Chicago magazine degernerated in disseminating the work of this precocious Imagist who demanded a more modern form of poetical expression. More frightening at the time was Harper's deleting two verses of George Sterling's "Night Sentries" so that it would fit on one page. Such occurrences furnished a sad commentary on the state of literature in America.[277] Equally distressing was the failure of Catholics to show an interest in the Catholic books in the public libraries.[278]

The stage, literature, and the advance of Catholicism obviously intriguged Charles Phillips. His paper bespoke his interests. A survey of his background revealed that his journalistic career was launched[279] under the guidance of Humphrey J. Desmond, Milwaukee's great Catholic editor. Desmond, essayist and editor, generally was interested in the Catholic advance; and, particularly, in promoting the reading circle and summer school movement. In fact, the early multiplication of the reading circles and summer schools encouraged his writing: "... our American Catholic population is exhibiting a

---

[275] Ibid., (February 8, 1913)
[276] Ibid., (May 3, 1913)
[277] The Monitor, (February 22, 1913)
[278] Ibid., (June 14, 1913)
[279] Julia R. Doyle, "Who's Who in Catholic Journalism," Extension, II (November, 1907) 9.

greater intellectual and literary activity than ever before, and one that gives promise of continuance and development."[280] The future looked brighter for author and publisher as the demand for books on Catholic subjects increased; however, much of the Catholic poetry was more or less a drug on the market. Yet, Dr. Parson's Lies and Errors of History, Father Zahm's scientific treatises and Bishop Spalding's essays indicated that the upward trend in Catholic literary marts was not confined to fiction alone.[281] The dying out of the literary snobbishness of certain Catholics, who assumed an air of condescension to all works of literature or art not appealing to Protestant audiences, was encouraging.[282] In a variation of this same theme, he wrote:

> There is one defect which we will take this advantage to call attention to, that is the disgustingly snobbish way in which Catholics who get recognition from non-Catholic sources are 'acclaimed.' It is an admission that Catholic taste is bad, and that the Catholic periodical has, in the eyes of the snobs no real position, since its appreciation counts for nothing unless bolstered by the Independent, The Atlantic or The Forum. We have had enough of this.[283]

Yet, it was evident, Catholic criticism was not above reproach. Too often, books and tracts written by Catholics against Catholics were characterized by narrow views and bad tempers. The Messenger of the Sacred Heart, for example, gave its bleak opinion of Dr. Zahm's Evolution and Dogma, "but it declines to write anything

---

[280]The Catholic Citizen, (January 4, 1896)
[281]The Catholic Citizen, (January 4, 1896)
[282]Ibid., (May 30, 1896)
[283]Ibid., (August 22, 1896)

like a review or this much discussed work."[284]

> Another difficulty in the way of the Catholic book, notably
> the Catholic book of fiction, is the lack of careful analy-
> sis and criticism. Some of the novels produced in our
> country by Catholics for Catholics have a permanent social
> value. But, not content to weigh properly what has been
> done, we call aloud for a new thing.[285]

Moreover, the high cost of publishing still curtailed the dissemi-
nation of much sound literature. There were plenty of poor, cheap
Catholic books (particularly, the premium book) and considerable
good, expensive ones; "but literature that is good, and sound and
truly Catholic, and cheap, not much."[286] The Catholic publisher had
not learned the art of helping his author, through the liberal[287]
advertising in the Catholic press, to gain a larger public.
(Perhaps, the unkindest cut of all was the refusal of the soap
companies to advertise in Catholic periodicals even though they had
a wider circulation and cheaper rates than some of the periodicals
so favored).[288] Abandoning advertising and its soapless inference,
Desmond made this demand:

> What is wanted nowadays is not treatises on dogma, not milk
> and watery devotional works, not lives of the saints, but
> strong, virile, common sense presentation of truth from the
> Catholic point of view.[289]

As for the work of the various Catholic authors, the Milwaukee
editor believed "that the children of our Church should know what

---

[284]Ibid., (July 25, 1896)
[285]Ibid., (October 17, 1896)
[286]The Catholic Citizen, (July 25, 1896)
[287]Ibid., (October 17, 1896)
[288]Ibid., (January 14, 1899)
[289]Ibid., (July 25, 1896)

members of the Catholic faith have done."290 This was the introduction to a lengthy column dealing with the accomplishments of
Charles Warren Stoddard. With this same attitude, he honored John
Gilmary Shea,291 Father Finn, and reviewed George Parsons Lathrop's
article on Orestes Brownson appearing in the June issue of The
Atlantic Monthly. Brownson, thought Desmond, had yet to receive the
measure of grateful appreciation which was his due.292

Father Finn, according to the Milwaukee paper, was the first
Catholic rival of the beloved author of youth, Oliver Optic.293
Father Finn's boys were not too pious and they represented the inland
youth, whereas Mrs. Sadlier's boys were limited to the New York,
Irish-American. Mrs. Sadlier's boys were always being persecuted,
but "I rather think we persecuted the 'Know Nothings' wherever we
found them."294 Maurice Francis Egan, who conducted a "corner" in
The Catholic Citizen, favored the novelists Christian Reid, Walter
Lecky, and Maurice Francis Egan.295 Equally unbiased was Egan's
high regard for the historians Johannes Janssens, Ludvig von Pastor,
and John Bach McMaster.296

Desmond, like Phillips, gave notice to the stage about him; so,
that the movements of Madame Modjeska297 and the playwright Minnie

290Ibid., (July 12, 1896)
291Ibid., (December 12, 1896)
292The Catholic Citizen, (July 4, 1896)
293Ibid., (January 11, 1896)
294Ibid., (May 2, 1896)
295Ibid., (November 28, 1896)
296Ibid., (May 30, 1896)
297Ibid., (October 16, 1897)

Andrews Snell and the death of Augustin Daly[298] were duly recorded.
Exceedingly objectionable, was the vile company currently headed by
a "variety ghoul named Jack."[299] Shun the average cheap theatre
came the sage advice. In the hope of reaching an even larger degree
of reform, The Catholic Citizen ran etiquette columns[300] indicating
the proper ballroom manners and the protecol involved in making a
social call. The object of this consolidated effort was ably stated
in Desmond's little volume, The New Laity and the Old Standards.

More and more, the conviction grew that the welfare of
Catholicity depended largely upon the cultivation and growth of an
intelligent, efficient, and loyal Catholic laity.[301] The desirable
qualities sought in the Catholic layman included intelligence, civic
patriotism, Catholic public spirit, and the knowledge and practice
of one's religion.[302] Catholics were urged to be more than mere
Mass goers and to be active in the congregation.[303] Some, frankly,
were too busy cultivating Protestants in the social swim;[304] more
were not ethical in their voting practices.[305] As to the relief of
the destitute and defective classes, it fell as a matter of civic
duty and justice "upon the State and not primarily on private

---

[298]Ibid., (June 17, 1899)
[299]Ibid., (September 28, 1897)
[300]The Catholic Citizen, (September 16,23, 1899)
[301]Humphrey J. Desmond, The New Laity and the Old Standards, p.1.
[302]Ibid., p.71.
[303]Ibid., p.65.
[304]Ibid., p.54.
[305]Ibid., p.75.

individuals or societies."[306] The realization was thrust upon the

Catholic layman that he was under an obligation to his fellow

Americans. It was the call to act:

> And not coldly, but sympathetically; not narrowly, but in
> the public spirit which recognizes the good thought of the
> whole Christian world; not hoping to solve the complex
> problem from the schoolmen, nor by sign posts pointing to
> medieval conditions, but recognizing the divine plan that
> God helps those who help themselves; recognizing that labor
> itself might find its own Moses, that the useful, practical
> expedients are apt to come, not from men trained in semina-
> ries, but from men close to working conditions, and grappling
> with the complex actualities of the great modern industrial
> problem.[307]

Desmond, in this manner, asked the Catholic laity to become a

vital part of American life, to be active and aggressive in the

projects promoting the welfare of their fellow men, their country,

and their church. This plea typified the American Catholic editor

From Monsignor Corcoran to Humphrey Desmond, the Catholic editor

contributed a helping hand to his co-religionists. Differing, at

times, in opinions and purposes, all, nevertheless, shared the

conviction that the United States provided a most excellent environ-

ment for the development of the individual Catholic and the growth

of the Church. To the American Catholic willing to learn and

study, these good editors gladly gave their encouragement and

advice.

---

[306] Ibid., p.85.
[307] Ibid., p.95.

CHAPTER VIII

ORGANIZING THE EFFORTS TO FORM THE
EDUCATED, PATRIOTIC, RELIGIOUS,
AMERICAN CITIZEN

The Catholic novelist, poet, essayist, and journalist, all
desiring to help their co-religionists to reach a more cordial and
cultivated existence on this earth, found that the background of
this period (1880-1915) was congenial to their plans. From the
various parts of the United States, the collected evidence indicated
that there were other people sharing in this belief of progress and
reform. Populist and Progressive, Suffragist and Socialist, and the
Temperance forces, too, had programs designed to improve their
country. Smaller groups, the learned societies for example, and
individuals like Edward Bellamy, Henry George, Thorstein Veblen, and
E. L. Godkin joined the "Muck-rakers" in aspiring for the better
day. Catholics, as individuals and in groups, contributed to this
improving, advancing impulse.

One year prior to the opening of this period (1880), an Italian
born priest died in Central City, Colorado. To this mining town,
booming and ghostless, Father Joseph M. Finotti had come to recover
his health. Father Finotti, in 1872, had published the first volume
of his Bibliographica Catholica,

... intended to be a catalogue of all the books published
in the United States, with notices of their authors and an
epitome of their contents.[1]

The first part covered America in its infancy to the year 1820;

while the second part, 1821-1875 was never finished although much of

the material had been compiled. Yet, Father Finotti, with his one

volume, displayed his special interest in the Catholic literary

history of America; just as Moses Coit Tyler, with his volumes,

attested to his liking for American literature.

When Father Finotti's ecclesiastical superior, Pope Leo XIII,

wrote his encyclical (1883) encouraging the study and writing of

history, the reaction in America took several forms. For example,

the Rev. Dr. Andrew A. Lambing, Scottdale, Pennsylvania, brought

forth a historical "publication which later became the American

Catholic Historical Researches."[2] Philadelphians, under the same

impetus, formed the American Catholic Historical Society, July 22,

1884.[3] The Very Rev. Dr. Thomas C. Middleton, O.S.A., was the first

president while the competent historian, Martin I. J. Griffin, "did

some of his best work under the influence of the society."[4] Later

in the year in December, the United States Historical Society was

established in New York, only its formation was attributed to a

[1] Edward P. Spillane, "Finotti, Joseph M.," The Catholic
Encyclopedia, VI (1913) 77,78.
[2] "Laetare Medal Conferred on Lawrence F. Flick, M.D., in the
Hall of the Society, 5 May 1920," Records of the American Catholic
Historical Society, XXXI (June, 1920) 121.
[3] Ibid.
[4] Ibid., p.123.

slightly different origin.

> ... The genesis of that society is traceable to the Third
> Plenary Council of Baltimore which recommended the preser-
> vation and study of the facts of our Catholic American
> History. On December 9, 1884, two days after the council
> closed, John Gilmary Shea and Richard H. Clarke, both of
> New Jersey, met in New York City and established the United
> States Historical Society.[5]

Clarke[6] became the first president. Shea, meanwhile, concentrated

on writing his four volume History of the Catholic Church in the

United States.

The genesis of the United States Historical Society, The Third

Plenary Council of Baltimore "was a turning point in the history of

the Church in America."[7] American attention was focused on this

council of Catholic bishops as it contemplated the problems

attending the rapid growth of the United States. From November 9

through December 7, 1884, the distinguished delegates presided over

by the Apostolic Delegate, Archbishop James Gibbons, deliberated the

religious, social, and economic changes making such an imprint upon

American life. "Beloved brethern," the Council warned, "a great

social revolution is sweeping over the world. Its purpose, hidden

or avowed, is to dethrone Christ and religion."[8] The defense

---

[5]Rev. John K. Sharp, "The Brooklyn Catholic Historical Society
and its founder Marc F. Vallette," Historical Records and Studies,
United States Catholic Historical Society, XXXVIII (1950) 99.

[6]Ibid., p.100.

[7]Mgr. James H. Moyninan, The Life of Archbishop John Ireland,
p.33.

[8]The Baltimore Publishing Company, The Memorial Volume, A
History of the Third Plenary Council of Baltimore, (November 9;
December 7, 1884) Pastoral Letter. 22.

suggested to contain this threat involved a general strengthening of
Catholic life all along the line. The education of the clergy was
to be more perfect; Catholic schools, increased and improved; secret
societies, shunned; and Catholic societies developed. The main line
of resistance, moreover, anchored on the home where the parents were
to shape the character and tastes of their children. In this
situation reading played a key role.

> ... no indelicate representation should ever be tolerated in
> a Christian home. No child ought to be subject to temptation
> by its own parents in its own home... See then that none but
> good books and newspapers as well as none but good companions
> be admitted to your homes. Train your children to a love of
> history and biography.[9]

The Council spoke and the Catholic body reacted. However, five
years elapsed before the laity's interest in the welfare of the
Church was proclaimed to all America. 1889 was a signal year in
American Catholicism for it witnessed the Centennial Celebration of
the establishment of the hierarchy in the United States, the assembly of the first Catholic Lay Congress in the United States, and the
opening of the Catholic University. Following the Centennial Celebration in the Baltimore Cathedral, the Lay Congress convened in
Baltimore, November 11, 12, 1889.

The Congress, in the mind of one of its chief promoters, Henry
F. Brownson, son of the great convert, was a significant indication
of the interest taken by the laity in the cause of religion.[10] The

[9]Ibid., p.20.
[10]William H. Hughes, (publisher), Three Great Events in the
History of the Catholic Church in the United States, p.v.

Organization Committee of the Congress felt that an assembly of the
Catholics in the United States "could not fail to be productive of
good results."

> It would demonstrate the union of the entire Catholic body
> in all that concerns the principles of our holy religion;
> the harmony, mutual attachment, and good will subsisting
> among the different orders of the church, the hierarchy,
> the clergy, and the laity, and it would moreover afford an
> opportunity to test in a public manner, the loyalty of the
> Catholics of the United States to the constitution and laws
> of the land, to which they have invariably been loyal in the
> past, and may, with equal confidence, be relied on to be
> faithful and devoted in the future.[11]

For two days, some of the most capable laymen expressed their
concepts for relating the Church to the age. Eighteen speeches, at
least, were presented to the delegates from more than thirty-five
states, Canada, England, and Ireland. Problems involving the United
States included the unequal distribution of capitalistic wealth and
taxes, educational systems, benevolent societies, temperance, and
Sunday observance. Of particular interest for Catholics were the
pleas for a more persistent usage of liturgical church music; the
stated aspirations of the young men's societies; and the evaluation
of the Catholic press and American Catholic literature. Conde
Pallen, who read the paper entitled, "Catholic American Literature,"
felt that such a literature was a province of the future; but, with
the optimism characteristic of that era, he advised: "... our
present conditions warrant us in coming forward and manifesting

---

[11]Ibid., p.xvii.

ourselves, declaring the truth that is in us, and revealing the
beauty of the face of the Son of Man."[12] Many of the other speakers
were the equal of Pallen in ability and reputation as the list[13]
counted John Gilmary Shea, Henry F. Brownson, Charles J. Bonaparte,
Peter L. Foy, George Dering Wolff, Henry J. Spaunhorst, Manly Tello,
Richard H. Clarke, and several others.

Such a Congress not only aired the opinions of an enlightened
Catholicism but it also provided the inspiration for Catholics to
try other things. In conjunction with the latter view, the
Cincinnati physician-editor and a leading advisor to the National
Catholic Press Association, Dr. Thomas P. Hart wrote:

> 'The first earnest and definite attempt to form a Catholic
> Press Association in the United States was inspired by a
> plank in the platform adopted by the First Catholic Congress
> held at Baltimore, Maryland, November 10 to 12, 1889. This
> plank said in part: "We not only recommend Catholics to
> subscribe more generally for Catholic periodicals; but we
> also look with eagerness for the establishment of a daily
> Catholic newspaper in our large cities, and a Catholic
> associated press agency."'[14]

At the same time and from the same source, another organization came
into being.

> As a result of the interest thus awakened in the matter by
> the Congress of Baltimore, the Catholic Truth Society was
> organized on the evening of March 1, 1890, in the arch-
> episcopal residence of St. Paul, Minn., with nine original
> members and its avowed object was to 'enable Catholic

---

[12]Ibid., p.67.
[13]Ibid., pp.19-84.
[14]Thomas F. Meehan, "Early Catholic Weeklies," United States
Catholic Historical Society, Historical Records and Studies,
XXVIII (1937) 248,249.

layman to perform their share of the work in the dis-
semination of Catholic truth, and the encouragement of
wholesome Catholic reading.'15

Another result of this Congress, of course, was that it prompted
the delegates assembled there to call for another one. The generous
Chicago layman, William J. Onahan, invited his co-religionists to
gather in the Windy City at the time of the next world's fair. The
delegates from St. Louis and Philadelphia objected that the fair
site had not been selected, to which Onahan correctly replied that
"there is no doubt in the minds of Chicagoans that the world's fair
will be held there."16

The Columbian Catholic Congress held in "the great and prosperous city of Chicago," September 4-19, 1893, reproduced the Baltimore
success on a larger scale. Cardinal Gibbons and a vast number of
the faithful gathered in the Windy City of Chicago to profess their
love of God and Country and to contemplate the various means for
better serving religion and the nation. One noticeable addition at
the Chicago convention was the presence of women delegates and
speakers. Among those speaking for the distaff side were Mrs. Rose
Hawthorne Lathrop, daughter of Nathaniel Hawthorne, Eleanor C.
Donnelly, Katherine E. Conway, Mary Onahan, Anna T. Sadlier, and
Elizabeth C. Cronyn of Buffalo, New York, a young woman vigorously
interested in popularizing adult education. Their male counterparts

---

15Progress of the Catholic Church in America and the Great
Columbian Catholic Congress of 1893, p.125.
16William H. Hughes, op.cit., p.82.

included many well known priests and laymen. Cardinal Gibbons,
Archbishops Corrigan and Patrick John Ryan, Bishop John J. Keane,
Father Walter Elliott, C.S.P., Henry L. Spaunhorst, Warren E.
Mosher, Richard E. Clarke, George Parsons Lathrop, and Maurice
Francis Egan gave well considered opinions[17] evaluating the Catholic
accomplishments in the United States and offered suggestions for
future improvement.

Among the resolutions passed by the Columbian Catholic
Congress, Number Twelve plainly expressed the desire to mold a
better informed American citizen.

> 12. We desire to encourage the Catholic Summer School of
> America, recently established on Lake Champlain, as a means
> of promoting education on university extension lines, and
> we also commend the forming of Catholic reading circles as
> an aid to the summer school, and an adjunct to higher
> education in general.[18]

The Catholic Summer School of America was the natural consequence of the reading circle movement promoted so successfully by
Warren E. Mosher in The Catholic Reading Circle Review and the
Paulist Fathers, The Catholic World. Like the Congresses, it demonstrated the cooperation of the clergy and laity necessary to bring
into existence the Catholic adaptation of the Chautauqua idea. The
Catholic Summer School at Cliff Haven, New York, provided summer
resort facilities and a galaxy of lecturers and teachers so that the

---

[17] Progress of the Catholic Church in America and the Great
Columbian Catholic Congress of 1893, pp.13-202.

[18] Ibid., p.200.

ambitious Catholic might acquire a sound education amidst pleasant
surroundings. Among the men and women supporting the program at
Cliff Haven and the other resort-educational centers under Catholic
auspices were many familiar names.[19] Brother Azarias, Marion
Crawford, Mary Catherine Crowley, Humphrey Desmond, Maurice Francis
Egan, Richard Malcolm Johnston, George Parsons Lathrop, Father James
F. Loughlin, John A. Mooney, Warren A. Mosher, William J. Onahan,
Conde Pallen, Father John Talbot Smith, Eliza Allen Starr, Doctor
James Joseph Walsh, and Father John A. Zahm, C.S.C., a veritable
Who's Who among Catholics, at one time or another lent their names
or services to the summer school idea.

The same impulse, which urged the forming of reading circles and
the gathering at summer schools, also prompted experienced readers
and librarians to compile or endorse lists of books suitable for
Catholic consumption. For example, the Jesuit priest, Father Thomas
Hughes, in the preface to A Directive List of Catholic Books and
Authors, told that the project was undertaken to show that there was
in existence "a mass of excellent literature on Catholic subjects,
or of books, at least by good Catholic authors."[20] Father John A.
Zahm, C.S.C., had a slightly different concept as he presented his
selections.

---

[19]James A. White, The Founding of Cliff Haven, Early Years of
The Catholic Summer School of America, pp.103-105.

[20]A Directive List of Catholic Books and Authors, p.2.

> "The hundred best books," as I take it should embrace the
> classics in the various departments of literature, and
> those that, of their very nature, are suggestive of other
> works of special merit.[21]

Obviously, the list contained the names of non-Catholic authors as
well as the Catholic, and, among the latter, the Americans favored
by Father Zahm were Father Louis A. Lambert, Christian Reid, John
Gilmary Shea, Eliza Allen Starr, John Boyle O'Reilly, and Orestes
Brownson.

Susan L. Emery, impressed with the number of Catholic books in
the Boston Public Library, made the plea:

> It would be gratifying if some such arrangement could be
> made by which one could know readily and thoroughly what
> we have, stowed away here and there on various shelves and
> in many alcoves, not always catalogues as to be easily
> found.[22]

Catholics, sharing the idea in other cities, brought forth the
required catalogues. Father John F. O'Donovan, S.J., compiled a
List of Catholic Books in the Pratt Free Library, Baltimore (1900).
Similar lists were prepared for the public libraries in New Haven,
Connecticut, (1905); Chicago, (1908); Seattle; and Cleveland,
(1911). In Buffalo, the Jesuit Fathers at Canisius College edited
A Comprehensive Catalogue of Catholic Books in the English and
German Languages. This work (1904) was based on the columns of the
Catholic Union and Times and of the Volksfreund and the list pre-
pared by the International Catholic Truth Society. According to the

---

[21]Notre Dame Scholastic, (May 21, 1887)
[22]Susan L. Emery, "Catholic Literature in Public Libraries,"
Donahoe's, XLII (September, 1899) 249.

author of this information, William Stetson Merrill, Catholic
literature needed to be "boomed" so that Catholics would demand
their co-religionists' books at the public libraries. The various
lists, it was hoped, would stimulate such a demand. In Merrill's
mind, Catholic societies could do no more noble work than to make
known what was available in the public libraries in their communi-
ties.[23] Emilie Louise Haley, who edited the Books by Catholic
Authors in the Cleveland Public Library, hoped that a list "of
standard books for Catholic readers including many non-Catholic
authors" would soon be prepared.[24]

While the members of the reading circles and summer schools and
the compilers of library lists worked to raise still higher the
cultural level of the American Catholic, some of their co-religionists faced the basic educational problem of dealing with the newly
arrived immigrant. Not even the McAroni verse of Thomas Daly could
soften the fact that the Italian immigrant from coast to coast was
a problem. The New York report found them huddled together in tenement squalor similar to the current crowding (1956) of the Puerto
Ricans on Gotham's streets. Not only were the Neapolitans poor, but
also they were in grave danger of losing their faith. Italian
priests were needed and it was equally important that the children

---

[23]William Stetson Merrill, "Catholic Literature in Public
Libraries," The Catholic World, LXXXIX (July, 1909) 507.
[24]Emilie Louise Haley, "Editorial Note," Books by Catholic
Authors in the Cleveland Public Library.

attended parochial schools. There was no improvement in the reality
that the Five Points House of Industry and the City Mission, "till
now mainly occupied with making Protestants of the children of
intemperate Irish parents,"[25] had shifted their attention to the
impoverished Italian children. Across the country, The Monitor in
San Francisco acknowledged:

> The Italian emigrant has become a big factor in the making
> of our country's population, but in too great a degree
> altogether he has 'got in all wrong.'[26]

The Monitor, worried over the great losses to the faith, the dire
want encouraging crime, and urged that the immigrant should be
settled in the rural areas.

The success of the "back to the land" plan was attested in a
letter from Father Peter Bandini to Father Hudson.

> I am very grateful and thankful to you for the paragraph
> you have given in the Ave Maria about my good people of
> Tontitown. If we can furnish some suggestions and be a
> help in trying to start other settlements with favorable
> conditions, spiritual and temporal, I think it will be a
> godsend to many Catholic immigrants that come to our land,
> and will be the best way to keep them faithful to their
> Church.[27]

Thus, the people of Tontitown, Arkansas, had one solution for a
vexing problem, back to the land, to the good, rural life. Yet,
urbanization increased its hold on American civilization, so that
the Italians were among the many committed "to the big city." Among

---

[25]Bernard J. Lynch, "The Italians in New York," The Catholic
World, XLVII (April, 1888) 73.
[26]The Monitor, (January 1, 1910)
[27]Rev. Peter Bandini to Rev. Daniel E. Hudson, C.S.C.,
(January 7, 1909) Hudson Papers. UNDA.

the larger cities, Chicago faced its responsibilities quite well.
There, a compassionate laity organized by the able Father Edward M.
Dunne, a native Chicagoan and an accomplished linguist, established
a mission in the midst of the Italian colony in the vicinity of
Jans Addams' Hull House. More than one hundred and twenty-five
teachers, men and women from every quarter of Chicago came to the
Holy Guardian Angels Mission

> ... to educate the ignorant and reclaim the erring, to bene-
> fit the body and save the soul, to form good Catholics and
> good citizens, to bring all under the loving care of the One
> Shepherd, within the safe confines of the One Fold.[28]

The Mission had a sewing class for three hundred and fifty children
as well as maintaining its own library for the pleasure of the more
advanced scholars. More important, perhaps, was the fact that one
absence brought the teacher to the absent one's home to check upon
the "spiritual and physical well-being of the family."[29]

The vitality attending the founding of The Mission was only one
instance of Chicago's coming of age. The city sparkled. Had not
confident promoters brought the World's Fair of 1893 to Chicago?
Still another topic of conversation was the Auditorium designed by
Louis Sullivan, the early skyscraper architect. Chicago's well-
being was more than physical, however. since Harriet Monroe's new
(1912) Poetry magazine and the spirited, Lincolnesque, "new poetry"
of Carl Sandburg, Vachel Lindsay, and Edgar Lee Masters gave rise to

---

[28]Kate Gertrude Prindeville, "Italy in Chicago," The Catholic
World, LXXVII (July, 1903) 457.
[29]Ibid., p.458.

the hope that Chicago might become the cultural center of the
Nation. Charles J. O'Malley, the poet and editor of The New World,
shared this feeling as he wrote, "... it is safe to predict that in
the years to come the great Catholic literary center of the United
States will be Chicago."[30] After one considered a population
exceeding one million and composed of

> Kelts, Teutons, Italians, Poles, Bohemians, French, Syrians,
> Greeks, Spaniards, the genius-producing races, in a word,
> and you may catch a glimpse of how glorious will be the
> noon of the present morning.[31]

As for the Catholic University necessary for such a development,
"In fifty years, the great institution of Notre Dame may be classed
as a suburb."[32] Among the Chicago writers, O'Malley considered
Father John E. Copus, S.J., to be the "coming Catholic novelist of
the country."[33] On the other hand, the convert novelist, Frank H.
Spearman was well established in the secular field. Art criticism,
long the province of Eliza Allen Starr, became the forte of another
Chicagoan, Mrs. Mary F. Nixon-Roulet. Even the mayor's wife,
Mrs. Carter Harrison, composed attractive juvenile stories as did
O'Malley's wife, Sallie. Numbered among the better journalists were
Father Thomas E. Judge and P. G. Symth. With the exception of
Father Leon M. Linden, the young women dominated the field of

---

[30]Charles J. O'Malley, "Catholic Literators of Chicago,"
The Rosary Magazine, XXVI (January, 1905) 19.
[31]Ibid., pp. 19,20.
[32]Ibid., p.19.
[33]Ibid., p.21.

poetry. The city editor of The New World, Mary J. Lupton, Katherine
A. Sullivan, and Mary Curtin Shepherd,[34] a relative of Jeremiah
Curtin, Sienkiewicz's translator, O'Malley regarded as poets of
promise. Further west, The Monitor reported that Father Thomas C.
Faggney had been chosen president of the Western Guild of Catholic
Writers, an organization devoted to uniting the Catholic publishers
and writers in the West. In this manner, Catholic writers were
enabled to find publication "without blue-penciling the best of
their efforts."[35] So, the feeling that the Catholic writers had
something important to say to his fellow Americans was not reserved
to Chicago alone.

Another new organization desirous of fostering a more distinct
Catholic expression was the American Ecclesiological Society, which
stated in its original prospectus that it proposed "to stimulate the
cause of Catholic Art in America."[36] It sought for architecture,
sculpture, and the decorative arts, a more worthy standard.

> Fortunately, the level of secular art, whose development
> was retarded by somewhat kindred conditions has not been until
> recent years so appreciably higher as to constitute a re-
> proach.[37]

To further the cause of church architecture, Charles D. Maginnis
wrote a concise, well illustrated article showing the advantages of

---

[34]Ibid., (February, 1905) p.117.
[35]The Monitor, (March 5, 1910)
[36]"The Reformation of Ecclesiastical Art," The Catholic World,
LXXI (July, 1900) 556.
[37]Ibid.

co-ordinating site, style, materials, masonry, mural and glass decorations to form an attractive structure.[38] To a generation brought up on House Beautiful and Architectural Forum, Maginnis' ideas seemed sound but simple, but, this was necessary advice for his contemporaries surrounded with horrible examples of poorly conceived buildings. The same reform was outlined by William Laurel Harris since "Church building which should be the most noble of the arts, often becomes the meanest."[39] Harris' analysis added the note that lasting results would not be obtained without the hearty support of the clergy.

Unfortunately, sculpture suffered in equal proportions. The effect was staggering. "Already a large number of our churches display in their frescoes and statuary a wearisome succession of stereotyped mediocrities whose production has been strictly mechanical."[40] There should be no place for "ready-made" statuary for "true art has to be achieved by real, personal, individual effort."[41] One step that would help restore Christian Art to its rightful sphere, was for the colleges and seminaries to give it "the attention it deserves."[42] The art critic, too, had caught the writer's urge "to do good."

[38]Charles D. Maginnis, "A Practical Talk on Church Building," The Catholic World, LXXVI (December, 1902) 369.

[39]William Laurel Harris, "A Modern Guild of Artists," The Catholic World, LXXVI (January, 1903) 438.

[40]Sadakichi Hartmann, "Ecclesiastical Sculpture in America," The Catholic World, LXXVII (September, 1903) 761.

[41]Ibid., p.767.

[42]Charles de Kay, "Christian Art: Its Status and Prospects in the United States," The Catholic World, LXXIV (October, 1901) 14.

Among the Catholics in the United States, the art critic, the writer, members of summer schools and reading circles, the teacher in the mission and the compiler of book lists, the convert made a notable contribution. With utmost zeal, the convert advanced the causes of the newly adopted faith. John Gilmary Shea recorded that the Oxford movement transferred to this country was responsible for influencing Bishop Levi Silliman Ives, Fathers Hecker and Hewit, and James A. McMaster to become Catholics.[43] Richard H. Clarke, in another complimentary article, praised the noted converts from Mother Elizabeth Seton and Fanny Allen through the years to the George Parsons Lathrops.[44] Ives with his New York Protectory for orphans and other distressed children; the literary contributions of Hecker, Hewit, McMaster, and Lathrop; and the sisterhoods established by Mother Seton and Rose Hawthorne Lathrop[45] illustrated several of the ways converts selected to serve their co-religionists. Among the literary figures presented earlier in this narrative, the converts included Orestes Brownson, Mrs. Dorsey, Christian Reid, Mary Agnes Tincker, Father Tabb, the Kilmers, Eliza Allen Starr, Charles Warren Stoddard, Frank H. Spearman and others.

---

[43]John Gilmary Shea, "Converts, their Influence and Work in this Country," American Catholic Quarterly Review, VIII (July, 1883) 522.

[44]Richard H. Clarke, "Our Converts," American Catholic Quarterly Review, XIX (January, 1894) 112-137.

[45]Rose Hawthorne Lathrop, following the death of her husband, George Parsons Lathrop, became Mother Alphonsa, foundress of the Sister Servants of Relief of the Third Order of St. Dominic, a society devoted to the caring of incurable cancer patients.

Equally interesting as these individual conversions, was the
reception of the Anglican Society of the Atonement into the Church.
The correspondence of Father Hudson revealed a part of the story.
From Graymoor, New York, early in April, 1908, Paul James Francis,
S.A., wrote to Father Hudson:

> Although I note a much more hopeful view of the subject of
> Corporate Reunion among later writers in the Catholic press,
> especially see (if you have not already done so) the very
> favorable recent articles in the Month, Tablet, and Ecclesias-
> tical Review. (sic.) I have often wondered why you, dear
> Rev. Father, more emphatically than any other of our Catholic
> Exchanges insist on the hopelessness of the Movement. In the
> present issue of the Ave Maria you say, 'The force may be
> expended in futile directions, not withstanding. It is only
> frankness to say that Rome will not, can not, minimize, or
> compromise. Anglicans are far more likely to enter the
> Church as individuals than in a body'. How can you be sure
> that Rome cannot compromise in matters of discipline, we are
> not asking compromises in doctrine.[46]

The next year, however, the same correspondent wrote that the
Society of the Atonement had been received into the Church; and,
then, he solicited Father Hudson's aid.

> It is the wish of those in authority that our two publica-
> tions, The Lamp and Rose Leaves, be continued. We shall
> no doubt suffer the loss of a large part of our Anglican
> constituency by the change, may I ask your help in more
> than retrieving this loss on the Catholic side. I hope to
> make The Lamp less controversial and more missionary in its
> character from now on, more a paper for lay folk; Rose
> Leaves will follow more in the footsteps of the Ave Maria,
> as particularly devoted to our Lady of the Atonement. Any
> advice as how to make either The Lamp or Rose Leaves more
> effective A.M.D.G. will be appreciated by me.[47]

---

[46]Paul James Francis, S.A., to the Rev. Daniel E. Hudson,
C.S.C.,(April 3, 1908) Hudson Papers. UNDA.
[47]Paul James Francis, S.A., to Rev. Daniel E. Hudson, C.S.C.,
(October 29, 1909) Hudson Papers. UNDA.

The Lamp and Rose Leaves were desirable publications. Moreover, in another field of endeavor, a most significant accomplishment in Catholic literary circles was the publishing of The Catholic Encyclopedia. Widely heralded at the time, it merited the recent approval of the Church historian of American Catholicism, Father John Tracy Ellis, who wrote:

> Finally, the greatest single monument to Catholic scholar-
> ship in the United States to date has undoubtedly been the
> Catholic Encyclopedia, and that magnificent achievement
> owes its existence, as it should have, to the combined
> efforts of a small group of learned laymen and priests,
> both secular and regular.[48]

Heading the editorial staff, which remained constant from beginning to end, was Dr. Charles G. Heberman,[49] librarian and Latin profes- sor at the College of the City of New York and a former president (1898) of the United States Catholic Historical Society. Two of his associates came from the Catholic University in Washington: Rt. Rev. Thomas J. Shahan, professor of Church History; and the Rev. Dr. Edward A. Pace, professor of Philosophy. The Jesuit editor, Father John J. Wynne, S.J., and Conde B. Pallen, Ph.D., completed the editorial board. Between January 11, 1905 and April 19, 1913, the Board held one hundred and thirty-four formal meetings; and, it was not until one year later that the Encyclopedia was completed.[50] However, the separate volumes were presented to the public as soon

---

[48]Rev. John Tracy Ellis, "American Catholics and the Intellectual Life," Thought, XXX (Autumn, 1955) 372,373.
[49]L.H., "Charles G. Hebermann," The Catholic Historical Review,
II (January, 1917) 440.
[50]The Catholic Encyclopedia and its Makers,   iii.

as they came from the press.

The need for a Catholic Encyclopedia was apparent. The Dolphin wrote that a carefully written encyclopedia published under Catholic auspices "would do all the work which half a dozen wide-awake Truth Societies can accomplish in the same direction."[51] Moreover, the secular encyclopedia contained an anti-Catholic bias, which even Catholic consulting editors could not remove. For example, Father Wynne took Appleton's to task for publishing biased articles allegedly having the approval of Mgr. John J. Keane. Father Wynne, in a letter to Father Hudson, declared that Appleton's were quite unjust

> ... to Mgr. Keane to emphasize his connections with the Cyclopedia as if he were really responsible for everything in it for and against the Catholic Church.[52]

Thus, The Catholic Encyclopedia came into existence to "give its readers full and authoritative information on the entire cycle of Catholic interests, action and doctrine."[53]

After editor Shahan became Bishop Shahan and rector of the Catholic University, he recalled his Encyclopedia work with pleasure and re-iterated its purpose.

> The work itself is destined to exert a great influence upon the non-Catholic people. By its use an evenly distributed leavening knowledge of the Catholic religion on the part of our Catholic press, our Catholic magazines, our Catholic

---

[51]The Dolphin, II (December, 1902) 731.
[52]Rev. John J. Wynne, S.J., to Rev. Daniel E. Hudson, C.S.C., (June 14, 1902) Hudson Papers. UNDA.
[53]The Catholic Encyclopedia and its Makers, iv.

laity, instructions and discussions, teachings of our
Sisters, all the vast amount of Catholic doctrine and
discipline will take on a certain even, regular, homo-
geneous character in the minds of our people. This is of
the greatest importance, if we are to do very great things
for the welfare of religion and particularly for the welfare
of the Catholic Church.[54]

This clarification of belief for Catholics and non-Catholics
alike also interested Georgina Pell Curtis, who wished to assist
"doubting souls" into the Church. The success of the English version of Roads to Rome, a collection of intimate stories relating
individual conversions, prompted her to solicit and edit[55] the
stories of American converts. Marked enthusiasm attended the publishing (1908) of Some Roads to Rome in America, so Miss Curtis
compiled a sequel (1914) Beyond the Road to Rome, which anticipated
some non-Catholic objections against the Church or the converts'
difficulties in adjusting to their newly found Faith.[56]

Wedged in between the "Roman Road" publication; was the appearance of The American Catholic Who's Who (1911). Miss Curtis, its
editor, stated

... that it is designed not to exploit the individual as such,
but to individualize him in order to show the concrete, to
each other and to the non-Catholic world, what Catholics have
done and are doing to add to the prestige, dignity, and power
of the Church.[57]

---

[54]Encyclopedia Day at Dunwoodie, New York, p.23.
[55]Georgina Pell Curtis, Some Roads to Rome in America, p.vii.
[56]Georgina Pell Curtis, Beyond the Road to Rome, p.viii.
[57]Georgina Pell Curtis, The American Catholic Who's Who,
Editor's Preface.

Judged from her editorial accomplishments, Miss Curtis worked
successfully to make Catholics and Catholicism better understood in
these United States. With a convert's zeal for further promoting
this understanding, she wrote to Father Hudson that her co-
religionists should enter the infant moving picture industry for the
good of all Americans, and especially the children. "Catholics
needed to step in, and take hold, and direct our share of it."[58]

Reviewing the individual and organizational efforts of this
period 1880-1915, the evidence indicated the Catholic participation
in the American desire for material and intellectual progress. The
Who's Who, Encyclopedia, summer schools, reading circles, and the
Catholic congresses demonstrated the ability of the clergy and
laity to provide a discipline productive of an educated, patriotic,
religious, American citizen.

---

[58]Georgina Pell Curtis to Rev. Daniel E. Hudson, C.S.C.,
(October 4, 1915) Hudson Papers. UNDA.

CHAPTER IX

CONCLUSION

Americans professing Catholicism, during the years 1880-1915, fashioned a quantity of literary work. In the happier days between the assassination of President Garfield and the sinking of the Lusitania, the American Catholics utilized the various literary forms to inspire, guide, and entertain their co-religionists. Fiction, poetry, essays and editorials came in abundance from their hearts and pens. The two acknowledged pioneer novelists, Mrs. Anna Hanson Dorsey and Mrs. Mary Anne Sadlier, revealed to their readers the beauties of their Faith and shared their advice regarding contemporary social problems. The assimilation of the Irish and German immigrants, the perils confronting both saloonkeepers and their patrons, and the converts' adjustment to their newly found religion were typical themes motivating the fiction of these good women.

The advance party, Mrs. Dorsey and Mrs. Sadlier, was joined later by the main body of Catholic women writers headed by Christian Reid and, perhaps, Mary Agnes Tincker. Unlike most of their female contemporaries, Christian Reid and Mary Agnes Tincker, at various times, attempted to write for the general public. Thus, they sublimated the goal of instruction to the one of entertainment with varied success. Entertainment, again, prompted the most widely heralded novelist of Catholic convictions, Francis Marion Crawford,

335

to write a novel a year, much to his fame and fortune. An excellent
story-teller, Crawford did not always satisfy the aspirations of
militant Catholics. Yet, Crawford served Catholicism well, particularly, when his desire to tell a good story did not conflict with
his religious belief, and thus had his admirers as well as his
critics among his co-religionists.

Several other converts followed in Crawford's direction. Henry
Harland wrote entertainingly of foreign Catholics; while Frank H.
Spearman treated of Catholicism in America, although his reputation
rested on the neutral ground of western and railroad stories. Still
another convert, Richard Malcolm Johnston, merited recognition as a
local colorist. However, the gracious "Colonel" Johnston, probably,
would have admitted that Kate Chopin, with her Creole and Acadian
short-stories, was the best Catholic writer of this school. Joel
Chandler Harris, although a convert in his lasy days on this earth,
did not figure in this estimation for his writings showed little to
indicate his drift toward Catholicism.

In another particular field, juvenile literature, Catholics
exhibited still more enthusiasm and competence. The famed Father
Finn presented an "ideal" to the American boy, so that they could be
influenced by healthy, fallible characters reacting to a Catholic
atmosphere. Father Finn and numerous other Americans bestowed their
approval upon Mrs. Mary T. Waggaman, whose attractive "juveniles"
entertained and edified so many Catholic children. Mrs. Waggaman
and Father Finn headed the list of juvenile fictionists. Many other

writers, whose talents were better adapted to other phases of
literature, wrote for the youngsters so important did they consider
the creation of desirable juvenile literature.

Among the other branches of literature, poetry received a full
measure of attention from the Catholics in America. Admittedly
mere verse-making passed for poetry, however, worthwhile poetry was
far from unknown. Together, poetry and verse-making were used to
honor the living and the dead and to praise or condemn existing
situations, as well as to express the true poetic muse. Patriotism
was the product of Father Abram Ryan, James Ryder Randall, and
Eleanor Cecelia Donnelly, so, that from their pens came praise for
the "Lost Cause," the injured state, and the departed American
Catholic heroes. For sheer patriotism, John Boyle O'Reilly was
their equal at any time. Moreover, he produced a penetrating
expression and a wider variety of experiences which enabled him to
reach many more of his American contemporaries. The popular appeal
of his subjects coupled to his vigorous expression were responsible
for his appearances in the better journals and upon the lecture
platforms. Still, O'Reilly's poetry lacked technical perfection.

This same criticism, however, was never levelled at the poetry
of Father Tabb and Louise Imogen Guiney. Father Tabb's quatrains
and sonnets exhibited his polished, precise technique, which presented his poems of nature and his religious poetry in such good
style. The courageous Miss Guiney, oblivious to popular appeal,
strove to present her feeling in the most perfect manner. True,

many of her expressions were archaic, mystical, beyond the ken of
her readers. Yet, she claimed distinction as a true minor poet inspired by the teachings of Catholicism. Joyce Kilmer, had he survived the war, might have surpassed both Father Tabb and Miss Guiney
as a positive influence. He shared their mutual regard for their
Faith and good poetry, while his interest in the common, everyday
things insured him of a greater audience appeal. Added to the works
of Tabb and Guiney and the potential of Kilmer were the effective
efforts of John Boyle O'Reilly, Thomas Daly, Eliza Allen Starr,
Eleanor Donnelly, Conde Pallen and Maurice Francis Egan to espouse
some worthwhile cause in the best verse possible. The beauty and
truth of Catholicism, the patriotism of Catholics, and the desire to
broaden the intellectual vistas of their co-religionists prompted
much versifying, the best of which might be considered poetry.

Even more suited to the critical appraisal of life in these
United States was the medium of the essay. Like many of their
Protestant neighbors, Catholics found numerous aspects of contemporary civilization to be particularly interesting. From warm
approval to acute disdain, the opinions varied. The best essayist
among the Catholics and, perhaps, all America, was the nimble
sharpshooter from Philadelphia, Agnes Repplier. She ranged all over
to criticize the sex-educationists and the defamers of New York City
as well as the parochial schools and controversial novels of her co-
religionists. Miss Repplier was not a "do-gooder;" however, she
was able to inject some thoughts of an American Catholic into the

general atmosphere of American Literature.

Two other women essayists approached the efforts of the talented Repplier. The versatile Katherine E. Conway, the journalist-poet associate of the colorful Boyle O'Reilly, used the fundamental approach to set her fellow Catholics right. Her little handbooks describing the social graces served as gentle reminders of the conduct to be expected from all ladies and gentlemen. Eliza Allen Starr, on the other hand, had a vast knowledge of the fine arts she wished to share with her fellow Americans. From her own St. Joseph's Cottage in Chicago, a pocket-sized art museum in itself, she came forth to lecture to interested mid-West audiences. This love for art and for the welfare of her audiences easily was discernible in her books and magazine articles.

Among the men, Brother Azarias, Conde Pallen, and Maurice Francis Egan composed essays of high calibre. The creator of a "how and what to read" handbook, Brother Azarias ably defended Christian literature and education so as to win the praise of the secular world. At the same time, the literary criticism of Egan and Pallen indicated to Catholics the knowledge, experience, and pleasure to be derived from the better books. On the defensive side, Dr. James J. Walsh and John A. Mooney were typical examples of well-grounded individuals ever willing to protect their religious principles from the slanders of an age. Two other specialists contributed to the cause of Catholic well-being. Father John Talbot Smith in the East and Charles Phillips in San Francisco examined every phase of the

American theatre to present a critical insight into the evils
threatening the stage. Every effort of the non-Catholic and Catholic
artist and producer to combat this trend was dutifully recorded.
Moreover, since many of the top-billings were of the Catholic persuasion, Father Smith and Editor Phillips gave particular notice not
only to their acts but also to their social life. In this fashion,
did they hope to remove the stigma attached to those working on the
"wicked, wicked stage." Equally valuable were their recommendations
promoting the work of the worthwhile actors and producers. Thus,
were these essayists and critics, aided by numerous others of their
co-religionists, able to present Catholic opinions regarding the
scenes about them.

As vocal as any laymen or priests, the high-ranking prelates
likewise advanced their counsel to those under their jurisdiction.
Usually, their writings concentrated on three objectives: the
creation of citizenship and patriotism among the faithful; the explanation of Catholicity and the defense of Christianity; and the
promotion of worthwhile cultural traits and educational systems. As
writers, Cardinal Gibbons, Archbishop Ireland, and Bishop Spalding
were the best known among the American hierarchy. While the literary
Cardinal Gibbons aspired for converts and the better training of his
beloved clergy and Archbishop Ireland's articles bore the stamp of
patriotism with a religious imprint, the Bishop of Peoria, John
Lancaster Spalding, was acknowledged the most talented of the
essayists among the hierarchy. As one interested in the cultural

advancement of his people, the perfection of schools, the rejection
of Socialism, and the achievement of harmony between capital and
labor, Bishop Spalding, in one thought-provoking essay after
another, fashioned an intellectual basis for a Catholic approach to
life in the United States. The other members of the hierarchy,
admittedly no Bishops Spalding in expression, nevertheless, lead
their fellow Catholics to make a positive contribution to the
civilization about them.

Another positive force shaping American opinion came from the
many laymen and priests editing and writing for Catholic periodicals.
Early in 1865, The Catholic World and the Ave Maria came into existence and have remained in operation until the present day. Each
was fortunate in having at its helm a talented priest-editor well-
in-touch with the pulsating civilization about him. Father Hecker
of The Catholic World brought the convert's zeal into full play as
he strove to make Catholicism better understood and its adherents
better informed.

In like manner, the Ave Maria's Father Hudson conducted a world-
wide correspondence as he encouraged Catholics to use their literary
talents. Soliciting articles, supplying advice and encouragement,
and advancing money to the closely budgeted writers, Father Hudson
gave support to and drew support from all Catholicism from a
cardinal like Gasquet to the poor unfortunate in jail. Happily,
there were other editors eager to match the distinguished pace set
by Father Hecker and Father Hudson. Monsignor Corcoran and his

associates, in The American Catholic Quarterly Review, published a
quality magazine. Securing the services of the more talented and
better informed Catholic writers, both here and abroad, The American
Catholic Quarterly Review expounded authoritative information regarding philosophy, theology, literature, science, religion, history,
and biography.

The conservative tone of The American Catholic Quarterly Review
was reproduced in the American Ecclesiastical Review. It was the
good intention of its founder and long-time editor, Father Heuser,
to furnish the clergy in America with a broad review of current
literature as well as to continue their technical education with
intriguing articles of particular interest to them. The quiet conservatism of The American Catholic Quarterly Review and the American
Ecclesiastical Review stood in sharp contrast to the sharp,
opinionated criticism created in the magazines of Thorne and Peruss.
Critical of their fellow Catholics and of each other, Thorne and
Preuss wasted no time in making known their likes and dislikes. Yet,
despite the vituperation generated by Thorne's Globe and Preuss'
Review, American Catholics had much to learn from their caustic
comment.

A much gentler and a more systematic program for learning was
devised by Warren E. Mosher, editor of The Catholic Reading Circle
Review. The fundamental aspects of myriad subjects were treated
within the pages of Mosher's magazine. Editor Mosher realized that
the simple, basic approach to literature and history and to science

and religion complied with educational status of many of his co-
religionists.

Other magazines hoped to continue this raising of the cultural
level, but, they considered it secondary to the devotional practices
they were cultivating. The Rosary, The Magnificat, and The
Messenger of the Sacred Heart belonged to the upper echelon of the
devotional magazines. Mention of The Messenger of the Sacred Heart
recalled the fact that it, in many ways, was responsible for the
creation of another fine Jesuit magazine, America. Given shape by
Father Wynne and continuity by the veteran Thomas Meehan, this news-
journal and review met the accelerated demands of American civilization by publishing a weekly commentary in length on current affairs
together with a brief survey of literary developments.

America, however, did not replace the Catholic newspapers
scattered about the United States. Edited by priests and laymen
equally desirous of informing and educating their fellow Americans,
these papers, oftentimes, portrayed a particular men's bias and
personality. The Western Watchman was Father Phelan. Critical of
the Germans and the Republicans, never hesitating to admonish all
Catholics from archbishops to the laity, the Western Watchman enjoyed a national reputation. The New World displayed William
Dillon's ever-present interest in politics and economics and Charles
O'Malley's literary bent. Charles Phillips' great liking for the
stage constantly erupted in The Monitor with praise and criticism
for plays and players. The title of Humphrey Desmond's paper, The

Catholic Citizen, gave the key to this man's fond desire of molding his co-religionists into being the first citizens of this republic.

The Catholic newspapers, in response to the stimuli about them, commented on temperance, women's rights, bimetallism, immigration, the latest literary contribution, the new play, and other conversation pieces. Among the better known papers observing these phenomena, Patrick Hickey's Catholic Review earned the bouquet of being a model Catholic newspaper much in advance of its time. The Boston Pilot developed by Patrick Donahoe, rose to a greater stature under the triumvirate of Boyle O'Reilly, Roche, and Miss Conway. The New York Freeman's Journal, during the various stages of its career, boasted of a capable, colorful editor whether it was James A. McMaster, Austin E. Ford, or Father Louis A. Lambert.

The Catholic magazine and newspaper promoted the sale and reading of works by their co-religionists, promulgated their views on current topics, and above all, defended the Church. At times, some editors were critical and a few unkind as they splintered the literary efforts of Catholics and non-Catholics alike. Certain works were labelled "terrible" and justly so, while others suffered from a wholesale condemnation. On the other hand, the better books survived such onslaughts, so, that the residue given to the Catholic reader constituted a more concentrated good reading. The Catholic editor was more of an individual than a type. Strong in opinion, if not always correct, each in his way, toiled diligently to make his co-religionists aware of the literature, religion, politics, and economic levels surrounding them all.

The supporting background attending this growth of Catholic writing included several worthwhile institutions. For example, certain scholars, librarians, and library associations compiled lists indicating the availability of Catholic books. The reading circles and summer schools provided an increasing body of educated men and women concerned with the intellectual growth of the Church in the United States. As a rule, the convert, too, was likely to be an educated person, driven by faith and knowledge to make his or her contemporaries aware of the beauty, literature, art, and architecture to be found in the Church. Men like John Gilmary Shea and Richard H. Clarke, so prominent in the founding of an early Catholic historical society, recognized and wrote of the converts' contributions.

Another phase of this background, the Baltimore Lay Congress of 1889 and the Columbian Catholic Congress of 1893 gave the entire country the opportunity to witness the assemblies of the more talented laymen and clerics, who considered their obligations and evaluated the Church's position with the welfare of all Americans in mind. Although the congresses, reading circles, and summer schools were notable achievements, the lasting creation of this era was The Catholic Encyclopedia. Highly praised then and now, this monumental work organized the many facts and facets of Catholicism so that they were easily accessible to the curious and the fair-minded. Nor should Georgina Pell Curtis be forgotten for her editing of the

American Catholic Who's Who as it forged another cuirass of intellectual armor.

Everything considered, these American writers and their sup-
porters made a grand effort to bring forth literary material stamped
in some way or another as Catholic. Unfortunately, they failed to
create an atmosphere attractive and stimulating enough to hold such
figures as F. Scott Fitzgerald, Theodore Dreiser, Eugene O'Neill,
Philip Barry, Ernest Hemingway, and Will Durant,[1] all of Catholic
birth and separated from the Church. In spite of this regrettable
short coming, The Era of Good Intentions recorded several
accomplishments.

For over thirty-five years, the men and women writing had the
good sense to promote the Catholic appreciation for life and literature. Some unlettered Catholics became more cultured in response to
the handbooks and essays pointing the way. In a more formal fashion,
the reading circles and summer schools brought them to a still
higher educational level. At the base of this drive for culture,
the Catholic novelists, poets, essayists, and editors provided the
hint, the insight, and even the cajolery necessary to arouse an
interest in the better books, the right picture, the true architecture, and the worthwhile play. Again, the realization was instilled
into the Catholic body that it was an integral part of a great and

---

[1]Rev. Calvert Alexander, S.J., The Catholic Literary Revival,
p.226.

growing nation and that its members were Americans with obligations
and opportunities.

Some of their creations have lasted. The Encyclopedia, The
Who's Who, and the records and studies of the various learned
societies have proven useful to later generations. Among the
fiction-makers, none, like Herman Melville, have been rediscovered.
They were not that good; but, in his day, Marion Crawford held his
own on the best-seller lists with the American Winston Churchills
and the Elinor Glynns. Kate Chopin's short-stories read well but
she lost the will to write far too soon.

Among true poets, more than a polite interest was evoked by the
mention of Father Tabb, Miss Guiney, and the promising Kilmer.
Miss Repplier lead a galaxy of essayists including laymen, priests,
and prelates. Moreover, the Catholic editor never received a
fraction of the rewards, monetary or otherwise, which should have
been his for creating an informative, attractive, opinionated
journalism. These Catholics wrote great quantities with flashes of
quality and genius. They were attuned to the buoyant, optimistic,
reforming milieu, which urged them to coerce their co-religionists
into becoming educated Americans and fervent Christians in THE ERA
OF GOOD INTENTIONS.

BIBLIOGRAPHY

UNPUBLISHED SOURCES

The following letters were written to the Reverend Daniel E. Hudson, C.S.C., and are presented with the Hudson Papers, University of Notre Dame Archives.

Bandini, Rev. Peter. January 7, 1909.
Benziger Brothers (Cincinnati), March 9, 1889.
Bradford, Gamaliel, Jr. February 6, 1913.
Brown, Mary Josephine. August 26, 1888.
Brownson, Henry F. March 14, 1903.
Crawford, Elizabeth Marion. May 29, 1909.
Curtis, Georgina Pell. October 4, 1915.
Dahlgren, Madeline Vinton. September 19, 1885.
Donnelly, Eleanor C. January 13, 1886.
Dorsey, Mrs. Anna Hanson. March 27, 1887; March 13, 1878;
    February 11, 1880; January 2, 1877; May 20, 1879; June 10,
    1879; June 27, 1879; March 13, 1886; March 1, 1886.
Dorsey, Ella Lorraine. July 18, 1890; September 2, 1888;
    September 10, 1910; August 19, 1914.
Egan, Maurice Francis. September 30, 1913.
Fanning,   A. April 27, 1908; May 8, 1908.
Fieg, Joseph F. February 13, 1908.
Francis, S. A., Paul James. April 3, 1908; October 29, 1909.
Furey, Francis. November 28, 1910.
Gasquet, Dom F. Aidan. January 8, 1908.
Guiney, Louise Imogen. January 22, 1909; July 13, 1911; March
    4, 1910; September 17, 1909.
Kennedy, Thomas F. June 4, 1910.
Kling, Lucile Nuncia. November 13, 1910.
Lindsey, Benjamin B. July 8, 1910.
Longhead, Flora Haives. April 4, 1908.
Lucasz, T.A.D. October 8, 1881.
Maes, Bishop Camillus P. Undated.
McCullagh, Francis. January 15, 1901.
The MacMillan Company. June 6, 1913.
McQuaid, Bishop Bernard J. February 18, 1908.
O'Shea, John J. April 23, 1910.
O'Shea, William J. September 4, 1909.
Putnam's, G.P. Sond. October 28, 1914; November 4, 1914.
Ryan, Mrs. John A. March 21, 1908.
Ryder, Eliot. January 30, 1886.
Sadlier, Anna. February 8, 1909.

Seawell, Molly Elliot. July 29, 1911.
Shahan, Rev. Thomas A. October 20, 1909.
Shippen, Eugene R. April 20, 1910.
Spalding, Bishop John Lancaster. January 21, 1901; August 18, 1901.
Spearman, Frank H. July 14, 1910; February 16, 1908; May 27, 1908.
Starr, Eliza Allen. March 6, 1879; March 23, 1881; July 16, 1882.
Stoddard, Charles Warren. January 26, 1901.
Tiernan, Frances Christine Fisher. February 9, 1886; February 27, 1909.
Waggaman, Mary T. December 7, 1911; December 12, 1912.
Walsh, Dr. James J. September 3, 1907.
Walsh, Thomas. January 9, 1908.
Ward, William Hayes. August 25, 1912.
Winter, L. P. March 25, 1913.
Wynne, S.J., Rev. John J. June 14, 1902.

Hecker, Rev. Isaac T. Letters to Orestes Brownson, August 26, 1869; January 30, 1871; January 8, 1872. Brownson Papers. University of Notre Dame Archives.
Hudson, Rev. Daniel E. Letters to Charles Warren Stoddard, December 26, 1905; December 4, 1906; April 27, 1907. Hudson Papers. University of Notre Dame Archives.
Kilmer, Joyce to Rev. Charles L. O'Donnell, C.S.C., April 23, 1914; December 19, 1914; May 8, 21, 1915; November 9, 1915; March 9, 1916; April 10, 1916; June 14, 1916; March 19, 1917.
Masters, Herman. Letter to Mary T. Waggaman, February 10, 1915. Hudson Papers. University of Notre Dame Archives.
Starr, Eliza Allen. Letter to James F. Edwards, April 6, 1886. Edwards Papers. University of Notre Dame Archives.

BOOKS, PAMPHLETS

A Directive List of Catholic Books and Authors. Baltimore: John Murphy and Co., 1893.
Alderman, Edwin Anderson; Harris, Joel Chandler; Kent, Charles William. Editors. Library of Southern Literature. 13 vols. New Orleans, Atlanta: Martin and Hoyt Co., 1909-1913. Vol. X.
Alexander, S.J., Rev. Calvert. The Catholic Literary Revival. Milwaukee: Bruce Publishing Co., 1935.
Allen, Gay Wilson. American Prosody. New York: American Book Co., 1935.
A Memorial of John Boyle O'Reilly from the City of Boston. Boston: By Order of the Common Council, 1890.

Baumgartner, Appolinaris W. Catholic Journalism, A Study of
    Its Development in the United States, 1879-1930. New York:
    Columbia University Press, 1931.
Becker, Kate Harbes. Biography of Christian Reid. n.p., n.d.
Beer, Thomas. The Mauve Decade. New York: A. A. Knopf, 1926.
Benziger Brothers. A Round Table of Representative American
    Catholic Novelists. New York: Benziger Brothers, 1896.
_____. The Best Stories by the Foremost Catholic Authors
    with an Introduction by Maurice Francis Egan. 10 vols. New
    York: Benziger Brothers, 1910. vol. I.
Brooks, Van Wyck. New England: Indian Summer. New York:
    E. P. Dutton, 1940.
Brown, S.J., Rev. Stephen J.; McDermott, Thomas. A Survey of
    Catholic Literature. Milwaukee: Bruce Publishing Co., 1945.
Browne, Francis Fisher. Bugle Echoes: A Collection of Poems of
    the Civil War, Northern and Southern. New York: White,
    Stokes and Allen, 1886.
Bugg, Lelia Hardin. The Correct Thing for Catholics. New York:
    Benziger Brothers, 1891.
Cavanaugh, C.S.C., Rev. John William. The Reverend John Talbot
    Smith. Notre Dame: n.p., 1924.
_____. Father Zahm. Pamphlet. New York: The Catholic
    World, 1922. Reprint.
Chatard, Bishop Francis Silas. Occasional Essays. New York:
    Catholic Publication Society, 1894.
Comerford, Thomas J. Souvenir of the Dual Jubilee; Consecration
    of the Rt. Rev. M. J. Hoban, D.D. (1896-1921), Erection of
    the Scranton Diocese (1868-1918). Scranton, Pa.: The
    International Text Book Press, 1922.
Conway, Katherine E. A Lady and Her Letters. Boston: Pilot
    Publishing Co., 1895.
_____. In the Footprints of the Good Shepherd. New York:
    Convent of the Good Shepherd, 1907.
_____. Making Friends and Keeping Them. Boston: John
    T. Flynn, 1895.
_____. On the Sunrise Slope. New York: Catholic
    Publication Society, 1881.
_____. Questions of Honor in the Christian Life. (2nd
    ed.) Boston: Pilot Publishing Co., 1895.
_____. The Christian Gentlewoman and the Social Apostalate.
    Boston: John T. Flynn and Co., 1904.
_____. The Color of Life. Boston: John T. Flynn and Co.,
    1927.
_____. The Way of the World and Other Ways. Boston:
    Pilot Publishing Co., 1900.
Coolbrith, Ina. Collector. Poems of Charles Warren Stoddard.
    New York: John Lane Co., 1917.

Cronin, Rev. Patrick. Memorial of the Life and Labors of St. Rev. Stephen Vincent Ryan, D.D., C.M. Second Bishop of Buffalo, New York. Buffalo: Buffalo Catholic Publication Society, 1896.

Crowley, Rev. Denis Oliver; Doyle, Charles Anthony. A Chaplet of Verse by California Catholic Writers. San Francisco: Diepenbrook and Co., 1889.

Crowley, Richard F. The Episcopal Silver Jubilee of the Most Reverend Patrick John Ryan, D.D., L.L.D., Archbishop of Philadelphia. Philadelphia: St. Dominic's Rectory, 1897.

Cullen, James B. The Story of the Irish in Boston. Boston: J. B. Cullen Co., 1889.

Curtis, Georgina Pell. Beyond the Road to Rome. St. Louis: B. Herder, 1914.

_____. Some Roads to Rome in America. 2nd ed., St. Louis: B. Herder, 1910.

_____. Editor. The American Catholic Who's Who. St. Louis: B. Herder, 1911.

Dahlgren, Madeline Vinton. The Social-Official Etiquette of the United States. 6th ed. Baltimore: John Murphy and Co., 1894.

Desmond, Humphrey J. A Reading Circle Manual. Milwaukee: The Citizen Co., 1903.

_____. The New Laity and the Old Standards. Philadelphia: John Joseph McVey, 1914.

Donnelly, Eleanor C. Crowned with Stars. Notre Dame, Indiana: Notre Dame University, 1881.

_____. Poems by Eleanor Donnelly with an Introduction by the Very Rev. Daniel I. McDermott. Philadelphia: H. L. Kilner, 1881.

Dorsey, Anna Hanson. Nora Brady's Vow. Philadelphia: J. B. Lippincott and Co., 1869.

_____. The Flemings. New York: P. O'Shea, 1869.

_____. The Old Gray Rosary. New York: P. O'Shea, n.d.

_____. The Oriental Pearl. Baltimore: John Murphy, 1848.

_____. Warp and Woof. Baltimore: John Murphy, 1887.

_____. Zoe's Daughter. Baltimore: John Murphy and Co., 1888.

Dorsey, Ella Lorraine. Jet the War Mule. Notre Dame, Indiana: Ave Maria, 1894.

_____. Midshipman Bob. Notre Dame, Indiana: Joseph A. Lyons, 1887.

Driscoll, Annette L. Literary Convert Women. Manchester, New Hampshire: The Magnificat Press, 1928.

Egan, Maurice Francis. A Gentleman. New York: Benziger Brothers, 1893.

_____. Lectures on English Literature. New York: W. H. Sadlier, 1889.

Egan, Maurice Francis. Recollections of a Happy Life. New
York: George H. Doran Co., 1924.
_____. The Ghost in Hamlet and other Essays in Comparative
Literature. Chicago: A. C. McClurg, 1906.
_____. The Watson Girls. Philadelphia: H. L. Kilmer,
1900.
Elliott, Maude Howe. My Cousin Marion Crawford. New York:
MacMillan, 1934.
Elliott, C.S.P., Rev. Walter. The Life of Father Hecker. New
York: The Columbus Press, 1891.
Ellis, Rev. John Tracy. The Life of James Cardinal Gibbons.
2 vols. Milwaukee: Bruce Publishing Co., 1952, vol. II.
Encyclopedia Day at Dunwoodie, February 4, 1918. New York:
The Encyclopedia Press, 1918.
The Catholic Encyclopedia and its Makers. New York: The
Encyclopedia Press, 1917.
Fahey, Rev. Martin E. Father Smith and the Catholic Actors
Guild of America. New York: Catholic Summer School of
America, 1924.
Farrelly, Sister M. Natalena. Thomas Francis Meehan (1854-1942),
A Memoir. New York: The United States Catholic Historical
Society, 1944.
Faulkner, Harold U. The Quest for Social Justice, 1898-1914.
New York: The MacMillan Co., 1931.
Frawley, S.S.J., Sr. Mary Alphonse. Patrick Donahoe. The
Catholic University of America Studies in American Church
History. Washington, D.C.: Catholic University of America,
1946.
Garvey, Literary Society. Mariale. Loretto, Pennsylvania:
St. Francis Seminary, 1930.
Gibbons, James Cardinal. A Retrospect of Fifty Years.
Baltimore: J. Murphy and Co., 1916.
_____. Discourses and Sermons for Every Sunday and
Principal Festivals of the Year. Baltimore: J. Murphy and
Co., 1908.
_____. Our Christian Heritage. Baltimore: J. Murphy and
Co., 1889.
_____. The Ambassador of Christ. Baltimore: J. Murphy and
Co., 1896.
_____. The Faith of Our Fathers. Baltimore: J. Murphy and
Co., 1892.
Guilday, Rev. Peter. Editor. The National Pastorals of the
American Hierarchy (1792-1919). Washington, D.C.: National
Catholic Welfare Council, 1923.
Guiney, Grace. Editor. Happy Ending. The Collected Lyrics of
Louise Imogen Guiney. New edition. Boston: Houghton-
Mifflin, 1927.
_____. Letters of Louise Imogen Guiney. 2 vols. New York:
Harper and Brothers, 1926.

Haley, Emilie Louise. Books by Catholic Authors in the
Cleveland Public Library. Cleveland: The Cleveland Public
Library, 1911.

Harland, Henry. The Cardinal's Snuff Box. New York: John
Lane, 1900.

_____. The Lady Paramount. New York: John Lane, 1902.

Hoehn, O.S.B., Rev. Matthew. Editor. Catholic Authors,
Contemporary Biographical Sketches, 1930-1947. Newark:
St. Mary's Abbey, 1948.

de Hovre, Rev. Franz. Catholicism in Education. Translated by
Rev. Edward B. Jordan. New York: Benziger Brothers, 1934.

Hubbell, Jay B. The South in American Literature, 1607-1900.
Durham, North Carolina: Duke University Press, 1954.

Hughes, William M. Publisher. Three Great Events in the History
of the Catholic Church in the United States. Detroit:
William H. Hughes, 1889.

Ireland, Archbishop John. The Church and Modern Society. 2 vols.
Chicago: D. H. McBride, 1896. St. Paul: Pioneer Press,
1904. vols. I,II.

Kunitz, Stanley J.; Haycroft, Howard. Editors. American
Authors, 1600-1900. New York: H. W. Wilson Co., 1938.

Laetare Medalist Dossier. Pamphlet. The Laetare Medal:
America's Golden Rose. Notre Dame, Indiana: University of
Notre Dame Archives.

La Farge, S.J., Rev. John. The Manner is Ordinary. New York:
Harcourt Brace, 1954.

Lavell, Mgr. Michael J. Monsignor Lavell's Eulogy. New York:
The Catholic Summer School of America, 1924.

Litz, Francis A. Father Tabb, A Study of His Life and Works.
Baltimore: Johns Hopkins Press, 1923.

_____. The Poetry of Father Tabb. New York: Dodd, Mead
Co., 1928.

Litz, Francis E. Letters: Grave and Gay and other Prose of
John Bannister Tabb. Washington, D.C.: Catholic University
of America Press, 1950.

Lord, Robert H.; Sexton, John E.; Harrington, Edward T. History
of the Archdiocese of Boston. 3 vols. Boston: Sheed and
Ward, 1944.

Manly, Louise. Southern Literature: From 1579-1895. Richmond,
Virginia: B. F. Johnson Publishing Co., 1895.

Maynard, Theodore. The Story of American Catholicism. New
York: The MacMillan Co., 1949.

McDermott, William A. Down at Caxton's. Baltimore: John
Murphy and Co., 1895.

McGovern, Rev. James. Editor. The Life and Letters of Eliza
Allen Starr. Chicago: The Lakeside Press, 1904.

Mott, Frank Luther. A History of American Magazines, 1865-1885.
3 vols. New York: D. Appleton and Co.; Harvard University
Press, 1938. vol. III.

Moynihan, Mgr. James H. *The Life of Archbishop Ireland*. New
  York: Harper, 1953.

Mullany, F.S.C., Brother Azarias. *Books and Reading*. New York:
  The Cathedral Library Association, 1896.

_____. *Essays Educational*. Chicago: D. H. McBride and Co.,
  1896.

_____. *Cloistral Schools*. Philadelphia: The Dolphin
  Press, 1906.

_____. *The Primary Schools in the Middle Ages*. Chicago:
  Catholic Truth Society, n.d.

Musser, Benjamin,Francis. *Franciscan Poets*. New York: The
  MacMillan Co., 1933.

O'Conor, S.J., Rev. J. F. X. *Reading and the Mind, with Something to Read*. New York: Benziger Brothers, 1893.

*Official Report of the Proceedings of the Catholic Congress Held
  at Baltimore, Md., Nov. 11th and 12th, 1889*. Detroit:
  William B. Hughes, 1889.

O'Neil, O.P., Rev. James Louis. *Why, When, How, and What We
  Ought to Read*. Boston: Thomas B. Noonan and Co., 1893.

O'Reilly, John Boyle. *In Bohemia*. Boston: The Pilot
  Publishing Co., 1886.

Pahorezki, O.S.F., Sr. M. Sevina. *The Social and Political
  Activities of William James Onahan*. Washington, D.C.:
  Catholic University of America, 1942.

Painter, Franklin Verzelius Newton. *Poets of the South*. New
  York: American Book Co., 1903.

Pallen, Conde. *Collected Poems*. New York: P. J. Kenedy and
  Sons, 1915.

Parks, Edd Winfield. *Southern Poets*. American Writers Series.
  New York: American Book Co., 1936.

Parrington, Vernon Louis. *The Beginnings of Critical Realism in
  America, 1860-1920*. Vol. III of *Main Currents in American
  Thought*. New York: Harcourt Brace and Co., 1930.

Pattee, Fred Louis. *The Development of the American Short
  Story*. New York: Harper and Brothers, 1923.

_____. *The New American Literature, 1890-1930*. New York:
  The Century Co., 1930.

Phelan, George F. *Gleanings From Our Own Fields Being
  Selections from American Catholic Poets*. New York: P.
  O'Shea, 1881.

Pine, M.S. *John Bannister Tabb, the Priest-Poet*. Washington,
  D.C.: Georgetown Visitation Convent, 1915.

*Progress of the Catholic Church in America and the Great
  Columbian Congress of 1893*. 4th ed. 2 vols. Chicago:
  John S. Hyland, 1897.

Quinn, Arthur Hobson. *American Fiction, An Historical and
  Critical Survey*. New York: D. Appleton Century and Co.,
  1936.

Rankin, Daniel S. *Kate Chopin and Her Creole Stories.*
Philadelphia: University of Pennsylvania Press, 1932.
Reid, Christian. *A Child of Mary.* Notre Dame, Indiana: Ave
Maria, 1885.
_____. *A Daughter of Bohemia.* New York: D. Appleton,
1873.
_____. *A Little Maid of Arcady.* Philadelphia: H. L. Kilner
and Co., 1893.
_____. *Armine.* New York: Catholic Publication Society,
1884.
_____. *Carmela.* Notre Dame, Indiana: Ave Maria, 1891.
_____. *Grace Morton.* Philadelphia: Peter F. Cunningham,
1888.
_____. *Heart of Steel.* New York: D. Appleton, 1882.
_____. *His Victory.* Notre Dame: Ave Maria, 1887.
_____. *Mabel Lee.* New York: D. Appleton, 1871.
_____. *Morton House.* New York: D. Appleton, 1871.
_____. *Secret Bequest.* Notre Dame: Ave Maria, 1915.
_____. *The Light of the Vision.* Notre Dame: Ave Maria,
1911.
_____. *Valerie Aylmer.* New York: D. Appleton, 1870.
_____. *Vera's Charge.* Notre Dame: Ave Maria, 1907.
Reilly, John T. *Collections and Recollections in the Life and
Times of Cardinal Gibbons.* 3 vols. Martinsburg, West
Virginia: Herald Print, 1892-1895. Vol. II.
Repplier, Agnes. *A Book of Famous Verse.* Boston: Houghton
Mifflin Co., 1892.
_____. *A Happy Half-Century and Other Essays.* Boston:
Houghton Mifflin Co., 1908.
_____. *Americans and Others.* Boston: Houghton Mifflin
Co., 1912.
_____. *Books and Men.* Boston: Houghton Mifflin Co.,
1888.
_____. *Compromises.* Boston: Houghton Mifflin Co., 1904.
_____. *Counter Currents.* Boston: Houghton Mifflin Co.,
1916.
_____. *Essays in Idleness.* Boston: Houghton Mifflin Co.,
1893.
_____. *Essays in Minature.* Boston: Houghton Mifflin Co.,
1892.
_____. *In Our Convent Days.* Boston: Houghton Mifflin
Co., 1905.
_____. *In the Dozy Hours and Other Papers.* Boston:
Houghton Mifflin Co., 1894.
_____. *Philadelphia, the Place and the People.* New York:
The MacMillan Co., 1898.
_____. *Points of View.* Boston: Houghton Mifflin Co.,
1891.

Repplier, Agnes. The Fireside Sphinx. Boston: Houghton
Mifflin Co., 1901.

_____. Varia. Boston: Houghton Mifflin Co., 1897.

Roche, James Jeffrey. Life of John Boyle O'Reilly. New York:
Cassell Publishing Co., 1891.

Ryan, Rev. Abram J. Poems: Patriotic, Religious, Miscellaneous. 1896 ed. New York: P. J. Kenedy and Sons, 1896.

Ryan, Marion Muir Richardson. Shadows of the Sunset and Other
Poems. By the author, 1918.

Ryder, Eliot. The Household Library of Catholic Poets from
Chaucer to the Present Day. Notre Dame, Indiana: Joseph A.
Lyons, 1881.

Sadlier, Mrs. James. The Knout, A Tale of Poland. Translated
by Mrs. James Sadlier. Philadelphia: Peter F. Cunningham,
1856.

_____. Aunt Honor's Keepsake. New York: D. and J.
Salier, 1890.

_____. Bessie Conway. New York: D. and J. Sadlier, 1885.

_____. Con O'Regan. New York: D. and J. Sadlier, 1885.

_____. New Lights or Life in Galway. New York: D. and J.
Sadlier, 1885.

_____. Old and New. New York: D. and J. Sadlier, 1885.

_____. The Blakes and the Flanagans. New York:
D. and J. Sadlier, 1873.

_____. The Fate of Father Sheehy. New York: D. and J.
Sadlier, 1863.

_____. The Young Ladies Reader, Compiled and Arranged for
Advanced Classes. New York: D. and J. Sadlier, 1885.

Schuster, George N. The Catholic Church and Current Literature.
New York: The MacMillan Co., 1930.

Schuster, J. Illustrated Bible History of the Old and New
Testaments for the Use of Catholic Schools. New York:
William H. Sadlier, 1889.

Seraphine, O. St. U., Mother. Immortelles of Catholic Columbian
Literature. Chicago: D. H. McBride, 1897.

Sharp, Mgr. John K. History of the Diocese of Brooklyn, 1853-
1953. 2 vols. New York: Fordham University Press, 1954.
Vol. I.

Smith, Albert E.; Fitzpatrick, Vincent de P. Cardinal Gibbons,
Churchman and Citizen. Baltimore: O'Donovan Brothers, 1921.

Smith, Rev. John Talbot. A Woman of Culture. New York:
William H. Young, 1897.

_____. Brother Azarias. New York: William H. Young, 1897.

_____. His Honor the Mayor and Other Tales. New York:
The Catholic Publication Society, 1892.

_____. List of Catholic Writers of Fiction. Pamphlet.
New York: Columbian Reading Union, 1892.

_____. Saranac. New York: William H. Young, 1897.

Smith, Rev. John Talbot. The Parish Theatre. New York:
Longmans, Green and Co., 1917.
Spalding, Bishop John Lancaster. Opportunity and Other Essays
and Addresses. Chicago: D. H. McClurg, 1900.
_____. Socialism and Labor and Other Arguments. Chicago:
D. H. McClurg, 1902.
_____. Thoughts and Theories of Life and Education.
4th ed. Chicago: D. H. McClurg, 1904.
Spearman, Frank H. Carmen of the Rancho. New York: Doubleday,
Doran, 1937.
_____. Flambeau Jim. New York: Scribner's, 1927.
_____. The Marriage Verdict. New York: Scribner's, 1923.
Starke, Aubrey Harrison. Sidney Lanier, A Biographical and
Critical Study. Chapel Hill: The University of North
Carolina, 1933.
Starr, Eliza Allen. Patron Saints. Baltimore: John B. Piet,
1881.
_____. Pilgrims and Shrines. 2 vols. Chicago: Union
Catholic Publication Society, 1883. By the Author, 1885.
Vols. I,II.
_____. Poems by Eliza Allen Starr. Philadelphia:
H. McGrath, 1867.
_____. The Archangels and the Guardian Angels in Art.
Chicago: By the Author, 1899.
Stedman, Laura; Gould, George M. The Life and Letters of Edmund
Clarence Stedman. 2 vols. New York: Moffat, Yard and Co.,
1910. Vol. II.
Tabb, Jennie M. Father Tabb, His Life and Work. Boston: The
Stratford Co., 1922.
Talbot, Rev. Francis X. The American Book of Verse. New York:
The American Press, 1928.
The Baltimore Publishing Company. The Memorial Volume, A
History of the Third Plenary Council of Baltimore November 9;
December 7, 1884. Baltimore: 1885.
T'Serclaes de Wommerson, Monseigneur Charles. The Life and
Labors of Leo XIII with a Summary of His Important Letters,
Addresses, Encyclicals Edited and Extended by Maurice Francis
Egan. Chicago: Rand, McNally, 1903.
Untermeyer, Louis. Editor. Modern American Poetry. 4th rev.
ed. New York: Harcourt, Brace and Co., 1930.
Wagenknecht, Edward. Calvalcade of the American Novel. New
York: Henry Holt and Co., 1952.
Weninger, Francis Xavier. Centennial Address to the Catholics
of the United States. New York: Hickey and Co., 1876.
White, James A. The Founding of Cliff Haven, Early Years of the
Catholic Summer School of America. New York: The United
States Catholic Historical Society, 1950.
Will, Allen Sinclair. Life of Cardinal Gibbons, Archbishop of
Baltimore. 2 vols. New York: E. H. Dutton, 1922. Vol. I.

Woillez, Madame. The Orphan of Moscow. Translated by Mrs.
James Sadlier. New York: D. and J. Sadlier, 1849.
Wood, Clement. Poets of America. New York: E. H. Dutton,
1925.
The Xavier Alumni Sodality. Fifty Years in Conflict and
Triumph, Golden Jubilee of Rev. John J. Wynne, S.J. New
York: The Loughlin Press, 1927.
Zwierlein, Frederick J. Life and Letters of Bishop McQuaid.
3 vols. Rochester, New York: The Art Print Shop, 1927.
Vol. III.

ARTICLES

"Again Facing the Twentieth Century," The Midland Review, IV
(1899), 18.
"Archbishop Ireland's Lafayette Address, July 4th 1900,"
Catholic World, LXXI (1900), 709-710.
"With Authors and Publishers," Ave Maria, LXXIII (1911),
95.
Baldus, S.A. "With Catholic Authors and Publishers," Extension,
January, 1915, p.22.
Barton, George. "A Story of Self Sacrifice," Records of the
American Catholic Historical Society of Philadelphia, XXXVII
(1926), 116.
Bascom, John. "The Orbit of Faith," The Dial, XXII (1897),
283-285.
Belloc, Hilaire. "The Need for Catholic History," American
Catholic Quarterly Review, XXXV (1910), 590-594.
Berrigan, S.J., Rev. Daniel J. "Forgotten Splendor," America,
LXX (1944), 605-606.
Bernard, Ronald L. "The Trend in Modern Catholic Poetry,"
Catholic World, CXLIX (1939), 430-435.
Beryl, "The New Catholic Poet," Ave Maria, XXXVIII (1894),
449-452.
Bisland, Elizabeth. "The Time-Spirit of the Twentieth Century,"
Atlantic Monthly, LXXXVII (1901), 15-22.
"Book Notes," The Dolphin, I (1902), 119,501.
"Book Review, The Constitution and Proceedings of the Catholic
Young Men's National Union," Catholic World, XXXV (1882),
135-137.
Bregy, Katherine. "American Catholic Essayists," Catholic
Builders of the Nation, IV (1923), 139-153.
_____. "The Poetry of Francis Thompson," Catholic World,
LXXXI (1905), 605-614.
Browne, William Hande. "John Bannister Tabb," Library of
Southern Literature," XII (1907-1910), 51-65.

Byrnes, James F. "Chauncey Olcott, the Actor and the Man,"
Extension, (January, 1909) p.6.
Bowerman, Sara G. "Tiernan, Frances Christine Fisher,"
Dictionary of American Biography, XVIII (1936), 531-532.
"Catholic Educational Union," Catholic Reading Circle Review, I
(1891) 396.
"Catholic Higher Education and The Dolphin," The Dolphin, I
(1902), 589-590.
"The Catholic Layman and the Future," Donahoe's Magazine, XXI
(1889), 24.
"Catholic Literature and the Catholic Public," Catholic World,
XII (1870), 399-407.
"Chronicles," American Catholic Historical Review, XII (1926),
128.
Clarke, Richard H. "Our Converts," American Catholic Quarterly
Review, XIX (1894), 112-137.
"Columbian Reading Union," Catholic World, LXXII (1900), LXXIV
(1901), LXXIV (1902), LXXVIII (1903).
Connor, D. J. "Father Tabb's Poetical Preferences," Catholic
World, CXV (1922), 242-248.
Conway, Rev. John. "Reading," Donahoe's Magazine, XVII (1887),
12.
Conway, Katherine E. "The Anecdotal Side of John Boyle
O'Reilly," Extension, (December, 1908), pp. 7, 23.
_____. "The Anecdotal Side of James Jeffrey Roche,"
Extension, (January, 1909), pp. 5, 23.
Curtis, Georgina Pell. "Ludwig van Beethoven," Catholic World,
LXXVII (1903), 515-521.
Daly, S.J., Rev. James J. "Louise Imogen Guiney," America,
XXIV (1920), 112-114.
_____. "Reading and Character," The Catholic Mind,
XIII (1915).
Dempsey, Patrick. "The Anecdotal Side of Father Tabb,"
Extension, (February, 1909), pp. 5, 25.
Dondore, Dorothy Ann. "Chopin, Kate O'Flaherty," Dictionary of
American Biography, IV (1930), 90-91.
Donnelly, Eleanor C. "The Cannon in the Convent Grounds,"
Ave Maria, XVII (1881), 227.
Doyle, Julia R. "Who's Who in Catholic Journalism," Extension,
(September, 1907), pp. 7, 27.
Dunne, Joseph W. "A Catholic Soldier Poet," The Month,
CLXXVIII (1942), 216-221.
Dwyer, Michael J. "Dr. Orestes A. Brownson," Donahoe's
Magazine, XIII (1885), 496-500.
Egan, Maurice Francis. "Christian Reid, A Southern Lady,"
America, XXIII (1920), 18-19.
_____. "James A. McMaster," Illustrated Catholic Family
Annual, (December, 1888), pp. 43-45.
Egan, Rose F. "The Basis of the Catholic Novel," Catholic
World, LXXVI (1902), 316-327.

Ellis, Rev. John Tracy. "American Catholics and the Intellectual Life," Thought, XXX (1955), 351-388.

Emery, Susan L. "Catholic Literature in Public Libraries," Donahoe's Magazine, XLII (1899), 244-249.

Farinholt, F. C.; Mullaney, Katherine F.; Dowd, Mary A.; Spellisy, Mary A. "The Public Rights of Women, A Second Round Table Conference," Catholic World, LIX (1894), 299-320.

Faust, A. J. "William M. Thackorary," American Catholic Quarterly Review, VIII (1883), 597-627.

Flick, Ella Marie. "Dr. James J. Walsh, 1865-1942," Catholic World, CLV (1942), 148-169.

Flower, Benjamin O. "The Last Century as a Utilitarian Age," The Arena, XXV (1901), 271-280.

Fremantle, Anne. "Four American Catholic Essayists," Commonweal XLIX (1948), 225-228.

Gavigan, Walter V. "Two Gentlemen of Georgia," Catholic World, CXLV (1937), 584-589.

Gibbons, Cardinal James. "The Character of Leo XIII," The Century, LXVI (1903), 793-795.

_____. "The Preacher and His Province," North American Review, CLX (1895), 513-524.

_____. "Personal Reminisces of the Vatican Council," North American Review, CLXVIII (1894), 385-400.

_____. "Benedits of Arbitration," The Independent, LII (1900), 2423-2424.

_____. "Catholic Christianity," North American Review, CLXXIII (1901), 78-90.

_____. "Divorce," The Century, LXXVIII (1909), 145-149.

_____. "Moral Aspects of Suicide," The Century, LXXIII (1907), 401-407.

_____. "Organized Labor," Putnam's, III (1907), 62-67.

_____. "Patriotism and Politics," North American Review, CLIV (1892), 385-400.

_____. "President McKinley," The Independent, LIII (1901), 2271-2272.

Goggin, Rev. James. "Christian Science and Catholic Teaching," Ave Maria, LXXII (1911), 577-582.

Guiney, Grace. "Louise Imogen Guiney, A Comment and Some Letters," Catholic World, CXXI (1925), 596-603.

Guiney, Louise Imogen. "On Catholic Writers and Their Handicaps," Catholic World, XC (1909), 203-215.

Hale, Jr., Edward E. "Miss Repplier's Essays in Idleness," Dial, XV (1893), 225-226.

Harris, William Laurel. "A Modern Guild of Artists Catholic World, LXXVI (1903), 426-442.

Hartley, Marsden. "Tribute to Joyce Kilmer," Poetry, XIII (1918), 149-154.

Hartmann, Sadakichi. "Ecclesiastical Sculpture in America." Catholic World, LXXVII (1903), 760-767.

Hassard, John R. G. "Literature and the Laity," Catholic World, XXXVI (1882), 1-8.

Herbermann, Elizabeth P. "John A. Mooney and His Literary Work, United States Catholic Historical Society, Historical Records and Studies, XIII (1919), 120-128.

Hecker, Rev. Isaac T. "Catholic Church in the United States," Catholic World, XXIX (1879), 433-456.

Hilton, A. J. "Advent," Ave Maria, LXXIII (1911), 714-715.

Hudson, C.S.C., Rev. Daniel E. "A Word in Defense of a Dead Author," Ave Maria, LXVIII (1909), 591-592.

Humiliata, IHM. Sr. Mary. "Religion and Nature in Father Tabb's Poetry," Catholic World, CLXV (1947), 330-336.

L. H. "Charles G. Herbermann," American Catholic Historical Review, II (1917), 436-441.

"Introductory," Catholic World, XXXI (1880), 1-4.

Ireland, Archbishop John. "The Marriage of Capital and Labor," Catholic World, LXXIV (1902), 531-535.

_____. "The Religion Condition in Our New Island Territory," (interview by Elbert F. Baldwin), The Outlook, LXII (1899), 933-934.

_____. "Rt. Rev. Matthias Toras, First Bishop of Dubuque," The Catholic World, LXVII (1898), 721-731.

_____. Theobald Matthew," The Catholic World, LII (1890), 1-8.

Jones Howard M. Book Review of Agnes Repplier: Lady of Letters by George Stewart Stokes (Philadelphia, Pa., 1949), Saturday Review of Literature, XXXII (April 30, 1949), 32.

de Kay, Charles. "Christian Art, Status and Prospects in the United States," Catholic World, LXXIV (1901), 9-16.

"Mr. Lawrence Kehor," Donahoe's Magazine, XVIII (1887), 284.

Kelley, M. E. "Women and the Drink Problem," Catholic World, LXIX (1899), 678-687.

Kelly, William D. "A Benefactress of Her Race," Notre Dame Scholastic, (March, 1895), pp. 405-408.

Kent, W. Hox. "The English Royal Commission on Divorce," Catholic World, XCVII (1913), 1-15.

Kerby, William J. "Catholicity and Socialism," American Catholic Quarterly Review, XXX (1905), 225-243.

_____. "Maurice Francis Egan," Catholic World, CXVIII (1924), 677-679.

Kessler, Emile. "Tabb and Wordsworth," Catholic World, CXLIII (1936), 572-576.

Kurth, Paula. "The Sonnets of Louise Imogen Guiney," America, XLIII (1930), 430-431.

"Laetare Medal Conferred on Lawrence F. Flick, M.D., in the Hall of the Society, 5 May 1920," Records of the American Catholic Historical Society of Philadelphia, XXXI (1920), 101-128.

La Forest, C.S.C., Brother Laurian. "Bishop Spalding's Views on Character Education," Catholic Educational Review, XLIX (1951), 524-531.

Landy, Joseph. "Poet in Another War," America, LXXI (1944), 456-457.

"Latest Books," Catholic World, LXXIX (1904), 111,255,399,547, 680,832.

Lathrop, George Parsons. "Was Tennyson Consistent?" American Catholic Quarterly Review, XVIII (1893), 101-121.

"In the Library," The Midland Review, IV (1899), 7.

"Literary Chat," Ecclesiastical Review, XXXIV (1906), 108-109.

Loughlin, Rev. James F. "The Higher and Lower Education of the American Priesthood," American Catholic Quarterly Review, XV (1890), 101-122.

"The Lounger," Critic, XLVII (1905), 204.

Lucey, S.J., Rev. William L. "Catholic Magazines: 1865-1880." Records of the American Catholic Historical Society of Philadelphia, LXIII (1952), 21-36.

_____. "Catholic Magazines: 1890-1893," ibid., 133-156.

_____. "Catholic Magazines: 1894-1900," ibid., 197-223.

Lynch, Bernard J. "The Italians in New York," Catholic World, XLVII (1888), 67-73.

MacAteer, William. "James Ryder Randall," Marials, VI (1930), 161.

McAvoy, C.S.C., Rev. Thomas T. "Americanism, Fact and Fiction," American Catholic Historical Review, XXXI (1945), 133-153.

_____. "Bishop John Lancaster Spalding and the Catholic Minority (1877-1908)," The Review of Politics, XII (1950), 3-19.

McCarthy, John. "Patrick Valentine Hickey," The Illustrated Catholic Family Annual, (January, 1890), pp. 43-46.

McDevitt, William. "Father Tabb at St. Charles College," Catholic World, CLVI (1943), 412-419.

McElrone, Hugh P. "Edmund Bailey O'Callaghan," Donahoe's Magazine, XXV (1891), 429,430.

McQuaid, Bishop Bernard J. "Relihion in Schools," North American Review, CXXXII (1881), 332-344.

_____. "Religious Teaching in Schools," Forum, VIII (1889), 377-390.

_____. "Seminaries," American Ecclesiastical Review, XVI (1897), 461-480.

Maginnis, Charles D. "A Practical Talk on Church Building," Catholic World, LXXVI (1902), 368-384.

Malloch, Archibald. "James J. Walsh," Science, XCV (1942), 522.

"Marietta, A Maid of Venice," The Critic, XL (1902), 178.

Meehan, Thomas F. "The Catholic Press," The Catholic Builders of the Nation, IV (1923), 219-234.

Meehan, Thomas F. "Early Catholic Weeklies," United States Catholic Historical Society, Historical Records and Studies, XXVIII (1937), 237-255.

_____. "The First Catholic Monthly Magazines," United States Catholic Historical Society, Historical Records and Studies, XXXI (1940), 137-144.

_____. "Mary Ann Madden Sadlier," The Catholic Encyclopedia, XIII (1912), 322,323.

"The Menace of Mormonism," Ave Maria, L (1900), 370-373.

Merrill, William Stetson, "Catholic Literature in Public Libraries," Catholic World, LXXXIX (1909), 500-507.

_____. "Eliza Allen Starr," Catholic World, LXXIV (1902), 607-613.

Meynell, Alice. "Father Tabb," Catholic World, XC (1910), 577-582.

Monroe, Harriet. "Comment," Poetry, XIII (1918), 33.

Mooney, John A. "Columbus and the Scientific School," American Catholic Quarterly Review, XVII (1892), 827-852.

_____. "Our Recent American Catholic Congress and Its Significance," XV (1890), 150-169.

_____. "Pius IX and the Revolution, 1846-48," American Catholic Quarterly Review, XVII (1892), 137-160.

_____. "Professor Janssens and Other Modern German Historians," American Catholic Quarterly Review, XII (1887), 424-451.

Mosher, Warren E. "Introduction," Catholic Reading Circle Review, I (1891), i-ii.

Mullany, Rev. John F. "Short Sketches of the Evangelists," Mosher's Magazine, XVII (1901), 397-399.

Neill, Charles P. "Economic Study," Mosher's Magazine, XVII (1901), 394-396.

"Notes and Remarks," Ave Maria, LXXIII (1911), 151.

"Notable New Books," Ave Maria, LXV (1907, 214. LXIX (1909), 631. LXXIV (1912), 376,825.

"Notes on Current Topics," Donahoe's Magazine, XVIII (1887), 91.

O'Donnell, C.S.C., Rev. Charles L. "Reading in Secondary Schools and Colleges," Catholic Educational Review, II (1911), 898-908.

O'Hagan, Thomas. "Study of American Literature," Catholic Reading Circle Review, IX (1896), 65-70.

O'Malley, Charles J. "Catholic Literators of Chicago," Rosary Magazine, XXVI (1905), 19-24.

_____. "The Catholic Literary Advance," The Midland Review, IV (1900), 6.

O'Malley, Sallie M. "The Brown Princess," Extension, II (1907), Serialized Fiction.

Onahan, William J. "General James Shields," Donahoe's Magazine, XVII (1887), 442-445.

O'Neill, S.J., Rev. George. "The Poetry of Louise Imogen Guiney," Studies, XX (1931), 575-582.

364

"One Who Loved Children," Commonweal, XIV (1931), 393.
Pallen, Conde. "A Chat by the Way," Catholic World, XLII (1885), 270-274.

_____. "American Manners," The Month, LVIII (1886), 60-65.

_____. "The Catholics and the Public Schools, the True Significance of 'Tolerari Potest,'" Educational Review, IV (1892), 456-462.

_____. "The Catholic Idea of Popular Summer Schools," Ecclesiastical Review, XV (1896), 61-70.

_____. "The Times that Lead Up to Dante," American Catholic Quarterly Review, XV (1890), 681-697.

"Conde Benoist Pallen," Commonweal, X (1929), 144.

Parsons, Wilfrid. "Dr. James J. Walsh," Commonweal, XXXV (1942), 550-551.

Patmore, Coventry. "The Toys," Ave Maria, XVII (1881), 441.

"Patrick Donahoe, Founder of The Pilot," Donahoe's Magazine, XXV (1891), 99-101.

Phillips, Charles. "The Year's Catholic Poetry," Catholic World, XC (1910), 445-461.

"A Plea for Reticence," Literary Digest, XLVIII (1914), 827-828.

"The Poems of Joyce Kilmer," Outlook, CXX (1918), 12.

Preston, Thomas B. "Cardinal Gibbons' Late Work," The Arena, I (1890), 336-342.

Prindeville, Kate Gertrude. "Italy in Chicago," Catholic World, LXXVII (1903), 452-461.

Purcell, Richard J. "Roche, James Jeffrey," Dictionary of American Biography, XVI (1935), 63.

_____. "Spalding, John Lancaster," Dictionary of American Biography," XVII (1935), 422-423.

_____. "Sadlier, Mary Ann Madden," Dictionary of American Biography, XVI (1935), 284.

"Recent Popular Books," The Dolphin, VIII (1905), 624-629.

"Reformation of Ecclesiastical Art," Catholic World, LXXI (1900), 556-560.

Reilly, Joseph J. "Stories by Kate Chopin," Commonweal, XXV (1937), 606-607.

Reily, L. W. "Henry George the Socialist," Donahoe's Magazine, XVIII (1887), 7.

Repplier, Agnes. "Andrew Lang," Catholic World, XCVI (1912), 289-297.

_____. "The Birth of the Controversial Novel," Catholic World, LXXXVII (1908), 30-38.

_____. "Catholicism and Authorship," Catholic World, XC (1909), 167-174.

_____. "Catholic Letters and The Catholic World," Catholic World, XI (1915), 31-37.

_____. "Christianity and the War," The Atlantic, (January, 1915), pp.6-14.

Repplier, Agnes. "The Choice of Books," Catholic World, LXXXIV (1906), 48-56.
_____. "A Commentary on Herr Delbruck," The Atlantic, (March, 1915), pp.426-428.
_____. "Our Lady Poverty," The Atlantic, (October, 1914), pp. 452-459.
_____. "Picturesqueness and Piety," Catholic World, XCII (1911), 720-738.
_____. "Popular Education," The Atlantic, (January, 1914), pp. 1-8.
_____. "Repeal of Reticence," The Atlantic, (March, 1914) pp. 297-304.
Rittenhouse, Jessie B. "The Charm of Louise Imogen Guiney," Bookman, LII (1921), 515-520.
_____. "Two Women Poets," Saturday Review of Literature, IV (1928), 758-759.
Robinson, Wilfrid J. "England's Catholic Revival," Ave Maria, III (1916), 7-12.
Russell, Matthew, "Our Poets. No. 25-Rev. Abram Ryan," Irish Monthly, XIX (1891), 629-639.
Ryan, Archbishop Patrick John. "Salutatory," American Catholic Quarterly Review, XV (1890), 385-389.
Sadlier, Anna T. "Christian Reid, A Tribute of a Fellow Worker," Ave Maria, XI (1920), 638-691.
Shuster, George N. "Finn, Francis James," Dictionary of American Biography, VI (1931), 392-393.
_____. "Father Tabb and the Romantic Tradition," The Month, CXLIV (1924), 516-525.
Shea, John Gilmary. "The Anti-Catholic Issue in the Late Election, the Relation of Catholics to the Political Parties," American Catholic Quarterly Review, VI (1881), 36-50.
_____. "The Catholic Church in American History," American Catholic Quarterly Review, I (1876), 148-173.
_____. "Converts, Their Influence and Work in this Country," American Catholic Quarterly Review, VIII (1883), 509-529.
de la Selva, Salomon. "Main Street and Other Poems," Poetry, XI (1918), 281-282.
Smith, Rev. John Talbot. "An Australian Singer," Donahoe's Magazine, LIV (1905), 417-425.
_____. "Augustin Daly," Donahoe's Magazine, XXXVI (1896), 47-56.
_____. "The Catholic Actor," Donahoe's Magazine, L (1903), 382-392.
_____. "The Catholic Actor in New York," Donahoe's Magazine, LV (1906), 51-59.
_____. "Catholics and the Stage," Catholic Builders of the Nation, IV (1923), 251-267.

Smith, Rev. John Talbot. "Catholic Plays and Players," Donahoe's Magazine, LV (1906), 636-644.
_____. "A Few Catholic Playwrights," Donahoe's Magazine, LV (1906), 133-142.
_____. "The Chance for Religious Drama," Donahoe's Magazine, LVII (1907), 146-155.
_____. "The Fiske Season in New York," Donahoe's Magazine, LII (1904), 350-356.
_____. "Foreign Plays on the American Stage," Donahoe's Magazine, LII (1904), 478-484.
_____. "Grand Opera for the People," Donahoe's Magazine, LVII (1907), 49-58.
_____. "Hades and Ibsen," Donahoe's Magazine, L (1903), 502-508.
_____. "Father Lambert and Robert Ingersoll," Ave Maria, LXXI (1910), 705-710.
_____. "Mary Agnes Tincker," Ave Maria, LXII (1909), 142-148.
_____. "The Morality of the Players," Donahoe's Magazine, LV (1906), 244-252.
_____. "The Poetic Drama," Donahoe's Magazine, LVII (1907), 282-290.
_____. "The Popular Play," American Catholic Quarterly Review, XXVIII (1903), 339-354.
_____. "Old Times in Catholic Journalism," Extension, (September, 1914), pp. 8,21.
"Some Books for Catholic Teachers," Ave Maria, LXVII (1908), 469.
"Some Philadelphia Converts," Records of the American Catholic Historical Society of Philadelphia, XXXIII (1922), 238-266.
"Sonnet to E.A.S.," Ave Maria, XVII (1881), 821.
Spalding, Bishop John Lancaster. "Catholics and Apaism," The North American Review, CLIX (1894), 278-287.
_____. "God in the Constitution, A Reply to Colonel Ingersoll," Arena, I (1890), 517-528.
_____. "Normal Schools for Catholics," Catholic World, LI (1890), 88-97.
_____. "Religion and Culture," American Catholic Quarterly Review, IV (1879), 389-414.
_____. "The Scope of Public School Education," Catholic World, LX (1895), 758-767.
_____. "Spalding on Americanism," The Independent, LII (1900), 2285-2287.
Spillane, Edward P. "Finotti, Joseph M." Catholic Encyclopedia, VI (1913), 77,78.
Stanley, Hiram. "Some Recent Books on Education," The Dial, XXIV (1898), 117-118.
Starr, Eliza Allen. "The Christian Interpretation of Art," Catholic Reading Circle Review, IX (1897), 322-326.

Swan, Caroline. "Christmas Morn," The Globe, XII (1902), 365.
_____. "Easter Glory," The Globe, XII (1902), 23.
_____. "A New Poet," The Globe, XI (1901), 29.
"Talk About New Books," Catholic World, LVIII (1893), LXI
    (1895), LXII (1896) LXIV (1897). LXVII (1898). LXX (1900).
    LXXI (1900). LXII (1901). LXXIII (1901). LXXIV (1902).
Taylor, Hannis. "Abram J. Ryan," Catholic Encyclopedia, XIII
    (1912), 282.
Thebaud, Augustus J. "Freemasonry," American Catholic
    Quarterly Review, VI (1881), 577-608.
Thorne, William Henry. "Rev. Dr. Brann and Co.," The Globe,
    IX (1899), 67-72.
_____. "Books and Authors," The Globe, XI (1901), 75-80.
_____. "Carnegie, Bellamy and Co.," The Globe, I (1890),
    295-306.
_____. "Catholic Journalism and Criticism," The Globe,
    IX (1899), 283-295.
_____. "Globe Notes," The Globe, IX (1899), 109, 123,
    499.
_____. "The Heroic and Commonplace in Art," The Globe, I
    (1889), 35,36.
_____. "A Lot of New Books," The Globe, IX (1899), 214-
    217.
_____. "Novels and Criticism," The Globe, I (1889), 74-
    84.
Tietjen, Eunice. "Trees and Other Poems," Poetry, V (1914),
    140-141.
"The Twentieth Century," The Century, LXI (1901), 473-474.
"Two New Novelists," Catholic World, XXXVIII (1884), 781-797.
deVere, Aubrey. "Wordsworth's Prophect," Ave Maria, XXXIX
    (1894), 449.
Wade, John D. "Eleanor Cecilia Donnelly," Dictionary of
    American Biography, V (1930), 369.
Waggaman, Mary T. "Billy Boy," Ave Maria, LXXII (1911),
    Serialized Fiction.
_____. "The Secret of Pocomoke," LXXIV (1912),
    Serialized Fiction.
Walpole, Hugh. "The Stories of Francis Marion Crawford," Yale
    Review, XII (1923), 673-691.
Walsh, Honor. "Eleanor Cecilia Donnelly," America, XVII (1917),
    143-144.
Walsh, James J. "Basil Valentine, A Great Pre-Reformation
    Chemist," American Catholic Quarterly Review, XXXI (1906),
    342-358.
_____. "Catholic School and Education," Extension,
    (December, 1907), pp. 36,39.
_____. "The Dark Ages in America," American Catholic
    Quarterly Review, XLIII (1918), 1-20.

Walsh, James J. "Geography and the Church in the Middle Ages," American Catholic Quarterly Review, XXXII (1907), 49-67.
_____. "In Memoriam: Conde Benoist Pallen," Commonweal, X (1929), 214-215.
_____. "John Gilmary Shea," American Catholic Quarterly Review, XXXVIII (1913), 185-203.
_____. "Jules Verne and the French Religious Situation," The Dolphin, VII (1905), 552-563.
_____. "Michael Servetus and Some Sixteenth Century Educational Notes," American Catholic Quarterly Review, XXVI (1901), 714-732.
_____. "Scientists and Faith," American Catholic Quarterly Review, XXXV (1910), 216-238.
"Dr. James J. Walsh," Catholic World, CLV (1942), 109-110.
"Was Washington an Irishman?" Donahoe's Magazine, XXV (1891), 141.
Whelpley, J.D.; Wilson, R.R. "Great Tasks of a New Century," World's Work, I (1901), 278-285.
Young, Alexander. "John Boyle O'Reilly," The Chautauquan, XII (1890), 339-343.
Zahm, C.S.C., Rev. John A. "Friends and Foes in Science," American Catholic Quarterly Review, XV (1890), 630-657.

PERIODICALS

America, LXVI (1942), 631.
American Catholic Quarterly Review, I (1876), 1-4.
Ave Maria, XVII (1881), 1, 255, 367. XXII (1886, vii. XXXI (1890), vii.
Catholic Reading Circle Review, II (1892), 715.
The Catholic World, XXXIII (1881). XLIV (1886), 284. XLV (1886), 285. LII (1890), 151.
Champlain Educator, XXIV (1905), 115.
Commonweal, XXXV (1942), 501.
Dial, XII (1891), 22. XX (1896), 103. XXIV (1898), 149.
Dolphin, I (1902), I.
Donahoe's Magazine, I (1878), 91. II (1879), Frontpiece.
Literary Digest, XXII (1901), 1-200.
Outlook, CXXXVI (1924), 170. CXX (1918), 12. LV (1897), 129, 130.
The Sign, National Catholic Magazine, XXXIV (1955), 65-66.

NEWSPAPERS

The Catholic Citizen (Milwaukee, Wis.), (1893). (1896). (1899).
The Catholic News (New York), 11 (1897). 12 (1897). 17 (1903).
    18 (1903).
The Catholic Review (New York), 24 (1883). 34 (1888). 43
    (1893).
The Catholic Telegraph (Cincinnati), 53 (1884). 63 (1894).
The Monitor (San Francisco), 52 (1910). 53 (1910). 42 (1907).
    43 (1907). 53 (1912). 54 (1912). 54 (1913). 55 (1913).
The New World (Chicago), 4 (1896). 5 (1897).
New York Freeman's Journal and Catholic Register, 44 (1883).
    64 (1897). 71 (1903).
New York Times, 79 (1929). 100 (1950).
The Pilot (Boston), 45 (1882). 49 (1886). 53 (1890). 56
    (1893). 57 (1894).
The Review (St. Louis), 6 (1899). 10 (1903). 11 (1904).
The Catholic Fortnightly Review (Successor to The Review), 14
    (1907).
Rochester Union and Advertising, June 28, 1892.
St. Louis Post-Dispatch, August 18, 1884.

UNPUBLISHED MATERIALS

Anastasia, C.S.C., Dr. M. "The Catholic Essay." Unpublished
    master's dissertation. English Department, University of
    Notre Dame, 1923.
Garland, O.P., Sr. M. Annella. "The Work of Bishop John
    Lancaster Spalding in the Diocese of Peoria 1877-1908,"
    Unpublished master's dissertation. History Department,
    University of Notre Dame, 1953.
Long, O.S.U., Sr. M. Callista. "Kate Chopin: Artistic Inter-
    preter of Creole, Arcadian, and Negro Culture," Unpublished
    master's dissertation. English Department, University of
    Notre Dame, 1941.

VITA

St. Theresa's Parochial School   Brooklyn, New York
                                                  1927-1930

Coudersport Public Schools   Coudersport, Penn ylvania
                                                  1930-1935

Cathedral Preparatory School   Erie, Pennsylvania
                                                  1935-1937

University of Notre Dame   AB. 1941

University of Notre Dame   MA. 1948

THE AMERICAN CATHOLIC TRADITION

An Arno Press Collection

Callahan, Nelson J., editor. **The Diary of Richard L. Burtsell, Priest of New York.** 1978

Curran, Robert Emmett. **Michael Augustine Corrigan and the Shaping of Conservative Catholicism in America, 1878-1902.** 1978

Ewens, Mary. **The Role of the Nun in Nineteenth-Century America** (Doctoral Thesis, The University of Minnesota, 1971). 1978

McNeal, Patricia F. **The American Catholic Peace Movement 1928-1972** (Doctoral Dissertation, Temple University, 1974). 1978

Meiring, Bernard Julius. **Educational Aspects of the Legislation of the Councils of Baltimore, 1829-1884** (Doctoral Dissertation, University of California, Berkeley, 1963). 1978

Murnion, Philip J., **The Catholic Priest and the Changing Structure of Pastoral Ministry, New York, 1920-1970** (Doctoral Dissertation, Columbia University, 1972). 1978

White, James A., **The Era of Good Intentions: A Survey of American Catholics' Writing Between the Years 1880-1915** (Doctoral Thesis, University of Notre Dame, 1957). 1978

Dyrud, Keith P., Michael Novak and Rudolph J. Vecoli, editors. **The Other Catholics.** 1978

Gleason, Philip, editor. **Documentary Reports on Early American Catholicism.** 1978

Bugg, Lelia Hardin, editor. **The People of Our Parish.** 1900

Cadden, John Paul. **The Historiography of the American Catholic Church: 1785-1943.** 1944

Caruso, Joseph. **The Priest.** 1956

Congress of Colored Catholics of the United States. **Three Catholic Afro-American Congresses.** [1893]

Day, Dorothy. **From Union Square to Rome.** 1940

Deshon, George. **Guide for Catholic Young Women.** 1897

Dorsey, Anna H[anson]. **The Flemmings.** [1869]

Egan, Maurice Francis. **The Disappearance of John Longworthy.** 1890

Ellard, Gerald. **Christian Life and Worship.** 1948

England, John. **The Works of the Right Rev. John England, First Bishop of Charleston.** 1849. 5 vols.

Fichter, Joseph H. **Dynamics of a City Church.** 1951

Furfey, Paul Hanly. **Fire on the Earth.** 1936

Garraghan, Gilbert J. **The Jesuits of the Middle United States.** 1938. 3 vols.

Gibbons, James. **The Faith of Our Fathers.** 1877

Hecker, I[saac] T[homas]. **Questions of the Soul.** 1855

Houtart, François. **Aspects Sociologiques Du Catholicisme Américain.** 1957

[Hughes, William H.] **Souvenir Volume. Three Great Events in the History of the Catholic Church in the United States.** 1889

[Huntington, Jedediah Vincent]. **Alban: A Tale of the New World.** 1851

Kelley, Francis C., editor. The First American Catholic Missionary Congress. 1909

Labbé, Dolores Egger. **Jim Crow Comes to Church.** 1971

LaFarge, John. **Interracial Justice.** 1937

Malone, Sylvester L. **Dr. Edward McGlynn.** 1918

The Mission-Book of the Congregation of the Most Holy Redeemer. 1862

O'Hara, Edwin V. **The Church and the Country Community.** 1927

Pise, Charles Constantine. **Father Rowland.** 1829

Ryan, Alvan S., editor. **The Brownson Reader.** 1955

Ryan, John A., **Distributive Justice.** 1916

Sadlier, [Mary Anne]. **Confessions of an Apostate.** 1903

Sermons Preached at the Church of St. Paul the Apostle, New York, During the Year 1863. 1864

Shea, John Gilmary. **A History of the Catholic Church Within the Limits of the United States.** 1886/1888/1890/1892. 4 Vols.

Shuster, George N. **The Catholic Spirit in America.** 1928

Spalding, J[ohn] L[ancaster]. **The Religious Mission of the Irish People and Catholic Colonization.** 1880

Sullivan, Richard. **Summer After Summer.** 1942

[Sullivan, William L.] **The Priest.** 1911

Thorp, Willard. **Catholic Novelists in Defense of Their Faith, 1829-1865.** 1968

Tincker, Mary Agnes. **San Salvador.** 1892

Weninger, Franz Xaver. **Die Heilige Mission** *and* **Praktische Winke Für Missionare.** 1885. 2 Vols. in 1

Wissel, Joseph. **The Redemptorist on the American Missions.** 1920. 3 Vols. in 2

The World's Columbian Catholic Congresses and Educational Exhibit. 1893

Zahm, J[ohn] A[ugustine]. **Evolution and Dogma.** 1896